PENGUIN  CLASSICS

THE PENGUIN BOOK OF EXORCISMS

JOSEPH P. LAYCOCK is an assistant professor of religious studies at Texas State University and a coeditor of the journal *Nova Religio*. He is the author or editor of several books about religion, including *Speak of the Devil*, *Spirit Possession Around the World*, and *The Seer of Bayside*, and has written for *Quartz* and *The New Republic*. He lives in Austin, Texas.

The Penguin Book of Exorcisms

Edited by
JOSEPH P. LAYCOCK

PENGUIN BOOKS

PENGUIN BOOKS

An imprint of Penguin Random House LLC
penguinrandomhouse.com

LIBRARY OF CONGRESS CATALOGING-IN-PUBLICATION DATA
Names: Laycock, Joseph, 1980– editor.
Title: The Penguin book of exorcisms / edited by Joseph P Laycock.
Other titles: Book of exorcisms
Description: 1st. edition. | New York : Penguin Books, [2020] |
Includes bibliographical references and index.
Identifiers: LCCN 2020018192 (print) | LCCN 2020018193 (ebook) |
ISBN 9780143135470 (paperback) | ISBN 9780525507147 (ebook)
Subjects: LCSH: Exorcism. | Demonology. | Spirit possession.
Classification: LCC BF1559 .P38 2020 (print) |
LCC BF1559 (ebook) | DDC 133.4/27—dc23
LC record available at https://lccn.loc.gov/2020018192
LC ebook record available at https://lccn.loc.gov/2020018193

Printed in the United States of America
2nd Printing

Set in Sabon LT Pro

Contents

THE PENGUIN BOOK OF EXORCISMS

THE ANCIENT NEAR EAST

THE GRECO-ROMAN WORLD

MEDIEVAL EUROPE

EARLY MODERN EUROPE AND AMERICA

JEWISH TRADITIONS OF EXORCISM

THE ISLAMIC TRADITION

SOUTH AND EAST ASIA

MODERN EXORCISMS

Introduction

The word "exorcism" is derived from the Greek word *exorkizein*, meaning "to bind by oath." But in practice, exorcism is not about exerting control over spirits so much as banishing unwanted spirits from people, places, or things. For many people today, the idea of possession and exorcism is defined by William Friedkin's film *The Exorcist* (1973). Regan MacNeil's possession by the demon Pazuzu in that film was based on a spectacular case that began in Maryland in 1949. However, this sort of possession in which a demoniac (known as an "energumen" in Christian literature) exhibits an alternate personality and manifests supernatural abilities is not typical of the types of situations in which exorcists intervene. If we look across cultures, there is almost no phenomenon, whether it be a behavior, an illness, a strange experience, or an act of nature that has not been attributed to spirits and treated using exorcism.

Animism—the belief in spirit beings such as gods, ghosts, or demons—can be found in nearly every culture on earth, and almost anything undesirable can be attributed to the influence of spirit beings. In many cultures exorcism is used as a way of treating illness. For example, the Gospels describe some individuals as "possessed" because they are blind and mute (Matthew 12:22) or crippled (Luke 13:10–13). Historian Moshe Sluhovsky suggests that in medieval Europe exorcism was primarily a means of curing the body, and that it was only in the wake of Protestantism and the Counter-Reformation that possession was reimagined as a disease of the soul. For this reason, anthropologist Erika Bourguignon concludes that when looking across cultures, spirit possession should be understood as a way of interpretation: It is a diagnostic model through which a culture makes sense of certain phenomena.

Techniques of exorcism vary across cultures and are nearly endless in variety. In addition to prescribed prayers or rituals, other strategies have included simply asking the spirit what it wants and appeasing it, transferring the spirit into a stone or an animal that is subsequently destroyed, having the patient consume blessed substances such as holy water or sacred writings, or even sending for someone possessed by a more powerful spirit who can frighten the other spirit away. The most dangerous forms of exorcism involve making the patient so uncomfortable that the spirit no longer wishes to inhabit their body. Such strategies can include beating the patient, fumigating them with noxious substances, burning them, or immersing them in water. Tragically, there are countless examples of would-be exorcists who have killed their patients using these strategies; those killed in this manner are nearly always children or young women.

Another common misconception about exorcism is that it is a relic of the Dark Ages that will soon fade away from the modern world. This belief is tied to the so-called secularization narrative, or the assumption that science will inevitably eradicate both belief in the supernatural and the social influence of religion. However, the secularization narrative has increasingly few supporters among social scientists today. In fact, exorcism is arguably more popular today than at any point in history, with the exception of sixteenth- and seventeenth-century Europe.

In the Western tradition, possession is almost completely absent from the Hebrew Bible, but demoniacs are everywhere in the New Testament. In Europe, the "Golden Age" of demonic possession was not the Middle Ages but in the two centuries following the Protestant Reformation. In the modern United States, exorcism was once extraordinarily rare: Protestants regarded it as superstitious and the Catholic Church regarded it as an embarrassment. All of this changed after 1973, when *The Exorcist* created a massive demand for exorcisms. Evangelicals and Pentecostals were already positioned to cater to this new market, often calling their services "deliverance ministries" rather than exorcisms. Protestant missionaries then helped to spread this new brand of spiritual warfare throughout the Global South (developing nations of Asia, Africa, South America, and the Caribbean), so that exorcism is now a standard practice in many churches throughout these areas. Eventually, the Catholic Church also embraced exorcism more openly and now offers courses at the Vatican to train more exorcists. Catholic advocates of exorcism, such as the late Father Gabriele Amorth (1925–2016), argued that more exorcisms were needed than ever before, because cultural trends such as yoga and the Harry Potter franchise were leaving millions vulnerable to demonic influence.

Historical analysis suggests that a good index of how prevalent exorcism is in a given culture is not the culture's level of scientific understanding but its level of religious, social, and political upheaval. At least in the Western tradition, the most famous cases of exorcism are always political: When people tell a story about a successful exorcism, it is usually to establish the authority of a religious figure or institution, or else to associate a rival religion or controversial social practice with the demonic. In sum, the ritual of exorcism seeks to establish, in dramatic fashion, who is good and who (or what) is evil. In this sense, it is not our understanding of the world that influences exorcism, but rather exorcism that shapes the way we see the world.

This anthology endeavors to show the range of stories, beliefs, and practices surrounding exorcism from across time and cultures. The documents assembled here include poetry and popular legends, treatises by physicians and theologians, letters and diary entries by clergy, reports from missionaries and colonial officers, scientific papers, and legal proceedings. While the collection emphasizes the Western tradition, documents and case studies have also been included from India, China, Japan, Tibet, Sudan, Haiti, and the Yakama nation. These examples lend perspective to the reader's understanding of exorcism as a cross-cultural phenomenon and may pique further interest in these traditions.

JOSEPH P. LAYCOCK

Suggestions for Further Reading

Blacker, Carmen. *The Catalpa Bow: A Study of Shamanistic Practices in Japan*. London: Routledge, 2004.

Boddy, Janice. *Wombs and Alien Spirits: Women, Men and the Zár Cult in Northern Sudan*. Madison: University of Wisconsin Press, 2014.

Bourguignon, Erika. *Possession*. New York: Chandler and Sharp, 1976.

Chajes, J. H. *Between Worlds: Dybbuks, Exorcists, and Early Modern Judaism*. Philadelphia: University of Pennsylvania Press, 2003.

Crapanzano, Vincent, and Vivian Garrison, editors. *Case Studies in Spirit Possession*. New York: Wiley, 1984.

Demos, John. *Entertaining Satan: Witchcraft and the Culture of Early New England*. New York: Oxford University Press, 2004.

Ferber, Sarah. *Demonic Possession and Exorcism in Early Modern France*. New York: Routledge, 2004.

Goodman, Felicitas D. *How About Demons? Possession and Exorcism in the Modern World*. Bloomington: Indiana University Press, 1988.

Levack, Brian. *The Devil Within: Possession and Exorcism in the Christian West*. New Haven, Conn.: Yale University Press, 2013.

Sluhovsky, Moshe. *Believe Not Every Spirit: Possession, Mysticism, and Discernment in Early Modern Catholicism*. Chicago: University of Chicago Press, 2007.

Acknowledgments

There are many people without whom this book would not have been possible. I would first like to thank the librarians, whose tireless and often thankless work maintaining archives makes books like this possible. Library staff at the Connecticut State Library, the University of Scranton, the University of Saint Mary of the Lake, Hennepin County Library, and Louisiana State University all assisted with gathering texts for this volume. This anthology would also not be possible without the numerous authors, translators, and descendants of authors who generously granted permission to reproduce excerpts here, especially Rob Martinez, Dan Ben-Amos, the Mariannhill Mission Society, the Rhine Research Center, Drew Sumrall, Daniel Métraux, Benno Pattison, and Father Michael L. Maginot. I would also like to thank the many experts whose consultation was helpful in preparing this book, especially A. Richard Heffron, who did an original Arabic translation; Rabbi Geoffrey Dennis, for his guidance with the Jewish tradition; librarian Gabe McKee for his help deciphering an eighteenth-century diary; choreographer Rebecca Whitehurst, for her insight into distinguishing super-ordinary gymnastics from supernatural levitation; and Pascale Dollfus, for her research on the Himalayan ritual of "Breaking the Stone." Finally, I would like to thank the staff at Penguin Classics who assisted me in this project, especially John Siciliano and Gretchen Schmid.

The Penguin Book of
Exorcisms

THE ANCIENT
NEAR EAST

AN EXORCISM FROM THE
LIBRARY OF ASHURBANIPAL[1]

SEVENTH CENTURY BCE

Ashurbanipal ruled Assyria from approximately 668 BCE to around 630 BCE. In the 1850s, thirty thousand cuneiform tablets and fragments were excavated from the site of his royal library in Ninevah. In addition to legal and historical texts, many of the tablets describe medical and magical practices, including exorcism. In the ancient Near East, exorcism was frequently used to treat the symptoms of disease, blurring the line between religious ritual and medicine. Demons were imagined as residing in the desert, and exorcism frequently involved ritually removing the spirit and returning it to the desert.

The exorcism below, written on two sides of a tablet, describes a man suffering from paralysis, pain, and loss of appetite. The first part of the exorcism describes the imagined cause of the symptoms: an evil spirit who prowls the desert. The exorcism invokes the god Marduk. In the Babylonian creation myth, the Enuma Elish, Marduk defeats the dragon Tiamat and her army of monsters. The exorcism also invokes Ea, a deity frequently associated with Marduk, whose domain includes civilization and water. Eridu, mentioned in the text, is a location in southern Mesopotamia that is sometimes described as the home of Ea.

The ritual itself involves sprinkling the patient with an herbal concoction. The ingredients of this medicine are unclear, although the translator suggests that šalalu may be an Indian herb akin to ginger. Next, an image of the patient is constructed "in dough," possibly a substance like cornmeal. The water is drained off the patient (or perhaps the dough image), taking the sickness with it, and

into a cup. The cup is then emptied "in broad places," es-
sentially returning the evil spirit to its natural habitat. The
final lines refer to the month in which the spirit began
causing problems. This is a common feature of ancient
Near Eastern exorcisms, as spirits were thought to oper-
ate within predictable patterns of time.

OBVERSE.

(Plate XXXI.)

Incantation:—

The evil Spirit hath lain in wait in the desert
    unto the side of the man [hath drawn nigh],
The evil Genius for ever is rampant
And none can [resist him],
The evil Ghost goeth furtively in the desert and
[Causeth] slaughter [among men].
The evil Devil prowleth in the city,
[It hath no rest?] from slaughtering men.
They smite the hero,
They lay low the maiden,
The little ones like a leek they tear in pieces,
They tear out the heart. . . .
Like a demon they envelop. . . .
They draw near. . . . .
[Where?] he sitteth they turn him back like
    a shut gate(?)[2]
Unto his house they drive him . . .
  . . . is estranged (?), he falleth in the marsh.
He cannot lift [his limbs], nor turn his side.
He hath no desire to eat food,
Nor drink water,
His members are dissolved, and his body is filled
    with pain.

Marduk hath seen him (etc.),
What I (etc.),
Go, my son (Marduk),
Fill a pot with water and
Binu the *maštakal*-plant, *suhuššu*, a stalk of
   šalalu, cypress,
And white cedar put therein and
Perform the Incantation of Eridu and
Make perfect the water of the Incantation and
Make perfect thy pure exorcism,
Sprinkle the man with the water and
Set *li'i*-food at his head and
Make the 'atonement' for the wanderer, the
   son of his god, and

REVERSE.

(Plate XXXII.)

Fashion a figure of him in dough,
Put water upon the man and
Pour forth the water of the Incantation;
Bring forth a censer (and) a torch,
As the water trickleth away from his body
So may the pestilence in his body trickle away.
Return these waters into a cup and
Pour them forth in the broad places,
That the evil influence which hath brought low
   (his) strength
May be carried away into the broad places,
That the spittle which hath been spat
May be poured forth like the water,
That the magic which mingleth with the
   spat-forth spittle
May be turned back,
By the magic of the Word of Ea,

The chanting lips which have uttered the ban,—
May their bond be loosened!
That this man may be pure, be clean!
Into the kindly hands of his god may he be
    commended.

Incantation:—Evil Spirit, evil Demon, evil Ghost,
    evil Devil, that bring evil at the beginning of an
    incomplete month.

THE BENTRESH STELA[1]

FOURTH CENTURY BCE

A stela is an upright stone slab with an inscription. In the ancient Near East, kings erected stele to commemorate law codes, military victories, and other accomplishments. The Bentresh Stela narrates the possession and exorcism of Princess Bentresh, daughter of the prince of Bakhtan. In the story, Bentresh's sister is the wife of the pharaoh Rameses II. The possessing spirit agrees to leave after the pharaoh sends a statue of the lunar god Khonsu to Bakhtan. Although the story is set during the reign of Rameses II, most scholars believe it was actually carved during the early Ptolemaic Period in the fourth century BCE. Physically, the stela consists of a block of black sandstone, approximately six and a half feet tall, engraved with twenty-eight lines of hieroglyphs. It was discovered in 1829 in a sanctuary near the Temple of Khonsu in Karnak, Egypt, and currently resides at the Louvre in Paris.

The purpose of the stela was almost certainly propaganda intended to communicate the power of the god Khonsu and the advantages of forming diplomatic alliances with Egypt. But there are also fascinating details about the culture of possession and exorcism during this period. The statue is the god Khonsu for all intents and purposes, and the possessing spirit yields to the god's power. Intriguingly, the statue is also described as "nodding violently," suggesting that it could move. Some have speculated that the statue was a kind of puppet that priests could animate using hidden apparatus.[2]

The story also suggests a theme of sibling rivalry. Although the symptoms of Bentresh's possession are not described, one can imagine that having her sister chosen as

the pharaoh's bride and taken away to live in the court of
a more powerful nation may have left her feeling jealous
or depressed. Possession could have been a socially ac-
ceptable way of expressing these feelings. When posses-
sion resulted in the arrival of an entourage from Egypt,
complete with feasting, this may have helped to appease
these feelings, causing the possession to cease.

INTRODUCTION

Horus: Mighty Bull, Likeness of Diadems, Abiding in Kingship,
like Atum; Golden Horus: Mighty of Strength, Expelling the
Nine Bows; King of Upper and Lower Egypt, Lord of the Two
Lands: Usermare-Setepnere; Son of Re, of his Body: Ramses-
Meriamon, beloved of Amon-Re, lord of Thebes, and all the
gods of Thebes. . . .

TRIBUTE IN NAHARIN

Lo, his majesty was in Naharin according to his yearly custom,
while the chiefs of every country came bowing down in peace,
because of the fame of his majesty. From the marshes was their
tribute; silver, gold, lapis lazuli, malachite and every sweet wood
of God's-Land were upon their backs, each one leading his
neighbor.

MARRIAGE OF RAMSES AND CHIEF
OF BEKHTEN'S DAUGHTER

Then the chief of Bekhten caused his tribute to be brought,
and he placed his eldest daughter in front thereof, praising his
majesty, and craving life from him. Now, she was exceedingly
beautiful to the heart of his majesty, beyond everything. Then
they affixed her titulary as: "Great King's-Wife, Nefrure." When

his majesty arrived in Egypt, she fulfilled all the functions of king's-wife.

ARRIVAL OF THE MESSENGER FROM BEKHTEN

When the year 23, the tenth month, the twenty-second day, came, while his majesty was in Thebes, the victorious, the mistress of cities, performing the pleasing ceremonies of his father, Amon-Re, lord of Thebes, at his beautiful feast of Southern Opet (Luxor), his favorite seat, of the beginning (of the world), came one to say to his majesty: "A messenger of the chief of Bekhten has come, bearing many gifts for the King's-Wife." Then he was brought before his majesty together with his gifts. He said, praising his majesty: "Praise to thee, Sun of the Nine Bows! Give us life from thee." So spake he, smelling the earth before his majesty. He spake again before his majesty: "I come to thee, O king, my lord, on account of Bentresh, thy great sister of the King's-Wife, Nefrure. Sickness has penetrated into her limbs. May thy majesty send a wise man to see her."

DISPATCH OF THE WISE MAN TO BEKHTEN

Then said his majesty: "Bring to me the sacred scribes and the officials of the court." They were led to him immediately. Said his majesty: "Let one read to you, till ye hear this thing. Then bring to me one experienced in his heart, who can write with his fingers, from your midst." The king's-scribe, Thutemhab, came before his majesty, and his majesty commanded that he go to Bekhten together with his messenger.

ARRIVAL OF THE WISE MAN
IN BEKHTEN

The wise man arrived in Bekhten; he found Bentresh in the condition of one possessed of a spirit. He found her unable to contend with him.

MESSAGE OF THE CHIEF OF
BEKHTEN TO RAMSES

The chief of Bekhten repeated in the presence of his majesty, saying: "O king, my lord, let his majesty command to have this god brought [. . . Here text has been lost between two fragments of the stela . . .]" Then the wise man whom his majesty had sent, returned to his majesty in the year 26, the ninth month, at the feast of Amon, while his majesty was in Thebes.

RAMSES' INTERVIEW WITH
THE TWO KHONSU'S

Then his majesty repeated (it) before Khonsu-in-Thebes-Beautiful-Rest, saying: "O my good lord, I repeated before thee concerning the daughter of the chief of Bekhten." Then they led Khonsu-in-Thebes-Beautiful-Rest to Khonsu-the-Plan-Maker, the great god, smiting the evil spirits. Then said his majesty before Khonsu-in-Thebes-Beautiful-Rest: "O thou good lord, if thou inclinest thy face to Khonsu-the-Plan-Maker, the great god, smiting the evil spirits, he shall be conveyed to Bekhten." There was violent nodding. Then said his majesty: "Send thy protection with him, that I may cause his majesty to go to Bekhten, to save the daughter of the chief of Bekhten." Khonsu-in-Thebes-Beautiful-Rest nodded the head violently. Then he wrought the protection of Khonsu-the-Plan-Maker-in-Thebes, four times.

DEPARTURE OF
KHONSU-THE-PLAN-MAKER

His majesty commanded to cause Khonsu-the-Plan-Maker-in-Thebes to proceed to a great ship, five transports, numerous chariots and horses of the west and the east.

ARRIVAL OF THE GOD IN BEKHTEN

This god arrived in Bekhten in a full year and five months. Then the chief of Bekhten came, with his soldiers and his nobles, before Khonsu-the-Plan-Maker. He threw himself upon his belly, saying, "Thou comest to us, thou art welcome with us, by command of the King Usermare-Stepnere (Ramses II)."

CURE OF BENTRESH

Then this god went to the place where Bentresh was. Then he wrought the protection of the daughter of the chief of Bekhten. She became well immediately.

CONCILIATION OF THE SPIRIT

Then said this spirit which was in her before Khonsu-the-Plan-Maker-in-Thebes: "Thou comest in peace, thou great god, smiting the barbarians. Thy city is Bekhten, thy servants are its people, I am thy servant. I will go to the place whence I came, to satisfy thy heart concerning that, on account of which thou comest. (But) let thy majesty command to celebrate a feast-day with me and with the chief of Bekhten." Then his god nodded to his priest, saying: "Let the chief of Bekhten make a great offering before this spirit." While these things were happening, which Khonsu-the-Plan-Maker-in-Thebes wrought with the spirit, the chief of Bekhten stood with his soldiers, and feared very greatly. Then he made a great offering before Khonsu-the-Plan-Maker-in-Thebes and the spirit; and the chief of Bekhten celebrated a feast day with them. Then the spirit departed in peace to the place he desired, by command of Khonsu-the-Plan-Maker-in-Thebes, and the chief of Bekhten rejoiced very greatly, together with every man who was in Bekhten.

RETENTION OF THE GOD IN BEKHTEN

Then he took counsel with his heart, saying: "I will cause this god to remain with me in Bekhten; I will not permit that he return to Egypt." Then this god tarried three years and nine months in Bekhten.

VISION OF THE CHIEF OF BEKHTEN

Then the chief of Bekhten slept upon his bed, and he saw this god coming to him, to forsake his shrine; he was a hawk of gold, and he flew upward toward Egypt. He (the chief) awoke in fright.

DEPARTURE OF THE GOD FOR EGYPT

Then he said to the priest of Khonsu-the-Plan-Maker-in-Thebes: "This god, he is still with us; let him depart to Egypt; let his chariot depart to Egypt." Then the chief of Bekhten caused this god to proceed to Egypt, and gave to him very many gifts of every good thing, very many soldiers and horses.

ARRIVAL OF THE GOD IN EGYPT

They arrived in peace at Thebes. Then came the city of Thebes and the-Plan-Maker-in-Thebes to the house of Khonsu-in-Thebes-Beautiful-Rest. He set the gifts which the chief of

Bekhten had given to him, of good things, before Khonsu-in-Thebes-Beautiful-Rest, (but) he gave not everything thereof into his house. Khonsu-the-Plan-Maker-in-Thebes arrived [at] his [plac]e in peace in the year 33, the second month, the ninth day, of King Usermare-Setepnere; that he might be given life like Re, forever.

THE GRECO-ROMAN
WORLD

HIPPOCRATES,
"ON THE SACRED DISEASE"[1]
400 BCE

"On the Sacred Disease," composed around 400 BCE, is a treatise from the Hippocratic Corpus. The physician Hippocrates is the putative author, although some scholars doubt this. The author describes a disease that many modern interpreters believe to be epilepsy and refutes the popular idea that the disease is caused by the gods or daimonia, lesser gods and spirits. Instead, the author argues that "the brain exercises the greatest power in man" and that the "sacred disease" is caused by defects of the brain that are often hereditary or acquired during childhood.

This text is significant for two reasons. First, it dispels the notion that ancient people were incapable of theorizing naturalistic explanations for mental disorders or invented ideas of spirit possession purely out of scientific ignorance. Significantly, the author does not deny the existence of the gods, only the idea that poorly understood diseases should be attributed to them. There is even a suggestion here of the idea of iatrogenic illness, or illness caused by medical treatment, as the author suggests that those who can relieve symptoms using incantations can also excite them. Second, the text provides an interesting insight into the kinds of beliefs and practices surrounding spirit possession that existed in ancient Greece.

It is thus with regard to the disease called Sacred: it appears to me to be nowise more divine nor more sacred than other diseases, but has a natural cause from which it originates like other affections. Men regard its nature and cause as divine from ignorance and wonder, because it is not at all like to other diseases. And this notion of its divinity is kept up by their inability to comprehend it, and the simplicity of the mode by which it is cured, for men are freed from it by purifications and incantations. . . . For whoever is able, by purifications and conjurations, to drive away such an affection, will be able, by other practices, to excite it; and, according to this view, its divine nature is entirely done away with. By such sayings and doings, they [magicians and exorcists] profess to be possessed of superior knowledge, and deceive mankind by enjoining lustrations and purifications upon them, while their discourse turns upon the divinity and the godhead [*daimon*]. And yet it would appear to me that their discourse savours not of piety, as they suppose, but rather of impiety, and as if there were no gods, and that what they hold to be holy and divine, were impious and unholy. This I will now explain. For, if they profess to know how to bring down the moon, and darken the sun, and induce storms and fine weather, and rains and droughts, and make the sea and land unproductive, and so forth, whether they arrogate this power as being derived from mysteries or any other knowledge or consideration, they appear to me to practise impiety, and either to fancy that there are no gods, or, if there are, that they have no ability to ward off any of the greatest evils. How, then, are they not enemies to the gods? For, if a man by magical arts and sacrifices will bring down the moon, and darken the sun, and induce storms, or fine weather, I should not believe that there was anything divine, but human, in these things, provided the power of the divine were overpowered by human knowledge and subjected to it. But perhaps it will be said, these things are not so, but, men being in want of the means of life, invent many and various things, and devise many contrivances for all other things, and for this disease, in every phase of the disease, assigning the cause to a god. Nor do they remember the same things once, but frequently. For, if they imitate a goat, or grind their teeth, or if their right side be convulsed, they say that the mother of the gods is the cause. But if they speak in a sharper and more intense tone, they resemble this state to a horse, and say that Posidon (*Neptune*) is the cause. Or if any excrement be passed, which is often the case, owing to the violence of the disease, the appellation of Enodius (*Hecate?*) is adhibited; or, if it be passed in smaller and denser masses, like bird's, it is said to be from Apollo Nomius. But if foam be emitted by the mouth, and the patient kick with his feet, Ares (*Mars*) gets the blame. But terrors which happen during the night, and fevers, and delirium, and jumpings out of bed, and frightful apparitions, and fleeing away—all these they hold to be the plots of Hecate, and the invasions of the Heroes, and use purifications and incantations, and, as appears to me, make the divinity to be most wicked and most impious. . . . But this disease seems to me to be nowise more divine than others; but it has its nature such as other diseases have, and a cause whence it originates, and its nature and cause are divine only just as much as all others are, and it is curable no less than the others, unless when, from length of time, it is confirmed, and has become stronger than the remedies applied. Its origin is hereditary, like that of other diseases. . . . But whoever is acquainted with such a change in men, and can render a man humid and dry, hot and cold by regimen, could also cure this disease, if he recognises the proper season for administering his remedies, without minding purifications, spells, and all other illiberal practices of a like kind.

LUCIAN OF SAMOSATA, THE SYRIAN EXORCIST[1]

150 CE

Lucian of Samosata was born in 125 CE in eastern Syria. He studied Greek and became an itinerant lecturer, traveling throughout the Roman Empire. He wrote about eighty works of short essays and dialogues, but is best remembered as a satirist. His work Philopseudes, *or* The Lover of Lies, *is a a dialogue in which a young man named Tychiades asks a friend why people are so fond of lies. Tychiades then describes a gathering he attended for a sick friend. The other guests were suggesting numerous folk remedies. When Tychiades suggested these would not work, the guests challenged his skepticism by telling increasingly fantastic stories. Tychiades's story of the party is a framing device through which Lucian presents folktales while simultaneously dismissing them as lies.*

In the passage below, a guest named Ion describes an exorcist. This passage can be taken as a plausible account of how people in the Roman Empire of the second century understood possession and exorcism. Lucian's skepticism, however, contradicts the popular narrative that ancient people believed in demonic possession because they simply could not imagine other causes for disease. The exorcist is a magician who charges money for his services, as was common at the time. The effects of possession in this account are not subtle, involving seizures and frothing at the mouth. The possessed also speaks in foreign tongues, an ability that is still considered a convincing sign of possession today. Significantly, Ion reports that he actually saw a spirit leaving someone's body and that it resembled smoke. This image of exorcised demons leaving the body as smoke appears in early modern European art as well as television shows like Supernatural *(2005–present).*

"I shall be glad, now, to hear your views on the subject of those who cure demoniacal possession; the effect of *their* exorcisms is clear enough, and they have spirits to deal with. I need not enlarge on the subject: look at that Syrian adept from Palestine: every one knows how time after time he has found a man thrown down on the ground in a lunatic fit, foaming at the mouth and rolling his eyes; and how he has got him on to his feet again and sent him away in his right mind; and a handsome fee he takes for freeing men from such horrors. He stands over them as they lie, and asks the spirit whence it is. The patient says not a word, but the spirit in him makes answer, in Greek or in some foreign tongue as the case may be, stating where it comes from, and how it entered into him. Then with adjurations, and if need be with threats, the Syrian constrains it to come out of the man. I myself once saw one coming out: it was of a dark smoky complexion."

TERTULLIAN,
THE NATURE OF DEMONS[1]

197 CE

Tertullian's Apologeticus, *composed in 197 CE, is a defense of Christianity arguing that Christians are not guilty of such charges as atheism, sacrilege, and treason, as well as more outlandish accusations such as incest, cannibalism, and murder. In responding to the accusation that Christians are atheists and do not honor the gods, Tertullian laid out one of the most important early treatises on Christian demonology.*

Tertullian did not claim that the pagan gods do not exist. Instead, he argued that they are actually daemons *or* daimonia, *a term from which the English word "demon" is derived. In the Greco-Roman world,* daimonia *were understood to be intermediary beings between gods and humans who could be either good or evil. In Plato's* Apology of Socrates, *Socrates tells the court that he has a* daimonium *that forbids him from acting unethically.* Daimonium *is a diminutive of* daimon, *or a "divine something." For Tertullian, though, Socrates was guided by a* daemon. *Unlike pagans, Tertullian argues that* daemons *are fallen angels who rebelled against the one true God and are enemies of humanity. They masquerade as gods to deceive humanity and receive blood sacrifices.*

In making this argument, Tertullian makes several claims about the nature of daemons *that are not apparent in the New Testament. For example, he states that all* daemons *have wings, as angels do. He describes them feasting on "the fumes and blood" of pagan sacrifices, suggesting that* daemons *eat food. Tertullian also explains what powers* daemons *have, and that they are actually quite limited.*

Daemons can be everywhere at once, which gives them a remarkable ability to gather information. They cannot actually predict the future, but can fake this ability because they have access to information that human beings do not: "Their velocity is believed to be divinity." Thus the prophecies of pagan oracles are nothing but daemonic deceptions. Similarly, the daemons pretend to heal disease by first making the patient sick and then ceasing this activity after pagan medicine is administered.

Possession and exorcism are essential to Tertullian's argument in these chapters. Tertullian describes how daemons can subtly corrupt the mind much as crops and flowers can be blighted by breezes and other factors that are otherwise undetectable. As the best proof that the gods are actually daemons, Tertullian challenges the reader to bring someone possessed by a daemon before a Christian, who can compel the daemon to confess its true nature. Notably, Tertullian is adamant that all Christians have the power to command daemons.

And we thus affirm the existence of certain spiritual substances; nor is the name a new one. The philosophers are acquainted with daemons; for Socrates himself waited upon the will of a daemon. And why not? When a daemon is said to have attended him from boyhood as a dissuader, doubtless from good. The poets are acquainted with daemons; even the untaught vulgar often make use of them in cursing; for they name also Satan, the chief of this evil race, in their word of execration, just as if from an innate consciousness of the soul. Angels, too, Plato also does not deny; and to the names of both the magicians, for example, are witnesses at hand. Moreover how from certain angels, corrupted of their own free will, a still more corrupt race of daemons has issued, condemned by God, along with the authors of the race and him whom we have spoken of as their chief, may be learnt in the sacred writings. It will be sufficient now to explain the method of their operation. Their business is the ruin of man; thus spiritual wickedness began to act from the very first for the destruction of man. Consequently they inflict on the body diseases and many grievous mishaps, and violently visit the mind with sudden and extraordinary aberrations. Their wonderful subtlety and tenuity gives them access to both parts of man. Spiritual agencies possess great powers; so that, being invisible and unperceived by the senses, they can be detected in the effect they produce rather than in their mode of producing it. If some hidden blight in the breeze unseasonably hastens forward any fruit or grain in blossom, nips it in the bud, or blasts it in maturity, and if the air, infected in some unseen way, pours forth its poisonous currents; then by the same obscure contagion the influence of daemons and angels brings about the corruption also of the mind with fury and foul madness, or with fierce lusts bringing various errors in their train; of which that is the most prevailing by which they commend these gods of yours to the enthralled and deluded minds of men, that so they may procure for themselves their own proper food of fumes and blood offered to effigies and images, and (what is a more acceptable banquet to them) turn mankind aside from reflecting upon the True Divinity by the deceptions of false divination.

And how they effect these very operations I will shew. Every spirit is winged. This both angels and daemons are. In a moment, therefore, they are everywhere. To them the whole world is one place: what is being done everywhere they know as easily as they declare it. Their velocity is believed to be divinity, because their real nature is unknown. So also they desire sometimes to be thought the originators of those events of which they merely bring the tidings; and indeed they are sometimes the causes of evil events, but of good ones never. Even the counsels of God, too, they formerly picked up from the addresses of the prophets; and now they gather them while their writings are being read aloud. And so gleaning by this means the knowledge of certain chance events, they enviously ape a divinity by stealing the divination. Moreover, how ingeniously they framed their equivocations in the oracles to suit either event, such men as Croesus and Pyrrhus are well aware. But it was in the way which I have just mentioned that the Pythian Apollo brought back word that a tortoise was being cooked with the flesh of a lamb; in a moment he had been in Lydia.[2] They are able, from inhabiting the air and from their proximity to the stars and from their intimate knowledge of the clouds, to know what the heavens are about to prepare, so that they can promise the rain of which they are already sensible. They are sorcerers also, truly, in respect of the cures of diseases. For they first cause the injury, and then, in order to make it seem like a miracle, prescribe remedies which are either new or absolutely opposed to the ordinary methods of treatment; after which they stop causing the injury, and are believed to have effected a cure.

There is little need for me to analyze their other ingenious devices, or even their powers of spiritual deception,—such as the apparitions of Castor, the water carried in a sieve, the ship drawn forward with a girdle, and the beard turned red at a touch,—so that stones should be believed to be divinities, and the True God not be sought after.

* * *

Further, if the magicians also call forth apparitions and dishonor the souls of those already dead; if they throw children into trances for the purposes of oracular response; if they palm off a number of miracles through fraudulent delusions; if they also send dreams, possessing, when once invited, the assistant power of angels and daemons, through whom both goats and tables are wont to be made instruments of divination;—how much more would that power be eager of its own accord and for its own purposes to devote itself with all its might to that same work which it performs to serve the business of another! Or if angels and daemons devote themselves to the same work as your gods, where in that case is the excellence of divinity, which surely ought to be believed to be superior to every other power? Will it not then be more becoming to assume that it is they themselves who make themselves gods, since they exhibit the same credentials as the gods, rather than to set down the gods as merely the equals of angels and daemons? The difference of places points the distinction, I suppose; so that you regard those as gods from their temples whom in another place you do not call gods; and it seems one sort of madness to leap from the sacred towers, and quite another kind to jump from a neighboring roof; and it is pronounced one kind of violence to mutilate oneself or to gash one's arms, and quite another to cut one's throat. The issue of the frenzy is the same in both cases, and so is the manner of the instigation.

So far we have dealt in words; now we come to an actual demonstration of fact, and by it we shall show that the nature of gods and daemons is one, though passing under different names. Let any one be brought before your tribunals, who it is agreed is possessed by a daemon. That spirit, when commanded to speak by any Christian you like to select, will as truly confess that he is a daemon, as elsewhere he will falsely claim to be a god. In exactly the same way let any one of those be produced who are deemed to be under the influence of a god—who, by inhaling over the altars, become the recipients of the divine influence from the fumes, who are bent double with choking, and prophesy panting. That very virgin Caelestis, the promiser of rains; that very Aesculapius, the inventor of medicine, who supplied life to Socordius, Thanatius, and Asclepiodotus,[3] men doomed to die again the next day—if these deities of yours do not confess themselves daemons, not daring to lie to a Christian, you may there and then shed the blood of that most insolent Christian. What could be plainer than a fact like this? What could be more trustworthy than a proof of this nature? The simplicity of truth is before your eyes; its own virtue attends it there; suspicion is altogether out of the question.

Will you say that this is done by magic or some deception of that kind, when you can use your own eyes and ears? What indeed can be objected against that which is transparently and openly displayed? If on the one hand they are truly gods, why do they lie by saying that they are daemons? Is it to gratify us? If so, then in that case the divinity you acknowledge is subject to the Christians; and that surely cannot be accounted divinity which is subject to man and (if it adds at all to the disgrace) to its own antagonists. If on the other hand they are daemons or angels, why do they elsewhere present themselves in the guise of gods? For just as they who are regarded as gods would naturally refuse to call themselves daemons, if they were truly gods, lest they should depose themselves from their own high dignity, so also those whom you know with direct knowledge to be daemons would not dare to elsewhere pose as gods, if those whose names they usurp were any sort of gods at all, since they would fear to abuse the high dignity of beings undoubtedly superior to them and deserving of dread. Thus, then, that divinity which you acknowledge is naught, because if it really existed it would neither be assumed by the daemons, nor denied by the gods. Since then each side competes in making the same confession, and denying its claim to godship, you must draw the conclusion that but one kind of beings exists, namely daemons.

PHILOSTRATUS,
THE LIFE OF APOLLONIUS OF TYANA[1]

210 CE

Apollonius of Tyana was a philosopher of the Pythagorean tradition who likely lived in the first century. Most of what is known about Apollonius today comes from the eight-volume work, The Life of Apollonius of Tyana, *written by the philosopher Philostratus at the request of the empress Julia Domna and completed in 210 CE. Philostratus portrays Apollonius as a wandering sage and miracle worker whose travels took him to Mesopotamia and as far away as India. Before his birth, miracles and a visit from the god Proteus signal that Apollonius will be a great man. Apollonius travels the world, teaching, performing miracles, and attracting a body of disciples. He is summoned to Rome by the emperor Domitian, who accuses Apollonius of crimes he did not commit. But Apollonius miraculously vanishes from the emperor's court, reappearing in Dicaerchia to rejoin his disciples. These details have caused numerous scholars to note the connections between the story of Apollonius and that of Jesus.*

Like Jesus, one of the signs of Apollonius's moral authority is his ability to perform exorcisms. Apollonius exorcised two young men—one a sulky teenager, the other a disorderly drunk. These stories of exorcism emphasize not only Apollonius's supernatural power, but also his authority as a pedagogue. In the first story, the possessing entity is not a demon, but the ghost of a fallen soldier who is possessing a young boy because he finds his body beautiful. The ghost appears both to be erotically attracted to

*the boy and to enjoy using his body "as a mask." Apollo-
nius does not conduct this exorcism in person but hands
the boy's mother a mysterious letter to deliver to the ghost.
The story implies that the letter contained threats that persuaded the ghost to depart.*

*In the second story it seems unclear whether the boor-
ish behavior of a "young dandy" is due to demonic possession or simply to being spoiled. But Apollonius orders
the spirit to give a sign of its departure, and it topples a
statue as it exits the youth. On seeing the statue inexplicably fall, the audience is persuaded that an exorcism has
really occurred. Note the similarity to Josephus, who also
witnessed an exorcism conducted during the Roman Empire. In that account, cups or basins of water were mysteriously knocked over, and this was cited as evidence that
a nonhuman entity had truly been present.*

This discussion was interrupted by the appearance among the
sages of the messenger bringing in certain Indians who were in
want of succor. And he brought forward a poor woman who
interceded in behalf of her child, who was, she said, a boy of
sixteen years of age, but had been for two years possessed by
a devil. Now the character of the devil was that of a mocker
and a liar. Here one of the sages asked, why she said this, and
she replied: "This child of mine is extremely good-looking, and
therefore the devil is amorous of him and will not allow him to
retain his reason, nor will he permit him to go to school, or to
learn archery, nor even to remain at home, but drives him out
into desert places. And the boy does not even retain his own
voice, but speaks in a deep hollow tone, as men do; and he
looks at you with other eyes rather than with his own. As for
myself I weep over all this, and I tear my cheeks, and I rebuke
my son so far as I well may; but he does not know me. And I
made up my mind to repair hither, indeed I planned to do so a
year ago; only the demon discovered himself, using my child as
a mask, and what he told me was this, that he was the ghost of

a man, who fell long ago in battle, but that at death he was passionately attached to his wife. Now he had been dead for only three days when his wife insulted their union by marrying another man, and the consequence was that he had come to detest the love of women, and had transferred himself wholly into this boy. But he promised, if I would only not denounce him to yourselves, to endow the child with many noble blessings. As for myself, I was influenced by these promises; but he has put me off and off for such a long time now, that he has got sole control of my household, yet has no honest or true intentions." Here the sage asked afresh, if the boy was at hand; and she said not, for, although she had done all she could to get him to come with her, the demon had threatened her with steep places and precipices and declared that he would kill her son, "in case," she added, "I haled him hither for trial." "Take courage," said the sage, "for he will not slay him when he has read this." And so saying he drew a letter out of his bosom and gave it to the woman; and the letter, it appears, was addressed to the ghost and contained threats of an alarming kind.

* * *

Now while he was discussing the question of libations, there chanced to be present in his audience a young dandy who bore so evil a reputation for licentiousness that his conduct had long been the subject of coarse street-corner songs. His home was Corcyra, and he traced his pedigree to Alcinous the Phaeacian who entertained Odysseus. Apollonius then was talking about libations, and was urging them not to drink out of a particular cup, but to reserve it for the gods, without ever touching it or drinking out of it. But when he also urged them to have handles on the cup, and to pour the libation over the handle, because that is the part at which men are least likely to drink, the youth burst out into loud and coarse laughter, and quite drowned his voice. Then Apollonius looked up and said: "It is not yourself that perpetrates this insult, but the demon, who drives you without your knowing it." And in fact the youth was, without knowing it, possessed by a devil; for he would laugh at things that no one else laughed at, and then would fall to weeping for no reason at all, and he would talk and sing to himself. Now most people thought that it was boisterous humor of youth which led him into excesses; but he was really the mouthpiece of a devil, though it only seemed a drunken frolic in which on that occasion he was indulging. Now, when Apollonius gazed on him, the ghost in him began to utter cries of fear and rage, such as one hears from people who are being branded or racked; and the ghost swore that he would leave the young man alone and never take possession of any man again. But Apollonius addressed him with anger, as a master might a shifty, rascally, and shameless slave and so on, and he ordered him to quit the young man and show by a visible sign that he had done so. "I will throw down yonder statue," said the devil, and pointed to one of the images which were there in the king's portico, for there it was that the scene took place. But when the statue began by moving gently, and then fell down, it would defy anyone to describe the hubbub which arose thereat and the way they clapped their hands with wonder. But the young man rubbed his eyes as if he had just woke up, and he looked towards the rays of the sun, and won the consideration of all who now had turned their attention to him; for he no longer showed himself licentious, nor did he stare madly about, but he had returned to his own self, as thoroughly as if he had been treated with drugs; and he gave up his dainty dress and summery garments and the rest of his sybaritic way of life, and he fell in love with the austerity of philosophers, and donned their cloak, and stripping off his old self modeled his life and future upon that of Apollonius.

ATHANASIUS, *THE LIFE OF SAINT ANTHONY*[1]

370 CE

Saint Anthony or Saint Anthony the Great was an Egyptian monk who lived approximately between 250 and 356 CE. At the age of twenty, he gave away his inheritance to become a hermit, living in the desert. He is often considered the father of Christian monasticism. Much of what we know about him comes from Athanasius, bishop of Alexandria (395–373 CE). Athanasius's biography of Anthony describes the hermit battling demons in the desert before returning to civilization and conducting exorcisms of his own. The trials described by Athanasius became a popular theme in Western art, with numerous paintings depicting Anthony being attacked by demons.

The Life of Saint Anthony is a heresiological text in that discussion of demons is used to critique both pagan religion and Arian Christianity, which Athanasius spent most of his career combating. It is also a demonological text that elaborates on the nature and powers of demons. In fact, Athanasius refers to his "vast knowledge" about demons. The purported source of this knowledge is the Holy Spirit, which grants the gift of discernment that allows Christians to identify the types of spirits, their goals, and the specific means of defeating them. Like Tertullian before him, Athanasius explains that demons are fallen angels who pose as pagan gods. They cannot actually see the future, but their preternatural speed allows them to convince people that they can. They are also masters of illusion. In an attempt to divert Anthony from his discipline, the demons assume the shapes of a beautiful woman, a young man, and dangerous animals. They also create

illusions of silver and gold in the hopes of distracting An-
thony.

Demons are jealous of humanity (and especially monks).
But for all their powers, they are largely helpless against
Christians. Athanasius refers to Satan's "feebleness." As
a hermit, Anthony claims more and more territory from
the demons by praying in places that are their traditional
abodes. In episodes that anticipate the modern phenom-
enon of ghost hunting, Anthony confronts the demons by
locking himself in a tomb and then retiring to an aban-
doned fortress. The enraged demons are able to beat An-
thony unconscious, but not kill him. Their attempts to
appeal to his lust, fear, and greed are equally futile against
Anthony's prayer and discipline. Anthony is described as
"an athlete" for his life of discipline and training. Ulti-
mately, the demons in this text are only a foil Athanasius
uses to display the triumph of Christians.

And when the Enemy, the hater of the virtues and the lover of
evil things, saw all this great perfection in the young man, he
could not endure it, and he surrounded himself with his slaves,
even as he is wont to do, and began [to work] on Anthony. At
the beginning of his temptings of the saint he approached him
with flattery, and cast into him anxiety as to his possessions,
and solicitude and love for his sister, and for his family, and for
his kinsfolk, and the love of money and lusts of various kinds,
and the [thought of the] rest [of the things] of the life of [this]
world, and finally of the hard and laborious life which he lived,
and of the weakness of body [which would come upon him]
with the lapse of time; and, in short, he stirred up in him the
power of the thoughts so that by means of one [or other] of
them he might be flattered, and might be made to possess
shortcomings and be caught in the net through his instigation.

Now when the Enemy saw that his craftiness in this matter was without profit, and that the more he brought temptation unto Saint Anthony, the more strenuous the saint was in

protecting himself against him with the armor of righteousness, he attacked him by means of the vigor of early manhood
which is bound up in the nature of our humanity. With the
goadings of passion he used to trouble him by night, and in the
daytime also he would vex him and pain him with the same to
such an extent that even those who saw him knew from his appearance that he was waging war against the Adversary. But
the more the Evil One brought unto him filthy and maddening
thoughts, the more Saint Anthony took refuge in prayer and in
abundant supplication, and amid them [all] he remained wholly
chaste. And the Evil One was working [upon him] every shameful deed according to his wont, and at length he even appeared
unto Saint Anthony in the form of a woman; and other things
which resembled this he performed with ease for such things
are a subject for boasting to him.

But the blessed Anthony knelt down upon his knees on the
ground, and prayed before Him Who said, "Before thou cri-
est unto Me, I will answer thee" (Isaiah 65: 24), and said, "O
my Lord, this I entreat Thee: let not Thy love be blotted out
from my mind, and behold, I am, by Thy grace, innocent before
Thee." And again the Enemy multiplied in him the thoughts of
lust, until Saint Anthony became as one who was being burned
up, not through the Evil One, but through his own lusts; but he
girded himself about with the threat of the thought of the Judgment, and of the torture of Gehenna, and of the worm which
dieth not. And whilst meditating on the thoughts which could
be directed against the Evil One, he prayed for thoughts which
would be hostile to him. Thus, to the reproach and shame of the
Enemy, these things could not be performed; for he who imagined that he could be God was made a mock of by a young
man, and he who boasted over flesh and blood was vanquished
by a man who was clothed with flesh.

* * *

And after these things he passed into another frame of mind,
and, having decided within himself that he would go forth from
the village, he departed and took up his abode in a tomb in the
cemetery, which was situated in a mountain which lay close by

the village; and he commanded one of his acquaintances to bring him a morsel of bread from time [to time]. And having done these things and entered into the tomb and shut the door upon himself, straightway the Adversary, together with a multitude of devils who were his associates, burst in upon him there, for he was afraid to let Saint Anthony go from the village altogether, and he began to say unto him, "How great is that which thou endurest! And to what limit wilt thou drive thyself? Thou hast come and hast entered into the place of our abode. What man is there who hath ever done the like? And when was it ever heard that men ought to live among the tombs? We have been driven out of the village, and we shall also be driven out from among the tombs. Now therefore will we take vengeance upon thee, for it is thou who hast made fools of us." Then they began to smite him with blows, and they smote him so severely that at length he fell [on the ground], and nothing but his breath was left in him; and Saint Anthony used to relate that the blows with which the devils smote him were more severe than those of the children of men. But God brought help unto him, and would not deliver him over to death, for He put it into the mind of him that used to visit him to come quickly, and to open [the door of] the tomb according to his wont, and he saw the blessed Anthony, who was like unto a dead man by reason of the blows; and straight way he lifted him up and brought him to the church in the village. And there collected about him no small number of people, and they gathered together and sat by his side as if he had been a dead man. Now by the sweet rest of sleep the blessed Anthony was refreshed, [and he was relieved] from his affliction, and he came to himself, and he turned round and saw that all the people were asleep, and that only his friend who was sitting watching by his pillow was awake; and he made a sign to him, and he drew nigh unto him, and Saint Anthony said unto him quietly, "Come, do [an act of] righteousness (or charity), lest the heart of the people should think and mankind should imagine that there is still power left in the Evil One, and should be afraid to lift up the heel against him."

And the man hearkened unto him, and whilst the people were quiet and asleep, he lifted him up and carried him to the tomb, and shut the door as usual. Then Saint Anthony prayed as he was lying down, for he had no power in him to stand up, and when he had multiplied [his] prayers, he said with a loud voice, "Where are ye, O children of Gehenna? Here am I, even I, Anthony, and I will not depart from this place until ye are destroyed in this place: for although ye multiply tortures, I shall not be remote from the love of Christ." And next he said with a loud voice, "Though a whole legion [of devils] encamp against me, my heart shall not fear": such were the words which this man, this athlete, proclaimed in his striving. Then the heart of the Enemy of righteousness melted within him, and he cried unto the dogs his kinsfolk, and spake, emitting smoke from himself as he did so, saying unto them, "Did ye not say unto me, What shall we do unto this man, this insolent fellow, who hath treated us wholly with contempt and disdain? His heart is not afraid of the quaking terror, his hearing is not perturbed by words (or voices), his eye is not terrified by visions, and his body hath no fear of blows. Who among you can give [me] counsel as to what shall be done [with him]?" And thereupon they contrived the following plan.

Now it is very easy for the Enemy to create apparitions and appearances of such a character that they shall be deemed real and actual objects, and [straightway] phantasms of this kind caused a phantom earthquake, and they rent asunder the four corners of the house, and entered therein in a body from all sides. One had the form of a lion, and another had the appearance of a wolf, and another was like unto a panther, and all the others were in the forms and similitudes of serpents, and of vipers, and of scorpions. The lion was roaring as a lion roareth when he is about to slay; the bull was ready to gore [him] with his horns; the panther was prepared to spring upon him; and the snakes and the vipers were hissing, and they appeared to be in the act of hurling themselves upon him; and the sounds which they made and the forms in which they showed themselves were terrible. Now the blessed man Anthony was not disturbed (or frightened) by their commotion, and his mind remained wholly undisturbed. And as he was lying down he laughed at these phantoms, and said, "Thus there is no power in you. Ye have taken unto yourselves the forms of wild beasts, and if there had been any power whatsoever to do harm in you, for one of you only to come [against me] would have been sufficient; but because our Lord hath cut off the things which incited you to attack me, and the goad of your wickedness hath no strength therein, ye lay plots and contrive snares, thinking that, peradventure, ye will be able to make men quake by fear only. And, moreover, whosoever hath had experience of your feebleness [knoweth] that ye have obtained as your helpers the mere forms and appearances of 'wild beasts.'"

* * *

Before this, however, it is proper for us to learn that the beings which are called devils were not created that they might be devils, for there is nothing evil in the works of God, and even they were created beautiful beings; but when they turned aside from the mind of righteousness, or from the heavenly understanding, they were removed to a distance from the place wherein they lived. And seeing that they were cast away by the exalted Will, they drew nigh and mingled themselves among the created beings of this world, and they made the heathen to go astray wholly according to their desire; and against us, because they have envy of us, they multiply their contendings that, peradventure, they may be able to turn us out of the way of the truth of the kingdom of heaven, and that we may not attain unto the country wherefrom they were swept out and fell. Therefore the labour of prayer and of abundant supplication is necessary for us, that through the Divine Providence, and through the gift which we have received from the Holy Spirit, we may be able to know what distinction existeth between the evil spirits, and what each one of them hath been commanded to [seek] after, and by what manner of means the destruction of every one of them is to be brought about. For their cunning is very great, and they spread abroad the mesh of their net in everything. Therefore the blessed Apostle and the rest of the righteous men, who like him had experience of and had tried the Tempter in every thing, and it is for this very reason that they have declared it, said, "The artifices of the Evil One shall not overcome us." And I will now narrate something of what I have endured from them, and a little of the vast knowledge which I have of them, and, like the beloved Prophets, I will tell what I understand about them.

The whole race of devils is beyond measure an envious one, and it is altogether jealous of all mankind, and particularly of the monks, for they cannot bear to see heavenly deeds wrought and heavenly lives led upon the earth, and they, therefore, make hidden pits and snares for us, as it is written, "They have laid their nets over my paths" (Psalm 57:7): now [the words] "their nets" mean thoughts of iniquity. Let us, however, be not afraid of their stirrings, and let us not be made lax by reason of their blandishments (or flatteries); but let us be constant in fasting and in prayer, and straightway they shall be vanquished and disappear. Now when they depart, let us not be confident and say, "Behold, they are put to shame, and we are freed from them", for this race of beings can never be put to shame, and they know not how to blush; for even whilst their temptations are being brought to naught on this side, they make an attack upon us on the other; and when they have examined and tried by what means our understanding may be flattered or terrified, they plan numberless schemes [to deceive us]. Now the devils are in the habit of leading men astray by declaring something such as the following: "Behold, we will inform you concerning the things which are about to take place," and then they show them mighty phantoms which reach up to the ceilings, so that by means of these similitudes they may lead astray those whom they are not able to injure in their minds.

MEDIEVAL EUROPE

CYNEWULF, "JULIANA"[1]

970–990

Saint Juliana of Nicomedia was a martyr who lived in what is now Italy and died around the beginning of the fourth century. The earliest reference to Juliana appears in the Martyrologium Hieronymianum, a list of Christian martyrs composed by Saint Jerome around the end of the fourth century. During the Middle Ages, Juliana became a popular saint, and the legend of her martyrdom grew. According to Saint Bede's account, composed in England in the eighth century, Juliana was betrothed to Eleusias, a pagan senator loyal to the emperor; Juliana had secretly converted to Christianity and refused the marriage, so Eleusias imprisoned and tortured her. When Juliana still spurned him, he had her beheaded.

Around the ninth century, an Anglo-Saxon poet named Cynewulf composed a poem called "Juliana" in Old English. The oldest surviving text of this poem dates to between 970 and 990. The text is damaged, so parts of the poem are lost to history. In Cynewulf's version of the story, after Juliana has been tortured and imprisoned, she is visited by a demon. The demon attempts to trick her into offering pagan sacrifices by pretending to be an angel. Juliana is not deceived and instead commands the devil to confess its evil deeds. Following this encounter, Eleusias attempts to boil Juliana in molten lead, but the lead miraculously fails to burn her. Finally, she is decapitated. Another account of Saint Juliana's encounter with the demon appears in The Golden Legend (Aurea Legenda), composed in 1265 by Jacobus de Voragine, archbishop of Genoa, demonstrating that this story was popular across Europe. By the Renaissance, there were several paintings

*of Juliana leading a humiliated devil by a chain around
his neck.*

*In Christian stories of exorcism, women are overwhelm-
ingly the ones in need of exorcism. Cynewulf's tale, which
was likely adapted from older Latin sources, is a rare account of a woman commanding and interrogating a demon.
Though a prisoner, Juliana is described by Cynewulf in
martial terms as "a valiant champion" and "bold in combat beyond all womankind." The demon confesses that
not even the patriarchs or the prophets exerted such power
over it.*

*Juliana's interrogation frames a demonological text out-
lining the nature of demons. The demon confesses first to
tempting people, then having influenced the villains of the
New Testament such as Herod and Simon Magus, and finally to killing people outright either directly or through
causing shipwrecks, drunken sword fights in the wine hall,
and other hazards common to Anglo-Saxon culture. There
is also some suggestion here of sympathy for the demon,
who begs for mercy and explains that demons who fail
Satan fear punishment in hell.*

Then was the door of the prison fastened with a bolt, the work
of the hammer. And within the holy maid endured faithful;
and ever in the prison, covered with darkness, in her heart she
praised the King of glory, the Lord of heaven, the Saviour of
men. And the Holy Ghost was a constant companion unto her.
Then suddenly came into the prison the Enemy of mankind,
skilled in evil; and he had the form of an angel. Wise was he in
afflictions, this enemy of the soul, this captive of hell, and unto
the holy maid he said:

"Why sufferest thou who art most dear and precious to the
King of glory, our God. This judge hath prepared for thee the
worst tortures, torment without end, if thou wilt not prudently
sacrifice and make propitiation unto his gods. Be thou in haste
when he bids thee be led outward hence, that thou make a

sacrifice, an offering of victory, before that death come upon thee, death in the presence of the warriors. In this wise shalt thou survive the anger of this judge, O blessed maid!"

But straightway did she, acceptable unto Christ, in no wise dismayed, ask whence he was come. And the outcast made answer unto her:

"I am an angel of God, come from above, His noble follower, sent unto thee in holiness from heaven. For thee cruel tortures, with woeful wounds, are prepared in punishment. The Lord bids thee, child of God, that thou avert them."

Then was the maid stricken with terror for the fearful message which the minister, the Enemy of heaven, declared unto her. And steadfastly in her youth and innocence she began to strengthen her heart and call upon God:

"Now, O Protector of man, Eternal and Almighty! do I entreat Thee by that noble creation which Thou, the Father of angels, didst establish in the beginning, that Thou let me not turn aside from the praise of Thy grace, as this messenger who standeth before me, declareth unto me—a fearsome message. Likewise, O Innocent One! I do entreat Thee that Thou make known to me, O Thou Glory of kings, Thou God of splendour, who this flying minister may be, that he doth urge me away from Thee upon the down-hill road!"

Then unto her spake a glorious voice from the clouds, and uttered this word:

"Do thou seize this vile one and hold him fast, till that he rightly declare unto thee his purpose, even from the beginning what his kinship may be."

And the heart of the glorious maid was glad; and she seized upon that devil. . . .

[. . .]

"to deliver up to death the King of all kings. And I wrought that the warrior wounded the Lord of hosts, while the army gazed upon it, until that blood and water together fell to the ground. I stirred up Herod in heart that he gave order to behead John, for that he reproved with words his love of wife, his unrighteous wedlock. Also with malice I taught Simon, so that he began to strive against the chosen followers of Christ, and with shame assailed those holy men, saying that they were wizards. With sharp wiles I dared to delude Nero so that he bade the followers of Christ, Peter and Paul, be given over unto death. By my teachings did Pilate formerly hang upon the cross the Ruler of the heavens, the mighty Lord. In like wise also did I incite Hegias, so that in his folly he bade the holy Andrew to be hanged to an high tree, and sent forth his spirit from the gallows, in a splendour of glory. Thus among my brothers I wrought many a deed of evil, of black sin, which I may not tell, nor fully relate nor know the countless number of my cruel, malicious thoughts."

Then by the grace of the Holy Ghost the blessed Juliana spake unto him:

"More fully yet, Enemy of man, shalt thou disclose thine errand; who sent thee unto me?"

And unto her the monster gave answer, dismayed, discovered, without hope of peace:

"Behold, my father, the king of the inhabitants of hell, sent me hither from that narrow home on this journey unto thee. And he in that abode of misery is more eager in every evil than I. When he sendeth us that we, through deceit, pervert the hearts of the righteous, and turn them from salvation, we are sad in heart, dismayed in mind. Nor is he a merciful lord unto us, but a terrible prince; and if we have done no evil, then dare we not enter in unto his presence. But he sendeth forth his ministers of darkness throughout the spacious earth, and biddeth them that they stir up violence, and if we are to be found upon the earthly path, or are come upon far or near, that they bind us and scourge us in torments of fire. And if through corruptions we pervert not the souls of the righteous, the hearts of the holy, then suffer we the hardest and most grievous punishments through painful blows. Now mayest thou know truly in thy heart that I was needs compelled unto this boldness, time and again afflicted, that I seek thee out."

Then still did the holy maid purpose to question the Enemy of man, the doer of evil, the contriver of sin: "Thou shalt more fully tell me, thou Enemy of souls, how thou, through sinful snares, dost work grievous harm unto the righteous, encompassed round about with malice."

Unto her the fiend replied, the faithless outcast: "I may easily make known unto thee the beginning of every evil, even unto the end, of those which I, on many a journey, have wrought with wounds of sin, that thou mayest thus more clearly know that this is truth and nowise false. For I hoped and deemed it certain in my heart that without difficulty I might, by my strength alone, turn thee from Salvation, so that thou shouldest withstand the King of heaven, the Lord of victories, and bow thee down to lesser gods, and sacrifice unto the Prince of evil. Thus in varied forms do I pervert the mind of the righteous man. When I find him establish his heart upon the will of God, then am I at once ready so that against him I bring manifold vices of the mind, cruel thoughts and secret errors. Through a multitude of snares I make sweet unto him the pleasures of sin, wicked desires of the heart, so that quickly given over unto unrighteousness, he hearkeneth unto my teachings. And I grievously inflame him with sin, so that, burning, he ceaseth from prayer and walketh insolently, nor may he steadfastly remain longer in the place of prayer, for the love of his sin. So I bring hateful error unto that man to whom I begrudge life and a clear belief. And he doth willfully hearken unto my teachings, and commit sin, and afterward, bereft of virtue, he slippeth away. But if I meet any courageous man, a valiant champion of the Lord against the sting of my arrows, who will not flee far thence from the battle, but, bold in heart, lifteth his shield against me, his holy buckler, a spiritual armour; who will not desert his God but, bold in prayer, standeth at bay in his course, then must I flee away from that place, humiliated, cut off from joy, and in the embrace of fire lament my sorrows, that I might not in battle, by cunning of strength, overcome. But I shall wretchedly seek out another less powerful man, under the banners of a slower champion, whom I may arouse by my incitements and impede in the warfare. And though spiritually he purpose some good thing, I am at once ready to read his every secret thought, to observe how his heart is strengthened within him, and how his resistance is wrought. And through sins I open the gate of this wall; when the tower is pierced, the entrance laid open, then I send into his breast by my arrows bitter thoughts, through various desires of the heart, so that it seemeth better to him to accomplish sins and lusts of the body, contrary to the worship of God. I am an eager teacher, that he may live after my evil fashions, turned openly from the law of Christ, corrupted in heart, for me to rule in the pit of sins. In this man I care more eagerly for the destruction of the spirit than of the flesh, which in a grave, hidden in the earth, shall become in the world a pleasure to the worm."

Then again the maid spake:

"Tell me, misshapen, unclean spirit, inciter of evils, how thou didst force thyself into the company of the more pure. Thou of old unfaithful didst strive and war with Christ, and didst plot against the holy. The pit of hell was digged below thee and there, driven by misery, for thy pride, thou didst seek out an abode. I deemed that thou wouldst be more wary and less bold in such an encounter against the righteous man, who through the King of glory hath oft withstood thy will."

And the miserable, accursed monster replied unto her and said:

"Do thou first tell me how thou bravely, by deep thought, became thus bold in combat beyond all womankind, so that thou hast thus firmly bound me with fetters, wholly powerless to resist. Thou didst put thy trust in the Eternal God sitting in glory, the Lord of mankind, as I establish my hope upon my father, the ruler of the dwellers in hell; and when I am sent forth against the righteous man, that in evil deeds I may pervert his heart and turn his soul from salvation, at times through resistance my will is denied to me, my hope at the hands of the holy, even as sorrow here came upon me in my journey. This I myself perceive, but all too late. Now shall I long, because of this evil-doing, suffer shame. Therefore, I entreat thee by the might of the Most High, by the grace of the King of heaven who suffered on the cross, the Prince of glory, that thou pity me in my distress, that I may not wholly perish miserably, though boldly and thus foolhardily I sought thee on this journey, when I aforetime expected no such plight as this."

Then the fair candle of splendour said unto that traitor:

"Thou shalt confess more deeds of evil, thou base spirit of hell, ere thou mayest go hence; what many deeds of wickedness thou hast accomplished with thy dark delusions for an injury to the children of men."

And to her the Devil made answer:

"Now by thy utterance I know that, constrained by hatred, I must needs lay bare my heart as thou biddest me, and endure compulsion. This plight is full hard, this calamity measureless. I shall suffer and endure everything in thy judgment, disclose the dark deeds of evil which I long have wrought. Oft I took away sight, and blinded countless numbers of the children of men with evil thoughts; and covered with a veil of mist, through a poisonous breath, and with dark showers, the light of the eye; and I destroyed the feet of some with snares. Some I sent into the fire, unto the embrace of the flames, which was the last visible sign of their footsteps. Eke for some I wrought it that their bodies spurted blood, and they suddenly gave forth their life through an outpouring of the veins. Some by my might upon the sea were drowned in the waters, upon their course on the ocean-stream, under the raging flood. Some I gave over to the cross, so that they miserably laid down their lives upon the high gallows. Some I induced by my evil devices to commit strife, so that they suddenly renewed old quarrels, drunk with beer. I poured out to them discord from the cup, so that they in the wine-hall, through the clash of swords, gave forth their lives from the body, and, doomed to death, hasted away, visited with pains. Some whom I found without God's token, neglected and unblessed, these I boldly slew with various deaths at my hands with malice. I may not tell, although I sit a long summer day, all the sorrows that early and late by treachery I have wrought, since first the heavens were lifted up, and the path of the stars, and the earth established, and the first men, Adam and Eve, whom I deprived of life and taught them, so that they forsook the love of the Lord of hosts, eternal grace and the bright prosperity of home; and misery came upon them both forever, and on their children, darkest of evil deeds. Why should I recount more of endless evil? I have brought forth all fierce crimes throughout the nations, which came to pass in the long ages from the beginning of the world, for mankind, for men on earth. No one of these there was who dared thus boldly, as thou hast now dared in thy holiness to touch me with thy hands; no man thus courageous upon earth in holy might, no one of the patriarchs, nor of the prophets; although the Lord of hosts, the King of glory, revealed unto them a spirit of wisdom and measureless grace, yet might I have approach unto them. No one of them so boldly covered me with bonds, or afflicted me with woes, before thou didst overcome and lay firm hold upon that great power, which my father, the enemy of mankind, gave unto me, when he, my prince, bade me go from out the darkness that I might make sweet unto thee sin. Then sorrow came upon me and heavy strife. After this sore distress I may not rejoice over this journey in the company of my fellows, when I miserably in my mournful home shall render up the penalty."

THOMAS AQUINAS, THE POWERS OF ANGELS AND DEMONS[1]

1274

Thomas Aquinas (1225–1274) was an Italian theologian and philosopher. His work integrated the work of Aristotle, as well as Arab philosophers, into a unified system of Christian thought. His magnum opus, The Summa Theologica, *remains a fundamental text of Roman Catholic theology. The* Summa *is a massive text, broken into three parts, in which Aquinas answers hundreds of questions about theology. Each question includes several articles in which he raises potential "objections" or areas of confusion the reader may have before presenting an answer supported by both Scripture and philosophical arguments. Aquinas was interested in angels and, by extension, demons, and dedicates several questions in Part I to explaining their nature and abilities. Although he rarely discusses possession and exorcism directly, several questions explore how angels and demons can influence the human mind.*

In Question 111, "The Action of the Angels on Man," Aquinas argues that while angels and demons cannot change human will, they are able to alter human senses and influence the human imagination. (But Aquinas specifies that they cannot inspire in the imagination anything that cannot be perceived by the senses. Thus, demons cannot cause a man born blind to imagine color.)

Question 114, "Of the Assaults of the Demons," explores the nature and purpose of demonic attacks on human beings, especially temptation. Like previous theo-

logians, Aquinas explains that the powers of demons are limited but that they enjoy convincing humans that their powers are godlike. God alone can perform true miracles; demons can perform miracles only in the sense of "rousing man's astonishment." Aquinas concludes this section by discussing whether demons who have been overcome by man may ever resume their assaults.

QUESTION 111:
THE ACTION OF THE ANGELS ON MAN

Whether the Angels Can Change the Will of Man?

Objection 1: It would seem that the angels can change the will of man. For, upon the text, *Who maketh His angels spirits and His ministers a flame of fire* (Heb. 1:7), the gloss notes that *they are fire, as being spiritually fervent, and as burning away our vices.* This could not be, however, unless they changed the will. Therefore the angels can change the will.

Obj. 2: Further, Bede says (*Super Matth.* 15:11), *that, the devil does not send wicked thoughts, but kindles them.* Damascene, however, says that he also sends them; for he remarks that "every malicious act and unclean passion is contrived by the demons and put into men" (*De Fide. Orth.* 2:4); in like manner also the good angels introduce and kindle good thoughts. But this could only be if they changed the will. Therefore the will is changed by them.

Obj. 3: Further, the angel, as above explained, enlightens the human intellect by means of the phantasms. But as the imagination which serves the intellect can be changed by an angel, so can the sensitive appetite which serves the will, because it also is a faculty using a corporeal organ. Therefore as the angel enlightens the mind, so can he change the will.

On the contrary, To change the will belongs to God alone, according to Prov. 21:1: *The heart of the king is in the hand of the Lord, whithersoever He will He shall turn it.*

I answer that, The will can be changed in two ways. First, from within; in which way, since the movement of the will is nothing but the inclination of the will to the thing willed, God alone can thus change the will, because He gives the power of such an inclination to the intellectual nature. For as the natural inclination is from God alone Who gives the nature, so the inclination of the will is from God alone, Who causes the will.

Secondly, the will is moved from without. As regards an angel, this can be only in one way—by the good apprehended by the intellect. Hence in as far as anyone may be the cause why anything be apprehended as an appetible[2] good, so far does he move the will. In this way also God alone can move the will efficaciously; but an angel and man move the will by way of persuasion, as above explained (Q[106], A[2]).

In addition to this mode the human will can be moved from without in another way; namely, by the passion residing in the sensitive appetite: thus by concupiscence or anger the will is inclined to will something. In this manner the angels, as being able to rouse these passions, can move the will, not however by necessity, for the will ever remains free to consent to, or to resist, the passion.

Reply Obj. 1: Those who act as God's ministers, either men or angels, are said to burn away vices, and to incite to virtue by way of persuasion.

Reply Obj. 2: The demon cannot put thoughts in our minds by causing them from within, since the act of the cogitative faculty is subject to the will; nevertheless the devil is called the kindler of thoughts, inasmuch as he incites to thought, by the desire of the things thought of, by way of persuasion, or by rousing the passions. Damascene calls this kindling *a putting in* because such a work is accomplished within. But good thoughts are attributed to a higher principle, namely, God, though they may be procured by the ministry of the angels.

Reply Obj. 3: The human intellect in its present state can understand only by turning to the phantasms; but the human will can will something following the judgment of reason rather than the passion of the sensitive appetite. Hence the comparison does not hold.

Whether an Angel Can Change Man's Imagination?

Objection 1: It would seem that an angel cannot change man's imagination. For the phantasy, as is said *De Anima* iii, is *a motion caused by the sense in act.* But if this motion were caused by an angel, it would not be caused by the sense in act. Therefore it is contrary to the nature of the phantasy, which is the act of the imaginative faculty, to be changed by an angel.

Obj. 2: Further, since the forms in the imagination are spiritual, they are nobler than the forms existing in sensible matter. But an angel cannot impress forms upon sensible matter (Q[110], A[2]). Therefore he cannot impress forms on the imagination, and so he cannot change it.

Obj. 3: Further, Augustine says (*Gen. ad lit.* 12:12): *One spirit by intermingling with another can communicate his knowledge to the other spirit by these images, so that the latter either understands it himself, or accepts it as understood by the other.* But it does not seem that an angel can be mingled with the human imagination, nor that the imagination can receive the knowledge of an angel. Therefore it seems that an angel cannot change the imagination.

Obj. 4: Further, in the imaginative vision man cleaves to the similitudes of the things as to the things themselves. But in this there is deception. So as a good angel cannot be the cause of deception, it seems that he cannot cause the imaginative vision, by changing the imagination.

On the contrary, Those things which are seen in dreams are seen by imaginative vision. But the angels reveal things in dreams, as appears from Matt. (1:20; 2:13, 2:19) in regard to the angel who appeared to Joseph in dreams. Therefore an angel can move the imagination.

I answer that, Both a good and a bad angel by their own natural power can move the human imagination. This may be explained as follows. For it was said above (Q[110], A[3]), that corporeal nature obeys the angel as regards local movement, so that whatever can be caused by the local movement of bodies is subject to the natural power of the angels. Now it is manifest that imaginative apparitions are sometimes caused in us by the local movement of animal spirits and humors. Hence Aristotle says (*De Somn. et Vigil.*), when assigning the cause of visions in dreams, that *when an animal sleeps, the blood descends in abundance to the sensitive principle, and movements descend with it,* that is, the impressions left from the movements of sensible things, which movements are preserved in the animal spirits, *and move the sensitive principle*; so that a certain appearance ensues, as if the sensitive principle were being then changed by the external objects themselves. Indeed, the commotion of the spirits and humors may be so great that such appearances may even occur to those who are awake, as is seen in mad people, and the like. So, as this happens by a natural disturbance of the humors, and sometimes also by the will of man who voluntarily imagines what he previously experienced, so also the same may be done by the power of a good or a bad angel, sometimes with alienation from the bodily senses, sometimes without such alienation.

Reply Obj. 1: The first principle of the imagination is from the sense in act. For we cannot imagine what we have never perceived by the senses, either wholly or partly; as a man born blind cannot imagine color. Sometimes, however, the imagination is informed in such a way that the act of the imaginative movement arises from the impressions preserved within.

Reply Obj. 2: An angel changes the imagination, not indeed by the impression of an imaginative form in no way previously received from the senses (for he cannot make a man born blind imagine color), but by local movement of the spirits and humors, as above explained.

Reply Obj. 3: The commingling of the angelic spirit with the human imagination is not a mingling of essences, but by reason of an effect which he produces in the imagination in the way above stated; so that he shows man what he [the angel] knows, but not in the way he knows.

Reply Obj. 4: An angel causing an imaginative vision, sometimes enlightens the intellect at the same time, so that it knows what these images signify; and then there is not deception. But sometimes by the angelic operation the similitudes of things only appear in the imagination; but neither then is deception caused by the angel, but by the defect in the intellect to whom such things appear. Thus neither was Christ a cause of deception when He spoke many things to the people in parables, which He did not explain to them.

Whether an Angel Can Change the Human Senses?

Objection 1: It seems that an angel cannot change the human senses. For the sensitive operation is a vital operation. But such an operation does not come from an extrinsic principle. Therefore the sensitive operation cannot be caused by an angel.

Obj. 2: Further, the sensitive operation is nobler than the nutritive. But the angel cannot change the nutritive power, nor other natural forms. Therefore neither can he change the sensitive power.

Obj. 3: Further, the senses are naturally moved by the sensible objects. But an angel cannot change the order of nature (Q[110], A[4]). Therefore an angel cannot change the senses; but these are changed always by the sensible object.

On the contrary, The angels who overturned Sodom, *struck the people of Sodom with blindness or* ἀορασία, *so that they could not find the door* (Gen. 19:11). The same is recorded of the Syrians whom Eliseus led into Samaria (4 Kings 6:18).

I answer that, The senses may be changed in a twofold manner; from without, as when affected by the sensible object: and from within, for we see that the senses are changed when the spirits and humors are disturbed; as for example, a sick man's tongue, charged with choleric humor, tastes everything as bitter, and the like with the other senses. Now an angel, by his natural power, can work a change in the senses both ways. For an angel can offer the senses a sensible object from without, formed by nature or by the angel himself, as when he assumes a body, as we have said above (Q[51], A[2]). Likewise he can move the spirits and humors from within, as above remarked, whereby the senses are changed in various ways.

Reply Obj. 1: The principle of the sensitive operation cannot be without the interior principle which is the sensitive power; but this interior principle can be moved in many ways by the exterior principle, as above explained.

Reply Obj. 2: By the interior movement of the spirits and humors an angel can do something towards changing the act of the nutritive power, and also of the appetitive and sensitive power, and of any other power using a corporeal organ.

Reply Obj. 3: An angel can do nothing outside the entire order of creatures; but he can outside some particular order of nature, since he is not subject to that order; thus in some special way an angel can work a change in the senses outside the common mode of nature.

QUESTION 114:
OF THE ASSAULTS OF THE DEMONS

Whether Demons Can Lead Men Astray by Means of Real Miracles?

Objection 1: It would seem that the demons cannot lead men astray by means of real miracles. For the activity of the demons will show itself especially in the works of Antichrist. But as the Apostle says (2 Thess. 2:9), his *coming is according to the working of Satan, in all power, and signs, and lying wonders.* Much more therefore at other times do the demons perform lying wonders.

Obj. 2: Further, true miracles are wrought by some corporeal change. But demons are unable to change the nature of a body; for Augustine says (*De Civ. Dei* 18:18): *I cannot believe that the human body can receive the limbs of a beast by means of a demon's art or power.* Therefore the demons cannot work real miracles.

Obj. 3: Further, an argument is useless which may prove both ways. If therefore real miracles can be wrought by demons, to persuade one of what is false, they will be useless to confirm the teaching of faith. This is unfitting; for it is written (Mark 16:20): *The Lord working withal, and confirming the word with signs that followed.*

On the contrary, Augustine says (Q[83]); *Often by means of the magic art miracles are wrought like those which are wrought by the servants of God.*

I answer that, As is clear from what has been said above (Q[110], A[4]), if we take a miracle in the strict sense, the demons cannot work miracles, nor can any creature, but God alone: since in the strict sense a miracle is something done outside the order of the entire created nature, under which order every power of a creature is contained. But sometimes miracle may be taken in a wide sense, for whatever exceeds the human power and experience. And thus demons can work miracles, that is, things which rouse man's astonishment, by reason of their being beyond his power and outside his sphere of knowledge. For even a man by doing what is beyond the power and knowledge of another, leads him to marvel at what he has done, so that in a way he seems to that man to have worked a miracle.

It is to be noted, however, that although these works of demons which appear marvelous to us are not real miracles, they are sometimes nevertheless something real. Thus the magicians of Pharaoh by the demons' power produced real serpents and frogs. And *when fire came down from heaven and at one blow consumed Job's servants and sheep; when the storm struck down his house and with it his children—these were the work of Satan, not phantoms*; as Augustine says (*De Civ. Dei* 20:19).

Reply Obj. 1: As Augustine says in the same place, the works of Antichrist may be called lying wonders, *either because he will deceive men's senses by means of phantoms, so that he will not really do what he will seem to do; or because, if he work real prodigies, they will lead those into falsehood who believe in him.*

Reply Obj. 2: As we have said above (Q[110], A[2]), corporeal matter does not obey either good or bad angels at their will, so that demons be able by their power to transmute matter from one form to another; but they can employ certain seeds that exist in the elements of the world, in order to produce these effects, as Augustine says (*De Trin.* 3: 8,9). Therefore it must be admitted that all the transformations of corporeal things which can be produced by certain natural powers, to which we must assign the seeds above mentioned, can alike be produced by the operation of the demons, by the employment of these seeds; such as the transformation of certain things into serpents or frogs, which can be produced by putrefaction. On the contrary, those transformations which cannot be produced by the power of nature, cannot in reality be effected by the operation of the demons; for instance, that the human body be changed into the body of a beast, or that the body of a dead man return to life. And if at times something of this sort seems to be effected by the operation of demons, it is not real but a mere semblance of reality.

Now this may happen in two ways. Firstly, from within; in this way a demon can work on man's imagination and even on his corporeal senses, so that something seems otherwise that it is, as explained above (Q[111], AA[3, 4]). It is said indeed that this can be done sometimes by the power of certain bodies. Secondly, from without: for just as he can from the air form a body of any form and shape, and assume it so as to appear in it visibly: so, in the same way he can clothe any corporeal thing with any corporeal form, so as to appear therein. This is what Augustine says (*De Civ. Dei* 18:18): *Man's imagination, which whether thinking or dreaming, takes the forms of an innumerable number of things, appears to other men's senses, as it were embodied in the semblance of some animal.* This not to be understood as though the imagination itself or the images formed therein were identified with that which appears embodied to the senses of another man: but that the demon, who forms an image in a man's imagination, can offer the same picture to another man's senses.

Reply Obj. 3: As Augustine says (QQ. 83, qu. 79): *When magicians do what holy men do, they do it for a different end and by a different right. The former do it for their own glory; the latter, for the glory of God: the former, by certain private compacts; the latter by the evident assistance and command of God, to Whom every creature is subject.*

Whether a Demon Who Is Overcome by Man, Is for This Reason Hindered from Making Further Assaults?

Objection 1: It would seem that a demon who is overcome by a man, is not for that reason hindered from any further assault. For Christ overcame the tempter most effectively. Yet afterwards the demon assailed Him by instigating the Jews to kill Him. Therefore it is not true that the devil when conquered ceases his assaults.

Obj. 2: Further, to inflict punishment on one who has been worsted in a fight, is to incite him to a sharper attack. But this is not befitting God's mercy. Therefore the conquered demons are not prevented from further assaults.

On the contrary, It is written (Matt. 4:11): *Then the devil left Him, i.e.* Christ Who overcame.

I answer that, Some say that when once a demon has been overcome he can no more tempt any man at all, neither to the same nor to any other sin. And others say that he can tempt others, but not the same man. This seems more probable as long as we understand it to be so for a certain definite time: wherefore (Luke 4:13) it is written: *All temptation being ended, the devil departed from Him for a time.* There are two reasons for this. One is on the part of God's clemency; for as Chrysostom says (*Super Matt. Hom. 5*), *the devil does not tempt man for just as long as he likes, but for as long as God allows; for although He allows him to tempt for a short time, He orders him off on account of our weakness.* The other reason is taken from the astuteness of the devil. As to this, Ambrose says on Luke 4:13: *The devil is afraid of persisting, because he shrinks from frequent defeat.* That the devil does nevertheless sometimes return to the assault, is apparent from Matthew 12:44: *I will return into my house from whence I came out.*

From what has been said, the objections can easily be solved.

EARLY MODERN
EUROPE AND
AMERICA

DESIDERIUS ERASMUS, "THE EXORCISM OR APPARITION"[1]

1518

Desiderius Erasmus (1469–1536) was a Dutch scholar, priest, and leading figure of Renaissance humanism. He studied and taught ancient Greek and Latin and encouraged a revival of the Greco-Roman classics in Europe. Erasmus was skeptical of the supernatural and encouraged reform of the medieval church. However, as the Protestant Reformation unfolded, he critiqued both the pope and Martin Luther.

The Colloquies of Erasmus was published in Latin in 1518. It consists of dialogues between characters on a range of topics, often delivered in an ironic tone. "The Exorcism or Apparition" is a dialogue between two friends, Thomas and Anselm (Tho. and Ans. in the text). Anselm is recounting how his friend Polus played an elaborate trick on a priest named Faunus, causing him to believe he had successfully exorcised a damned spirit. Needless to say, Erasmus seems highly skeptical of claims about exorcism. Whereas skeptics often attribute stories of exorcism to a misunderstanding of mental illness or other natural phenomena, Erasmus suggests that these stories are more often the result of conscious deception. Significantly, Polus has no discernible motive for deceiving the priest: he does it because "His Fancy lies that Way." Faunus compounds the deception by retelling the story and adding even more fantastic details: People lie to us and we lie to ourselves.

This colloquy contains some interesting insights into the culture of exorcism during the Renaissance. The rite of exorcism found in The Ritual Romanum *would not be formalized for another century. Instead, the priest performs a ritual using sacred objects while standing inside a magical circle. The text also describes a belief that the Devil knows everyone's sins, but that sins that have been admitted during the sacrament of confession are "struck out of the Devil's memory." This belief is presented in the works of modern demonologists such as Ed and Lorraine Warren, but Erasmus shows it dates back at least to the Renaissance.*[2]

Tho. I know the Humour of the Man well enough. But to the Story of the Apparition.

Ans. In the mean Time, one Faunus a Priest (of those which in Latin they call Regulars, but that is not enough, unless they add the same in Greek too, who was Parson of a neighbouring Parish, this Man thought himself wiser than is common, especially in holy Matters) came very opportunely to pay a Visit to Polus.

Tho. I understand the Matter: There is one found out to be an Actor in this Play.

Ans. At Supper a Discourse was raised of the Report of this Apparition, and when Polus perceiv'd that Faunus had not only heard of the Report, but believ'd it, he began to intreat the Man, that as he was a holy and a learned Person, he would afford some Relief to a poor Soul that was in such dreadful Torment: And, says he, if you are in any Doubt as to the Truth of it, examine into the Matter, and do but walk near that Bridge about ten a-Clock, and you shall hear miserable Cries; take who you will for a Companion along with you, and so you will hear both more safely and better.

Tho. Well, what then?

Ans. After Supper was over, Polus, as his Custom was, goes a Hunting or Fowling. And when it grew duskish, the Darkness having taken away all Opportunity of making any certain Judgment of any Thing, Faunus walks about, and at last hears miserable Howlings. Polus having hid himself in a Bramble Hedge

DESIDERIUS ERASMUS, "THE EXORCISM OR APPARITION"   63

hard by, had very artfully made these Howlings, by speaking through an earthen Pot; the Voice coming through the Hollow of it, gave it a most mournful Sound.

Tho. This Story, as far as I see, out-does Menander's *Phasma.*[3]

Ans. You'll say more, if you shall hear it out. Faunus goes Home, being impatient to tell what he had heard. Polus taking a shorter Way, had got Home before him. Faunus up and tells Polus all that past, and added something of his own to it, to make the Matter more wonderful.

Tho. Could Polus keep his Countenance in the mean Time?

Ans. He keep his Countenance! He has his Countenance in his Hand, you would have said that a serious Affair was transacted. In the End Faunus, upon the pressing Importunity of Polus, undertakes the Business of Exorcism, and slept not one Wink all that Night, in contriving by what Means he might go about the Matter with Safety, for he was wretchedly afraid. In the first Place he got together the most powerful Exorcisms that he could get, and added some new ones to them, as the Bowels of the Virgin Mary, and the Bones of St. Winifred. After that, he makes Choice of a Place in the plain Field, near the Bramble Bushes, from whence the Voice came. He draws a very large Circle with a great many Crosses in it, and a Variety of Characters. And all this was perform'd in a set Form of Words; there was also there a great Vessel full of holy Water, and about his Neck he had a holy Stole (as they call'd it) upon which hung the Beginning of the Gospel of John. He had in his Pocket a little Piece of Wax, which the Bishop of Rome used to consecrate once a Year, which is commonly call'd Agnus Dei.[4] With these Arms in Times past, they were wont to defend themselves against evil Spirits, before the Cowl of St. Francis was found to be so formidable. All these Things were provided, lest if it should be an evil Spirit it should fall foul upon the Exorcist: nor did he for all this, dare to trust himself in the Circle alone, but he determined to take some other Priest along with him. Upon this Polus being afraid, that if he took some sharper Fellow than himself along with him, the whole Plot might come to be discover'd, he got a Parish-Priest thereabout, whom he acquainted before-hand with the whole Design; and indeed it was necessary for the carrying on the Adventure, and he was a Man fit for such a Purpose. The Day following, all Things being prepared and in good Order, about ten a-Clock Faunus and the Parish-Priest enter the Circle. Polus had got thither before them, and made a miserable Howling out of the Hedge; Faunus begins his Exorcism, and Polus steals away in the Dark to the next Village, and brings from thence another Person, for the Play could not be acted without a great many of them.

Tho. Well, what do they do?

Ans. They mount themselves upon black Horses, and privately carry Fire along with them; when they come pretty near to the Circle, they shew the Fire to affright Faunus out of the Circle.

Tho. What a Deal of Pains did this Polus take to put a Cheat upon People?

Ans. His Fancy lies that Way. But this Matter had like to have been mischievous to them.

Tho. How so?

Ans. For the Horses were so startled at the sudden flashing of the Fire, that they had like to have thrown their Riders. Here's an End of the first Act of this Comedy. When they were returned and entered into Discourse, Polus, as though he had known nothing of the Matter, enquires what was done. Faunus tells him, that two hideous Cacodaemons⁵ appear'd to him on black Horses, their Eyes sparkling with Fire, and breathing Fire out of their Nostrils, making an Attempt to break into the Circle, but that they were driven away with a Vengeance, by the Power and Efficacy of his Words. This Encounter having put Courage into Faunus, the next Day he goes into his Circle again with great Solemnity, and after he had provok'd the Spirit a long Time with the Vehemence of his Words, Polus and his Companion appear again at a pretty Distance, with their black Horses, with a most outragious Noise, making a Feint, as if they would break into the Circle.

Tho. Had they no Fire then?

Ans. No, none at all; for that had lik'd to have fallen out very unluckily to them. But hear another Device: They drew a long Rope over the Ground, and then hurrying from one Place to another, as though they were beat off by the Exorcisms of Faunus, they threw down both the Priest and holy Water-Pot all together.

Tho. This Reward the Parish-Priest had for playing his Part?

Ans. Yes, he had; and for all that, he had rather suffer this than quit the Design. After this Encounter, when they came to talk over the Matter again, Faunus tells a mighty Story to Polus, what great Danger he had been in, and how couragiously he had driven both the evil Spirits away with his Charms, and now he had arriv'd at a firm Persuasion, that there was no Daemon, let him be ever so mischievous or impudent, that could possibly break into this Circle.

Tho. This Faunus was not far from being a Fool.

Ans. You have heard nothing yet. The Comedy being thus far advanc'd, Polus's Son-in-Law comes in very good Time, for he had married Polus's eldest Daughter; he's a wonderful merry Droll, you know.

Tho. Know him! Ay, I know him, that he has no Aversion for such Tricks as these.

Ans. No Aversion, do you say, nay he would leave the most urgent Affair in the World, if such a Comedy were either to be seen or acted. His Father-in-Law tells him the whole Story, and gives him his Part, that was, to act the Ghost. He puts on a Dress, and wraps himself up in a Shrowd, and carrying a live Coal in a Shell, it appear'd through his Shrowd as if something were burning. About Night he goes to the Place where this Play was acted, there were heard most doleful Moans. Faunus lets fly all his Exorcisms. At Length the Ghost appears a good Way off in the Bushes, every now and then shewing the Fire, and making a rueful Groaning. While Faunus was adjuring the Ghost to declare who he was, Polus of a sudden leaps out of the Thicket, dress'd like a Devil, and making a Roaring, answers him, "You have nothing to do with this Soul, it is mine"; and every now and then runs to the very Edge of the Circle, as if he would set upon the Exorcist, and then retired back again, as if he was beaten back by the Words of the Exorcism, and the Power of the holy Water, which he threw upon him in great Abundance. At last when this guardian Devil was chased away,

Faunus enters into a Dialogue with the Soul. After he had been
interrogated and abjured, he answers, that he was the Soul of
a Christian Man, and being asked his Name, he answered Faunus. Faunus! replies the other, that's my Name. So then they
being Name-Sakes, he laid the Matter more to Heart, that Faunus might deliver Faunus. Faunus asking a Multitude of Questions, lest a long Discourse should discover the Fraud, the Ghost
retires, saying it was not permitted to stay to talk any longer,
because its Time was come, that it must go whither its Devil
pleased to carry it; but yet promised to come again the next
Day, at what Hour it could be permitted. They meet together
again at Polus's House, who was the Master of the Show. There
the Exorcist relates what was done, and tho' he added some
Lies to the Story, yet he believed them to be true himself, he
was so heartily affected with the Matter in Hand. At last it appeared manifestly, that it was the Soul of a Christian who was
vexed with the dreadful Torments of an unmerciful Devil: Now
all the Endeavours are bent this Way. There happened a ridiculous Passage in the next Exorcism.

Tho. Prithee what was that?

Ans. When Faunus had called up the Ghost, Polus, that acted
the Devil, leap'd directly at him, as if he would, without any
more to do, break into the Circle; and Faunus he resisted stoutly
with his Exorcisms, and had thrown a power of holy Water,
the Devil at last cries out, that he did not value all this of a
Rush; "you have had to do with a Wench, and you are my own
yourself." And tho' Polus said so in Jest, it seemed that he had
spoken Truth: For the Exorcist being touched with this Word,
presently retreated to the very Centre of the Circle, and whispered something in the Priest's Ear. Polus seeing that, retires,
that he might not hear what it was not fit for him to hear.

Tho. In Truth, Polus was a very modest, religious Devil.

Ans. He was so, otherwise he might have been blamed for
not observing a Decorum, but yet he heard the Priest's Voice
appointing him Satisfaction.

Tho. What was that?

Ans. That he should say the glorious 78th Psalm, three Times over, by which he conjectured he had had to do with her three Times that Night.

Tho. He was an irregular Regular.

Ans. They are but Men, and this is but human Frailty.

Tho. Well, proceed: what was done after this?

Ans. Now Faunus more couragiously advances to the very Edge of the Circle, and challenges the Devil of his own Accord; but the Devil's Heart failed him, and he fled back. You have deceived me, says he, if I had been wise I had not given you that Caution: Many are of Opinion, that what you have once confess'd is immediately struck out of the Devil's Memory, that he can never be able to twit you in the teeth for it.

Tho. What a ridiculous Conceit do you tell me of!

Ans. But to draw towards a Conclusion of the Matter: This Dialogue with the Ghost held for some Days; at last it came to this Issue: The Exorcist asking the Soul, If there was any Way by which it might possibly be delivered from its Torments, it answered, it might, if the Money that it had left behind, being gotten by Cheating, should be restored. Then, says Faunus, What if it were put into the Hands of good People, to be disposed of to pious Uses? The Spirit reply'd, That might do. The Exorcist was rejoic'd at this; he enquires particularly, What Sum there was of it? The Spirit reply'd, That it was a vast Sum, and might prove very good and commodious: it told the Place too where the Treasure was hid, but it was a long Way off: And it order'd what Uses it should be put to.

Tho. What were they?

Ans. That three Persons were to undertake a Pilgrimage; one to the Threshold of St. Peter; another to salute St. James at Compostella; and the third should kiss Jesus's Comb at Tryers; and after that, a vast Number of Services and Masses should be performed in several great Monasteries; and as to the Overplus, he should dispose of it as he pleas'd. Now Faunus's Mind was fixed upon the Treasure; he had, in a Manner, swallowed it in his Mind.

Tho. That's a common Disease; but more peculiarly thrown in the Priests Dish, upon all Occasions.

Ans. After nothing had been omitted that related to the Affair of the Money, the Exorcist being put upon it by Polus, began to put Questions to the Spirit, about several Arts, as Alchymy and Magick. To these Things the Spirit gave Answers, putting off the Resolution of these Questions for the present, promising it would make larger Discoveries as soon as ever, by his Assistance, it should get out of the Clutches of its Keeper, the Devil; and, if you please, you may let this be the third Act of this Play. As to the fourth Act, Faunus began, in good Earnest, everywhere to talk high, and to talk of nothing else in all Companies and at the Table, and to promise glorious Things to Monasteries; and talk'd of nothing that was low and mean. He goes to the Place, and finds the Tokens, but did not dare to dig for the Treasure, because the Spirit had thrown this Caution in the Way, that it would be extremely dangerous to touch the Treasure, before the Masses had been performed. By this Time, a great many of the wiser Sort had smelt out the Plot, while Faunus at the same Time was every where proclaiming his Folly; tho' he was privately cautioned by his Friends, and especially his Abbot, that he who had hitherto had the Reputation of a prudent Man, should not give the World a Specimen of his being quite contrary. But the Imagination of the Thing had so entirely possess'd his Mind, that all that could be said of him, had no Influence upon him, to make him doubt of the Matter; and he dreamt of nothing but Spectres and Devils: The very Habit of his Mind was got into his Face, that he was so pale, and meagre and dejected, that you would say he was rather a Sprite than a Man: And in short, he was not far from being stark mad, and would have been so, had it not been timely prevented.

Tho. Well, let this be the last Act of the Play.

Ana. Well, you shall have it. Polus and his Son-in-Law, hammer'd out this Piece betwixt them: They counterfeited an Epistle written in a strange antique Character, and not upon common Paper, but such as Gold-Beaters put their Leaf-Gold in, a reddish Paper, you know. The Form of the Epistle was this:

"Faunus, long a Captive, but now free. To Faunus, his gracious Deliverer sends eternal Health. There is no Need, my dear Faunus, that thou shouldest macerate thyself any longer in this Affair. God has respected the pious Intention of thy Mind; and by the Merit of it, has delivered me from Torments, and I now live happily among the Angels. Thou hast a Place provided for thee with St. Austin, which is next to the Choir of the Apostles: When thou comest to us, I will give thee publick Thanks. In the mean Time, see that thou live merrily.

"From the Imperial [Empyrian] Heaven,[6] the
  Ides of September, Anno 1498.
    Under the Seal of my own Ring."

This Epistle was laid privately under the Altar where Faunus was to perform divine Service: This being done, there was one appointed to advertise him of it, as if he had found it by Chance. And now he carries the Letter about him, and shews it as a very sacred Thing; and believes nothing more firmly, than that it was brought from Heaven by an Angel.

Tho. This is not delivering the Man from his Madness, but changing the Sort of it.

Ans. Why truly, so it is, only he is now more pleasantly mad than before.

Tho. I never was wont to give much Credit to Stories of Apparitions in common; but for the Time to come, I shall give much less: For I believe that many Things that have been printed and published, as true Relations, were only by Artifice and Imposture, Impositions upon credulous Persons, and such as Faunus.

Ans. And I also believe that a great many of them are of the same Kind.

A POSSESSED WOMAN
ATTACKED BY
A HEADLESS BEAR[1]

1584

In 1584, an anonymous pamphlet appeared in England entitled A true and most dreadfull discourse of a woman possessed with the devill, at Dichet, in Sommersetshire: a matter as miraculous as ever was seen in our time. Although the pamphlet's protagonist, Margaret Cooper, exhibited traditional symptoms of possession such as foaming at the mouth, the tale describes her being assaulted by a headless bear, who contorted her into a hoop and rolled her around the house. Her husband and brother-in-law finally repelled the creature by invoking the Holy Trinity. The end of the pamphlet names six witnesses to this event. In 1614, another pamphlet appeared entitled A Miracle of Miracles: as fearful as ever was seen or heard in the memory of man. The story was the same except that the date, May 9, 1584, had been changed to September 9 "last past" (i.e., 1613 or 1614). There was a third pamphlet, in 1641, entitled Most Fearefull and Strange Newes from the Bishippricke of Durham, Being a True Relation one Margaret Hooper. Here the date has changed again, to November 15, 1641, and the woman's name has changed from Cooper to Hooper[2] (perhaps because the bear rolled her into the shape of a hoop). Several pamphlets feature illustrations of the headless bear.

These pamphlets seem more concerned with inculcating pious behavior in the reader than relating an actual event. The list of witnesses in the original pamphlet should not be taken overly seriously—it is likely that fraudulent *names and dates were often added to wonder tales to give them greater verisimilitude. Shakespeare pokes fun at this tradition in* A Winter's Tale, *where Autolycus offers to sell a ballad about a woman who was transformed into a singing fish and who appeared on "Wednesday the fourscore of April." When asked whether the ballad is true, he answers, "Five justices' hands at it, and witnesses more than my pack will hold."*

Wild bears were long extinct in Britain by this period, but headless bears were apparently a horror trope in early modern England. A 1583 edition of Actes and Monuments by English historian John Foxe contains a cryptic reference to one William Web, who "set the image of a headless bear in the tabernacle of St. Roke."[3] In Christopher Marlowe's Doctor Faustus, *performed in 1592, the devil Belial assumes the shape of a bear. In* A Midsummer Night's Dream, *written a few years later, Puck the faerie describes taking the shapes of "a hog, a headless bear, sometime a fire." The preface to Robert Burton's* Anatomy of Melancholy *(1621) contains the lines, "my phantasie Presents a thousand ugly shapes / Headless bears, black men, and apes." Finally, the Puritan divine Richard Baxter's book* The Certainty of the World of Spirits *(1691) contains the following tale:*

Simon Jones, a strong and healthful man of Kederminster (no way inclined to melancholy, or any fancies), hath oft told me, that being a souldier of the king in the war against the parliament, in a clear moon-shine night, as he stood sentinel in the Colledge Green at Worcester, something like a headles bear appeared to him, and so affrighted him, that he laid down his arms soon after, and returned home to his trade, and while I was there afterward, which was fourteen years, lived honestly, religiously, and without blame, and I think is yet living which mindeth me of that which followeth, though to me not known.[4]

The headless bear appears to have existed just on the edge of the English imagination, being too fantastic to fully believe in, yet plausible enough that stories about it were used to instill moral behavior.

Upon the ninth day of May last past, Anno. 1584, there was a Yeoman of honest reputation, dwelling in the town of Dichet, which is about three miles of Bruton (the most ancient town within Sommersetshire) whose name is *Stephen Cooper* (a man of good wealth and well-beloved of his neighbors) who being sick and living in a weak state, sent his wife (whose name was *Margaret Cooper*) upon the ninth day of May last past into Gloster-shire, to take order concerning a farm which he hath in a Village called *Rockhampton, alias Rockington*, at whose coming thither, it seemed all things were not according to her mind. Thus continuing there one day and something more, she returned home to her husband, partly aggrieved at such changes as she thought her husband might reform if God lent him life. Now when she was come home again to Dichet, she found her husband recovered to an indifferent health: to whom she began to use very much idle talk, as well concerning the same farm, as also concerning an old groat [a coin] which her son (being a little boy) had found about one week before. Thus she continued (as it were one that had been bewitched or [harried?] with some evil spirit) until Tuesday at night following, which night she took her rest something indifferently until towards the morning: at which time she began with much vain speech to disquiet her husband, and to use much idle talk: but her husband seeing her in such a mind, and finding that she was as it were one that were desperate, he persuaded her to call upon God, and that being the creature of God she should not forget to call upon her Creator in the day of trouble: wherefore he counseled her to pray with him, and to say the Lord's Prayer after him, which she partly did: Yet the devil who always both builds his Chapel so near as he may to bere God's Church, began to withdraw her from Prayer, and put her in mind to call in most fearful sort for the groat which her son had lately found, as also for her Wedding ring, desiring to see them with all speed: her husband made no great haste thereunto, but continued in prayer, that it would please God to send her a more quiet spirit, and to strengthen her, that faith might speedily vanquish such vanity in her. But the more he praised and persuaded her to Praise, the more she seemed to be as it were troubled with some evil Spirit, calling still for the old groat which her husband neglected to show her: whereat she began with a very stern and staring countenance to look on her husband in most wonderful sort, as that he was sore frightened with the same. Then he called for her Sister, for that he was not able to keep her in the bed: which when her Sister and Brother were come to the Chamber, they kept her down violently in the bed: and forthwith she was so sore tormented that she foamed at the mouth, and was shaken with such force that the Bed and the Chamber did shake and move in most strange sort: her husband continued praying for her deliverance: so that within one half hour after her shaking was left, she began to tell them that she had been in Town to beat away the Bear which followed her into the Yard when she came out of the Country, which to her thinking had no head. Then her husband and friends persuaded her to leave those vain imaginations, persuading her that it was nothing but the lightness of her brain which was become idle for want of rest. Wherefore her husband and friends persuaded her to say the Lord's Prayer with them, which she did, and after took some small rest: and thus they remained until the Sunday following: in which time she continued raging as it were bestraught of her memory, which came by fits, to the great grief of her husband, friends, and neighbors. Upon the Saturday following there was good hope of her recovery, for that she in the night before had taken some reasonable rest: her friends and neighbors came to comfort her, but sometimes she would talk somewhat idly to them, which came by small fits. And upon the Sunday she seemed very patient and conformable to reason, until midnight: at which time the Candle which was set up burning in the same Chamber was burned out: She then suddenly waking called to her husband and cried out, saying, that she did see a strange thing like unto a Snail, carrying fire in the most wonderful sort: Whereat her husband was amazed: and seeing the Candle was clean burned out, called to his Brother and her Sister (which were in house with other of their friends watching and sitting up, to comfort her if her extreme fit should any way molest her) who hearing her husband call, came in and brought a Candle lighted and set it on the table, which stood near where the woman lay: She began then to ware as one very fearful, saying to her husband and the rest, do you not see the Devil: whereat they desired her to remember God and to call for grace, that her faith might be only fixed upon him to the vanquishing of the Devil, and his assaults. Well (quoth she) if you see nothing now, you shalt see something by-and-by: and forthwith they heard a noise in the street as it had been the coming of two or three Carts, and presently they in the Chamber cried out saying: Lord help us what manner of thing is this that commeth here. Then her husband looking up in his bed espied a thing come to the bed much like unto a Bear but it had no head nor tail, half a yard in length and half a yard in height: her husband seeing it come up to the bed, rose up and took a joined stool and struck at the said thing, the stroke sounded as though he had broken upon a featherbed: then it came to the woman and struck her three times upon the feet, and took her out of the bed, and so rolled her to and fro in the Chamber, and under the bed: The people there present to the number of seven persons were so greatly amazed with this horrible sight, that they knew not what to do, yet they called still upon God for his assistance: but the Candle was so dim that they could scarcely see one another. At the last this Monster which we suppose to be the Devil, did thrust the woman's head between her legs and so rolled her in a round compass like a hoop through three other Chambers down a high pair of stairs in the hall, where he kept her the space of a quarter of an hour: Her husband and they in the Chamber above dared not come down to her, but remained in prayer weeping at the stairs' head, grievously lamenting to see her so carried away. There was such an horrible stink in the hall, and such fiery flames, that they were glad to stop their noses with cloths and napkins. Then the woman cried out calling to her husband, now he is gone: then (quoth he) in the name of God come up to me, and so even upon the sudden she was come so quickly that they greatly marveled at it. Then they brought her to bed, and four of them kept down the clothes about the bed, and continued in Prayer for her. The Candle in the Chamber could not burn clear but was very dim, and suddenly the woman was got out of the bed, and the window at the bed's head opened, whether the woman did unpin the window, or how it cameth to pass they knew not, but it was opened, and the woman's legs after a marvelous manner thrust out at the window, so that they were clasped about the post in the middle of the window between her legs: The people in the Chamber heard a thing knock at her feet as it had been upon a Tub, and they saw a great fire as it seemed to them at her feet, the stink whereof was horrible: The sorrowful husband and his brother emboldened themselves in the Lord, did charge the Devil in the name of the Father, the Son, and the holy Ghost, to depart from her and to trouble her no more: then they laid hands on her and cried to the Lord to help them in that their great need, and so pulled her in again and set her upon her feet: Then she looked out at a window and began to say: O Lord (quoth she) methinks I see a little child, but they gave no regard to her: These words she spake two or three times: so at the last they all looked out at the window: and lo they espied a thing like unto a little child with very bright shining countenance, casting a great light in the Chamber, and then the Candle burned very brightly, so that they might one see another, then fell they flat to the ground and praised the Lord that he had so wonderfully assisted them, and so the child vanished away. Then the woman being in some better feeling of herself was laid in her bed and asked forgiveness at God's hands, and of all that she had offended, acknowledging that it was for her sins that she was tormented of the evil Spirit. And so God bethanked she hath ever since been in some reasonable order, for there hath been with her many godly learned men, as Maister Doctor Cottington, Parson of the same Town, and Maister *Nicholles* Preacher of *Bruton*, with other chief Preachers from divers places of the Country.

FINIS.

These be the names of the Witnesses, that this is most true:

Steven Cooper.
John Cooper.
Ales Easton.
John Tomson.
John Anderton.
Myles Foster.

with divers others.

"A TRUE DISCOURSE UPON THE MATTER OF MARTHE BROSSIER"[1]

1599

Martha Brossier, a peasant girl from Romorantin, France, is remembered as a famous fraud after she was investigated by a team of medical doctors in Paris. Whatever Brossier was actually experiencing, her status as a demoniac made her a pawn in the political intrigue of the French court. In 1598, King Henry IV signed the Edict of Nantes, granting substantial autonomy to the Huguenots, France's Protestant minority. The edict was unpopular with radical French Catholics, especially the recently formed Capuchin Order of Friars. Historian Sarah Ferber suggests that Brossier was "sponsored" by radical Catholics for political purposes: As a demoniac, her opposition to the Huguenots and the edict carried certain supernatural authority that could be used to challenge the king.[2] As such, Brossier's arrival in Paris shortly before Easter 1599 presented something like a national crisis.

Brossier was twenty-six in 1598. Most of what we know about her before she arrived in Paris comes from a letter sent by one "Anne Chivrou" to Henri de Gondi, bishop of Paris, in mid-March 1599. Chivrou claimed to have been a neighbor of Brossier's in Romorantin, and had been incarcerated after Brossier accused her of witchcraft. Chivrou urged the bishop not to believe her claims of demonic possession. It seems that Brossier had been seeking an escape from the life of an unmarried daughter. She tried to leave town once wearing her father's clothes and with her hair cropped. She had also tried unsuccessfully to join a

convent. Chevrou implies Brossier was inspired by an out-
break of possessions and a witch trial in Romorantin. She
had also read a book about Nicole Orby, a woman who
had undergone public exorcisms in Laon in 1566. In es-
sence, she had made a study of possessed women and
learned to copy them.

Early in 1598, the curé of Romorantin began performing public exorcisms of Brossier. Almost immediately the
public began using these exorcisms to consult Brossier as
a kind of oracle: Her demons would answer questions
about whether dead loved ones were in heaven or purgatory, whether enemies would go to hell, etc. Brossier's
demons excoriated anyone who doubted her possession,
calling them Huguenots or apostates.

In February 1598, Brossier began traveling to other
towns with her father, two sisters, and a canon from Romorantin. Brossier's exorcisms became a sort of traveling
show, possibly as a way for the family to earn money.
As they traveled, they collected "certificates" from local
clergy attesting that they had observed Brossier and that
she was indeed possessed. Brossier eventually collected
twenty-five such certificates. According to one account,
the exorcists identified three devils inhabiting Brossier:
Beelzebub, described as old and cruel, a "merry devil"
named "Acalon, the Jester of Hell," and one called the
Skullion of Hell.

In March 1598, a group of experts from the University
of Orléans tested Brossier—possibly because her public
attacks against Huguenots were seen as a threat to the
peace. They read from a Latin grammar book, which
Brossier reportedly misinterpreted as an exorcism and reacted accordingly. They also employed a technique from
Italian exorcist Giralomo Menghi's book Flagellum Dae-
monum, or The Whip Against Devils (1576). This involved
tying her to chair and burning noxious herbs under her
nose. These events are described in the excerpts below.
On March 17, Church authorities in Orléans and Cléry
revoked her certificates and prohibited all clerics in the

diocese from exorcising her. However, Brossier traveled from Orléans to Clery, where she was exorcised continually, in violation of the ban, until May. Brossier's father even managed to finagle a new certificate of possession from Orléans and resumed the traveling public exorcisms.

In March 1599, Brossier arrived in Paris. Ferber suggests that the Capuchins may have arranged for her to come to the city while the king was away visiting his palace in Fontainebleau. Almost immediately, Brossier went to the Abbey of Sainte-Geneviève and began denouncing the Huguenots as being in league with the devil. In response, Bishop Henri de Gondi called a commission of doctors and theologians that began examining Brossier on March 30. By April 1, the overwhelming majority of the doctors determined that she was not possessed. Although supporters demanded that a new panel be convened, the Parlement and the king ordered that she be taken into custody. On April 5, Brossier was imprisoned in the Châtelet (a fortress). She remained there for nearly two months, in relative comfort. She was regularly visited by doctors and other members of high society curious about her condition. On May 24 the Parlement issued a decree that guards would escort Brossier and her family back to Romorantin and that her father was to ensure she never left "upon paine of Corpororall Punishment." The following summer, King Henri IV commissioned Michel Marescot, the senior physician of the Paris committee that examined Brossier, to write a pamphlet exposing Brossier as a fraud. This was published anonymously as "A True Discourse Upon the Matter of Marthe Brossier," and the following fall it was translated into English.

However, this was not the last to be heard of Brossier. In December 1599, the prior of a Capuchin monastery "abducted" her (the abduction may have been a pretense to spare her father from punishment) and took her on another anti-Huguenot tour. Eventually the group began heading toward Rome to see Pope Clement VIII. This alarmed Henri IV, who pressured diplomats and Church

officials to prevent Brossier from reaching Rome. It is not
known what ultimately became of Brossier; however, there
are reports of her in Italy until at least 1604.³

In the excerpts below, Michel Marescot recounts his
inspection of Brossier in Paris from March 30 to April 5.
He then supplements this with reports from other clergy,
including those who tested Brossier in Orléans in 1598. He
includes an excerpt from Menghi's Flagellum Daemo-
num, *describing the "parfume" used to exorcise Brossier.*
Marescot seems to regard this formula as self-evidently
absurd. Marescot suggests that clergy "trained" Brosssier
how to be possessed. At one point in his pamphlet, she
states, "There were fifteene moneths spent in carying of
her too and fro, like an Ape or Beare to Angers, Saulmur,
Clery, Orleans, and Paris; in which time they taught her
to practice all these gambalds." He does emphasize that
demonic possession is a real phenomenon described in
the Bible; however, he frames Brossier as a fraud who un-
dermines the Church by deceiving "the simple people."

On Tuesday the xxx. of March 1599. at the commandement
of the right Reverend, the Bishop of Paris, there met together,
Marescot, Ellain, Hautin, Riolan, and Duret, within the Abbie
of Saint Genevesua, in the hall of my Lord Abbat, where was
brought before them one Martha Brossier, who (they said) was
possessed of a wicked Spirit: and this was in the presence also
of the said Lords the Bishop and the Abbat, and many other
persons of Note. By the commandement of the said Lord Bishop,
Marescot (as the ancientest of the rest) questioned with her in
Latin: (for the rumour went, that she spake all manner of languages) but she answered not a word. Then said the Abbat, She
will not answer, unlesse my Lord Bishop commaund her. Then
the Bishop commaunded the Devill to speake, saying, A*diuro te*
per Deum viuum, vt respondeas Domino Marescoto. I adjure
thee by the living God, that thou answere Master Marescot.
But both the woman and the Devill were mute. She was againe

questioned withall in Latin by Marescot the Phisitian, and in Greeke by Master Marius Doctor of Divinitie, and the King's Reader of Greeke Philosophie: but she answered not a word. Then the Bishop being very desirous and curious to discover the trueth: (because the said Martha had said, that this was no place to answere in) commaunded that she should be caried into a Chappell. Wherein, a number of Tapers being lighted, one Priest accompanied with two others, all apparelled in decent and Priestly garments, in the presence of the said Lord Bishop and the Abbat, and many other persons of qualitie, all being together in great devotion and at their praiers, began to exorcise her. She, being upon her knees praying to God, and making the signe of the Crosse, presently tumbled her selfe backward, first upon her buttocks, then upon her backe and upon her shoulders, and then softly upon her head. Whilest she lay upon her back, fetching her breath very deepe, and quaking in her flankes, (like a horse after he hath runne) she turned her eyes in her head, blared out her tongue, and tolde the Bishop that he had not his Miter, and bid him that he should goe and fetch it. Then they caused certen Reliques of the very true Crosse to bee brought unto her, which she indured to be put in her mouth. They presented also unto her a Doctor's whood, which shee stoutly rejected, as though the whood of a Divine, or the Miter of a Bishop had more vertue and more Divinitie in them, then the Reliques of the very Crosse. These things being done, and many other, which would bee to no purpose to rehearse, the Lord Bishop commaunded, that the Phisitians would tell him what they thought of it. Who after that they had maturely deliberated together, and considered all that they thought fit to bee considered, reported to the Bishop with the consent of them all, and by the mouth of the said Marescot, the ancientest of them all, what their opinion was, and that in few words, *Nihil à Daemone: Multa ficta: Amorbo pauca. Nothing of the Devill: Many things counterfeited: and a few things of sicknesse.* And indeed all these actions were counterfeit, as hereafter shall be shewed. But in trueth her tongue was red, and they perceived some little rumbling under her short ribs on the left side, proper to those that are subject to the Spleene.

The day following, which was Wednesday the last day of March, Ellain and Duret met together: and when the Exorcismes or Conjurations were againe repeated, the said Martha fell downe at the rehearsall of certaine words, raised her selfe up againe very lustily, made moves upon the Exorcists even to their faces, and nothing else was then done, saying that Duret pricked her with a pin, betweene the thumbe and the forefinger. After these actions diverse times reiterated untill Noone, the Bishop demaunded of Ellain and Duret, what they deemed of it. But they intreated the Bishop, it might stand with his good pleasure, that the other Phisitians, which had seene her the day before, might be called, and others also with them, to the end they might more maturely deliberate of the matter: especially considering, that the said Martha Brossier, being commaunded to give some tokens of her possession by the Devill, had made answere, To morrowe: which request the Bishop found to bee very reasonable.

Upon Thursday the first day of Aprill, all mysteries were imployed and used: none of the remedies were forgotten, that are proper to the driving out of Devils. They setled themselves to prayers: She blared out her tongue, turned her eyes, and at the pronouncing of certaine words, (*Et homo factus est: Verbum caro factum est: Tantum ergo Sacramentum*: that is, *And he was made man: The word was made flesh: Therefore so great a Sacrament*) she fell as before, and used such motions, as they doe that are troubled with a Convulsion. Yet all these actions seemed to the Phisitians to be meerly counterfeit: and therefore they would have been gone. But my Lord the Bishop intreated them, that they would bestow yet a little more time for the publike benefit. The Exorcismes or Conjurations were begun againe: and then the woman hearing the words, (*Et homo factus est, And he was made man*) she labored with all her strength and forces to make her gambals, and being upon her backe, in foure or five skips removed her selfe from the Altar to the Chappell-dore: which indeed did astonish all the companie. Father Seraphin [n.b. A Capuchin Frier] waxed somewhat angrie, and said: *If there be any here that is incredulous, and will trouble her, the Devill will carie him away in the ayre.* Then

Marescot growing impatient at that cousinage, said, *I will take that hazard and perill upon me: let him carie me away, if he can.* And so set his knee upon her knee, took her by the gorge, and commanded her to bee quiet. She being not able to stirre her selfe, and seeing her cousinage to bee discovered, said, *He is gone: he hath left me.* The good Seraphin approching neere unto her, said, *Indeede this is nothing but Martha: the Devill is departed. Then have I made him runne away,* quoth Marescot. The Bishop being very desirous to know the trueth, and doubting some counterfeiting, said: *Let us begin againe, and pray to God, that he would learne us the trueth: let us see if the Devill will torment her againe.* Then they sung Veni Creator, and the Apostles Creede. At this word, *Et homo factus est, And he was made man,* she did not fall, nor was tormented any more: yea, when they shewed her the holy Sacrament, she neither was troubled, nor tumbled any more: but seeing Marescot, Hautin, and Riolan behinde her, she said, *Meddle thou with thy Phisicke.* Marescot answered her: *If thou doe stirre, and play the foole againe, I will handle thee well enough.* In the meane while they persevered in their prayers to God. She thinking that Marescot was departed, fell againe upon her backe, plaied her old trickes, and used her ordinarie motions. Then Marescot, Hautin, and Riolan held her, and staied her very easily. The Bishop began to say to Father Seraphin the Exorcist, *Good Father, command her to rise.* The good Father cried unto her with a lowd voyce, *Raise thy selfe upon thy feete, raise thy selfe upon thy feete.* Marescot said, *The Devill riseth not in our presence:* and withall, because few people should take offence, he spake alowd in Greeke, Μηδὶν παρὰ φυσιν, μηδὶν παρὰ φύσιν. And it is not to bee marveiled at, that the said Marescot, Hautin, and Riolan were not afraid, because they knew her dissembling, and beleeved in Jesus Christ, who is the terror of all Devils.

Riolan, at the commaundement of the Bishop, spake unto her in Latin, as followeth: *Misera, quous perges nobis illudere? Nunquámne cessabis plebeculam ludificare? Agnosce culpam, & veniam deprecare. Patent enim tuae fraudes: & nisi hoc feceris, breui tradêris in manus Iudicis, qui quaestione veritatem extorquebit: Thou wretched woman, how long wilt thou pro-ceede to delude us? Wilt thou never cease to deceive the simple people? Acknowledge thy fault, and crave pardon. For thy guiles are discovered: and unlesse thou doe so, thou shalt shortly bee delivered into the hands of the Judge, who by torture will wrest out the trueth.* She being demaunded, whether she understood this or no, answered in good sooth, *She did not.* It was thought, that now all this businesse was done: and the Bishop withdrew himselfe, and went out of the Chappell, with diverse men of good Note, and commaunded the Phisitians, then being present, freely to tell him their opinion and advise. One of them assured him for certaine, that she had the Devill in her bodie, because she had blared out her tongue very farre, and had indured the pricking of a pinne. Another amongst them said, that undoubtedly hee had seene very many signes of counterfeiting: but yet his advise was, that they should stay three moneths longer, to the end they might be assured, whether she had the Devill in her bodie or no. For Master Fernelius, as he writeth in his Second booke *De abditis rerum causis, Of the secret causes of Nature,* could not certainly know a certaine sicke gentleman to bee possessed with a Spirit, till the end of three moneths.[4] Sixe others there were, that very confidently and constantly said for certaine, all these actions of Martha were fained and dissembled, as it was reported on the Tuesday before. And therefore it was thought that they were now at the end of this businesse.

But upon the Friday and Saturday following, being the fourth and fifth daies of Aprill, they called other Phisitians, (omitting the greatest part of those which had seene her before) and then they began a new combat with this Fantasticall Devill. One spake certaine Greeke wordes unto her: and she answered in French. Another spake in English: shee answered in French, but yet (as some say) somewhat to the purpose. They observed her most violent and sudden motions to be without any change, either in pulse, or in breath, or in colour. The Phisitians then present, made report in many words and magnificall termes, that Martha was possessed with a Devill, and signed it with their hands. Which report wee will write out hereafter, word for word, as it is in the Originall.

While all this was in doing, the Parliament fearing, that this concourse of people, which came to see this new Devill, might breede some new Monster of Sediition, (whereunto were are all too much inclined) made a Decree, That Martha Brossier should be committed into the hands of Monsieur Lugoly, the Lieutenant Criminall. Hereat, the Ecclesiasticall persons repined, and said, that this cause, of a woman pretended to be possessed, belonged unto the[m]. The Preachers cried out alowd at the matter. And the King, being then at Founteyne-Bell'-eau [Fontainbleau], and fearing also, that of this sparke there might be kindled a great flame, commanded the like. And for the performance thereof, Martha was caried into the Chastelet, where she continued and lived almost for the space of two moneths, not as a prisoner, but being entertained very mildly, and well lodged: viewed and visited by Bishops, Abbats, and other Ecclesiasticall persons, Councellors of the Court, Advocates, Gentlemen, and many Ladies and Gentlewomen, as many times and as often as any was desirous to see her. Besides, she was viewed by many Phisitians, that is to say, by my Masters De la Riviere, the chiefe Phisitian, Laurence the Kings ordinarie Phisitian, Laffilé the auncient Deane of the Facultie in Paris, Le Feure, Marescot, Ellain, Hautin, Lusson, Pietre, Renard, Heroüard, Cousinot, D'Amboise, Palmier, and Marcés: all which did say, and signed it with their hands, that they had not seene nor observed any thing, that was above the common lawes of Nature. And yet many there were, who being still infected with the old Leaven, had scattered it abroad throughout the Citie, that in the Chastelet she had plaied many of her Devillish trickes: which was afterward found to be false.

The said Martha, being shriven on the morow after Easter-day, and absolved by the Curate of Saint Germaines, or the Vicar there, received the Holy Sacrament, without making any stirre, or signe, or apparance of a person possessed by a wicked Spirit. In the end, when all sorts of informations were most diligently searched, and all things well considered, the Great

Parliament of Paris set downe a Decree, with great prudence and clemencie, which wee will deliver you in the end of this discourse. We have declared unto you the whole Historie as in trueth it was: and now wee must shew, by what reasons we were induced, firmely to beleeve, that Martha Brossier neither was, nor is possessed of a wicked Spirit: and afterwards wee will signifie unto you, how sleight their reasons are, which held the contrary opinion, to the end we may cleere a matter of so great weight and of such consequence. But first we would have every man to understand, that we were not any way assistant in this action, but only being called and commanded there-unto, by the right Reverend, the Bishop of Paris: and that wee had none other scope therein, save only God and our Con-science, not regarding what many might say thereof, nor the harme that might redound to us thereby. And touching the Thesis and Generall Proposition, there was never any doubt of it. For we doe beleeve, according to the Christian Faith, that there are Devils: that they enter into men's bodies: and that they torment them in sundrie sorts: and all, whatsoever the Catholike Church hath determined of their creation, Nature, Power, effects and Exorcismes, wee hold to bee true, firme and stable, as the Pole of Heaven. But touching the Hypothesis, that is to say, that Martha Brossier is, or hath been possessed of a Devill, we say, it is absurd, false, and without any likeli-hood. And to prove it, we will conclude by this generall Syllo-gisme.

> Major. Nothing ought to be attributed to the Devill, that hath not something extraordinarie above the lawes of Nature:
> Minor. The actions of Martha Brossier are such, as have nothing extraordinarie above the lawes of Nature.
> Conclusio. And therefore the Actions of Martha Brossier ought not to be attributed to the Devil.

* * *

The following excerpt describes the testing of Brossier at Orléans in March 1598.

After certaine dayes he caused common ordinarie water, (not hallowed) to be brought unto her in a Holy-water stocke: and then Martha seeing the Holy-water-stocke, layed her selfe downe, fell to her brabling, and made her wonted Apes-faces. Afterwards, the Lord Bishop told her that he had a peece of the True Crosse. Hee tooke a key of Iron, wrapped it worshipfully in Taffata like a Relike, and offered it Martha to kisse: and presently she began to play her Devilish trickes. A little while after, when he sayde, *Let one bring me my great booke of Conjurations*, they caused a Virgil to be brought unto him: and he began to reade, *Arma virumque cano* [The first line of Virgil's *The Aeneid*.] By and by, she thinking them to be words of Conjuration, fell downe upon the ground, and tormented her selfe in the best manner she could. At the last, her counterfeiting being discovered, the Lorde Bishop sent her away, and would not prophane those holy Mysteries of Exorcisme, to drive away a Counterfeit Devill. Others may imitate and folow the wisedome of this Prelate.

And what was done at Clery and at Orleans? The Officiall there, being well assisted with the wisest of the Clergie, did forbid all Priests of the Diocesse of Orleans, to Exorcise Martha, upon paine of Suspension from Divine Service. It would be a long matter, if we should goe about to rehearse all that was done at Orleans, for the discovering of this cousinage of the sayde Brossier: wee will onely tell you two of the pretiest of them. First, there was brought unto her a great thicke Grammar of Despanterius, bound after the old fashion with boords, and with claspes of Copper: it was opened and given her to reade. Shee lighted upon this place, *Nexo, xui, xum vult: Texo, xuit, indeque Textum* [conjugation of the Latin verb "Nexo"]. Which words Martha thinking to be Diabolical, began to fall backward, (but softly enough, as we tolde you before) and to fetch her ordinarie friskes and gambaldes. Another pretie tricke was, that my Masters of the Clergie in Orleans, would needes make experiment of the graund Remedie to drive away the Devill, and that is called the Parfume. They did set fire to this Parfume, and offered those villanous and stinking vapours to her Nose, she in the meane while

being bound to a chayre, but her feete at libertie to play withall: and then began shee to crie out, *Pardon me, I am choaked,
He is gone away.*

* * *

THE DESCRIPTION OF THE DIABIOLICAL PERFUME, TAKEN OUT OF THE BOOKE INTITULED, FLAGELLUM DAEMONUM, THE WHIP OF DEVILS: AND IS THIS.

Take Brimstone, Assafoetida, Galbanum, S. Johns-Worte, and
Rue; all these things being hallowed according to their owne
proper and peculiar benediction, must bee cast upon the fire,
and the smoake thereof applyed to the Nosthrils of the possessed.

This is an excellent Remedie ad fugandos & fumigandos
Daemones, to drive and smoake away Devils.

Of the vertue of this Remedie, I will say nothing; but I am
greatly amazed, that they mene to drive out Devils with such
stinking Odours and Smels, considering that Porphyrie &
Psellus, who are Philosophers of Plato's Sect, doe say that such
Parfumes are the Devil's Dainties.

DES NIAU, *THE HISTORY OF THE DEVILS OF LOUDUN*[1]

1634

The possession of an entire convent of Ursuline nuns in the French town of Loudun in 1634 is one of the most famous and spectacular cases of exorcism in history. The events in Loudun inspired Aldous Huxley's 1952 book, The Devils of Loudun, *as well as a Broadway play, an opera, and the 1971 film* The Devils. *Fueling the case was the trial of the priest Urbain Grandier, who was ultimately burned at the stake for witchcraft. Because statements of the possessed were used as evidence in a legal trial, historians have numerous primary sources by witnesses and exorcists, including an autobiography by Jeanne des Anges, the convent's mother superior. This material has provided ample fodder for analysis and interpretation.*

Urbain Grandier's arrival in Loudun disrupted the small community, earning him numerous enemies. He was handsome, highly educated, and a charismatic preacher. He was also a lothario who wrote a treatise on why priestly vows of celibacy cannot be honored. He allegedly had many affairs and fathered a child with Philippa Trincant, the daughter of the king's solicitor in Loudun.

In September 1632, the seventeen nuns in the town's convent began experiencing supernatural "disturbances." Some of the alleged activity may have been pranks put on by the nuns out of boredom. However, Grandier's enemies saw an opportunity. Canon Jean Mignon, the director of the convent, was also Philippa's cousin and an enemy of Grandier's. Mignon began performing exorcisms on all of the nuns, which seems to have greatly worsened their symptoms. In doing so, he elicited confessions that Grandier had bewitched them. Jeanne des Anges, in particular, described sexual fantasies about Grandier, which she attributed to his sorcery.

The exorcisms were held in public and lasted for months. More priests arrived to assist in the exorcisms, and they became a sort of tourist attraction. The focus of the exorcisms was less to deliver the nuns and more to indict Grandier. In the year 1610, a committee of theologians from the Faculty of Paris had warned about using possessed people in this manner, writing: "One must never admit the accusation of demons, still less must one exploit exorcisms for the purpose of discovering a man's faults or for determining if he is a magician . . . the devil being always a liar and the Father of Lies."[2] However, Grandier's enemies were adamant that demons bound by exorcism could not lie and were a reliable source of information. One of Grandier's supporters argued that this policy "turns Christians into idolaters," because they are executing people based on the sayings of demons.[3]

Grandier was arrested and tortured. By repeatedly stabbing him with a needle, inquisitors discovered four "devil's marks" that they said were immune to pain. A written pact was also produced that was allegedly signed by Grandier and several demons, proving he was a sorcerer. At one point, several nuns recanted their confessions, but the recantations were dismissed as the lies of demons. In August 1634, Grandier was burned at the stake.

The possessions did not end with Grandier's death. Jeanne des Anges insisted that she was possessed by seven demons, much like Mary Magdalene. In December 1634, the Jesuit Jean-Joseph Surin was summoned to Loudon. Surin formed a close relationship with des Anges, and they became lifelong friends. At one point, Surin reported that a demon had come out of des Anges and possessed him, a trope that appears in William Peter Blatty's The Exorcist.

Surin instructed des Anges to combat the demon herself using quiet prayer and spiritual exercises. This proved far more effective than the theatrical and humiliating public exorcisms that des Anges had previously undergone. In 1637, des Anges declared that she was delivered from all seven demons. Afterward, she gained a reputation as a holy woman and traveled throughout France.

There are numerous interpretations of the events at Loudun. Several physicians who observed the exorcisms were skeptical and diagnosed the nuns as suffering from furor uterinus—a discredited medical notion that agitation of the uterus could cause a range of emotional and mental problems for women, including disordered sexuality. However, there may have been something about the social psychology of convent life combined with the spiritual worldview of early modern Europe that lent itself to the experience of demonic possession. Historian Moshe Sluhovsky found forty-five cases of mass possession in convents across Europe and the New World colonies between 1435 and 1690.[4]

The excerpt below is from The History of the Devils of Loudun, *attributed to Monsieur des Niau, a counselor from La Fléche who observed the exorcisms. Des Niau's assumption is that the possessions were genuine and that Grandier was indeed a sorcerer. However, his description of the symptoms of exorcism is interesting. He claims the nuns could speak different languages—even those of indigenous people in the New World. He also describes feats such as levitation, although more often these were "near levitations." For example, des Anges is described as balancing on one elbow, a position someone might have been able to hold for a few seconds, especially with practice or if they had another appendage on the floor, concealed by a habit.[5] Significantly, des Niau reports that the nuns seemed healthier than before the exorcisms began. It seems likely the regimen of thrashing and contortions during daily exorcisms made them quite fit.*

* * *

As the church, at its birth, gained great credit through similar events, so again, in this case, did they serve to revive the faith of true believers, and so it will be again in future times.

Loudun was fated to behold events of this nature, and they were to produce their ordinary effect, viz., to enlighten those whose consciences, though distorted, had preserved some remnants of original good, and to blind souls darkened with pride, and hearts full of perversity.

As usually happens, the extraordinary phenomena displayed in the persons of the nuns were taken for the effects of sexual disease. But soon suspicions arose that they proceeded from super natural causes; and at last they perceived what God intended every one to see.

Thus the nuns, after having employed the physicians of the body, apothecaries and medical men, were obliged to have recourse to the physicians of the soul, and to call in both lay and clerical doctors, their confessor no longer being equal to the immensity of the labour. For they were seventeen in number; and everyone was found to be either fully possessed, or partially under the influence of the Evil One.

All this could not take place without some rumors spreading abroad; vague suspicions floated through the city; had the secret even been kept by the nuns, their small means would soon have been exhausted by the extraordinary expenses they were put to in trying to hide their affliction, and this, together with the number of people employed in relieving them, must have made the matter more or less public. But their trials were soon increased when the public was at last made acquainted with their state. The fact that they were possessed of devils drove everyone from their convent as from a diabolical residence, or as if their misfortune involved their abandonment by God and man. Even those who acted thus were their best friends. Others looked upon these women as mad, and upon those who tended them as visionaries. For, in the beginning, people being still calm, had not come to accuse them of being imposters.

Their pupils were first taken from them; most of their relations discarded them; and they found themselves in the deepest poverty. Amidst the most horrible vexations of the invisible spirit, they were forced to labour with their hands to earn their bread. What was most admirable was that the rule of the community was never broken. Never were they known to discontinue their religious observances, nor was divine service ever interrupted. Ever united, they retained unbroken the bonds of charity which bound them together. Their courage never failed, and when the seizure was past, they used to return to their work or attend the services of the Church with the same modesty and calmness as in the happy days of yore. I know that malice will not be pleased at such a pleasing portraiture. But this base feeling, too natural in the human heart, should be banished thence by all men of honor, who know its injustice and only require that history should be truthful. Probability itself is in favor of our statements. For when God permits us to be attacked so violently by our common enemy, it is as a trial to ourselves, to sanctify us and raise us to a high degree of perfection, and simultaneously He prepares us for victory, and grants us extraordinary grace, which we have only to assimilate and profit by.

It became necessary to have recourse to exorcisms. This word alone is for some people a subject of ridicule, as if it had been clearly proved that religion is mere folly and the faith of the church a fable. True Christians must despise these grinning impostors. Exorcisms, then, were employed. The demon, forced to manifest himself, yielded his name. He began by giving these girls the most horrible convulsions; he went so far as to raise from the earth the body of the Superior who was being exorcised, and to reply to secret thoughts, which were manifested neither in words nor by any exterior signs. Questioned according to the form prescribed by the ritual, as to why he had entered the body of the nun, he replied, it was from hatred. But when, being questioned as to the name of the magician, he answered that it was Urbain Grandier, profound astonishment seized Canon Mignon and his assistants. They had indeed looked upon Grandier as a scandalous priest; but never had they imagined that he was guilty of Magic. They were therefore not satisfied with one single questioning: they repeated the interrogatory several times, and always received the same reply.

* * *

As regards the presence of Devils in the possessed, the Church teaches us in its ritual, that there are four principal signs, by which it can be undoubtedly recognized. These signs are the speaking or understanding of a language unknown to the person possessed; the revelation of the future, or of events happening far away; the exhibition of strength beyond the years and nature of the actor; and floating in the air for a few moments.

The Church does not require, in order to have recourse to Exorcisms, that all these marks should be found in the same subject; one alone, if well authenticated, is sufficient to demand public exorcism.

Now, they are all to be found in the Nuns of Loudun, and in such numbers that we can only mention the principal cases.

Acquaintance with unknown tongues first showed itself in the Mother-Superior. At the beginning, she answered in Latin the questions of the Ritual proposed to her in that language. Later, she and the others answered in any language they thought proper to question in.

M. de Launay de Razilli, who had lived in America, attested that, during a visit to Loudun, he had spoken to them in the language of a certain savage tribe of that country, and that they had answered quite correctly, and had revealed to him events that had taken place there.

Some gentlemen of Normandy certified in writing that they had questioned Sister Clara de Sazilli in Turkish, Spanish, and Italian, and that her answers were correct.

M. de Nismes, Doctor of the Sorbonne, and one of the chaplains of the Cardinal de Lyon, having questioned them in Greek and German, was satisfied with their replies in both languages.

Father Vignier, Superior of the Oratory at La Rochelle, bears witness in his Latin Narrative, that, having questioned Sister Elizabeth a whole afternoon in Greek, she always replied correctly and obeyed him in every particular.

The Bishop of Nimes commanded Sister Clara in Greek to

raise veil and to kiss the railings at a certain spot; she obeyed, and did many other things he ordered, which caused the prelate to exclaim that one must be an Atheist or lunatic not to believe in "possession."

Some doctors questioned them also as to the meaning of some Greek technical terms, extremely difficult to explain, and only known to the most learned men, and they clearly expressed the real signification of the words.

Lastly, Grandier himself being confronted with them, his Bishop invested him with the stole to exorcise the Mother Superior, who, he declared, knew Latin; but he did not dare to question her or the others in Greek, though they dared him to it; whereon he remained very embarrassed.

As to the Revelation of hidden matters or of events passing afar off, proofs are still more abundant. We will only select a few of the most remarkable.

M. Morin, Prior of St. Jacques de Thouars, having requested M. Morans, Commissioner appointed by the Bishop of Poitiers to watch over the possessed, and to assist in the trial of Grandier, to allow some sign to be given proving *actual infernal possession*, whispered to M. de Morans that he wished one of the possessed to bring him five rose leaves. Sister Clara was then away in the refectory; M. de Morans ordered, in his thoughts, the Demon who possessed her to obey the wish of M. Morin, for the greater glory of God. Thereupon the Nun left the refectory, and went into the garden, whence she brought first a pansy and other plants, and presented them with roars of laughter, saying to M. de Morans: "Is that what you wish, father? I am not a Devil, to guess your thoughts." To which he replied simply: "*Obedias*," obey. She then returned to the garden, and after several repetitions of the order, presented through the railings a little rose branch, on which were six leaves. The Exorcist said to her: "*Obedias punctualiter sub paena maledictionis*," obey to the letter under penalty of malediction; she then plucked off one leaf, and offered the branch saying: "I see you will only have five; the other was one too many." The Prior was so convinced by what he saw, that he went out with tears in his eyes. An official report of the fact was drawn up.

Madame de Laubardemont also tried the same experiment, in order to convince many skeptics who were present; and she was equally successful.

The *Lieutenant-Criminel* of Orleans, the President Tours, Lieutenant-General de S. Maixant, and myself also had our curiosity gratified. I desired that Sister Clara should bring me her beads, and say an *Ave-Maria*. She first brought a pin, and then some aniseed; being urged to obey, she said: "I see you want something else," and then she brought me her beads and offered to say an *Ave-Maria*.

M. Chiron, Prior of Maillezais, desiring to strengthen his belief in demoniacal possession, begged M. de Morans to allow him to whisper to a third party the sign he required; and he thereon whispered to M. de Fernaison, Canon and Provost of the same Church, that he wished the nun to fetch a missal then lying near the door, and to put her finger on the introit of the mass of the Holy Virgin, beginning "Salve, Sancta parens." M. de Morans, who had heard nothing, ordered Sister Clara, who was likewise ignorant of what had been said, to obey the intentions of M. Chiron. This young girl then fell into strange convulsions, blaspheming, rolling on the ground, exposing her person in the most indecent manner, without a blush, and with foul and lascivious expressions and actions, till she caused all who looked on to hide their eyes with shame. Though she had never seen the prior, she called him by his name, and said he should be her lover. It was only after many repeated commands, and an hour's struggling, that she took up the missal, saying: "I will pray." Then, turning her eyes in another direction, she placed her finger on the capital S at the beginning of the introit aforesaid, of which facts reports were drawn up.

M. de Milliere, a gentleman of Maine, certified that, being present at the Exorcism of Sister Clara, and on his knees, the Devil asked him whether he was saying a *De Profundis* for his wife, which was the case. The Marquis de la Mothe, son of M. de Parabel, governor of Poitou, certified that sister Louise de Nogeret had disclosed his most secret faults in the presence of Father Tranquille, and of Madame de Neuillant, his aunt.

The same M. de la Mothe also asked an Exorcist to make

Sister Clara, who was in the convent, come out, kneel down, and say an Ave Maria; she came after repeated commands, and obeyed.

Chevalier de Meré, who was present, asked the Devil on what day he had last confessed. The Devil answered Friday. The Chevalier acknowledged this to be correct; whereupon Sister Clara withdrew. But as he wished to try the Devil again, he begged the exorcist to make her return, and whispered some words to the Marquis and the Monk, for the nun to repeat. The exorcist refused, as the words were indecent. He changed them, therefore, into *Pater, et Filius el Spiritus Sanctus!* He whispered these words so low, that the exorcist could hardly hear them. The nun, who was in another room, came at the command of the Father, and addressing the Chevalier, first said the indecent words the monk had refused, and then repeated several times *Gloria patri et filio et Spiritui Sancto.* She was ordered to say the words exactly as she had been desired, but she said she would not.

The Bishop of Nimes, being present at an exorcism by Father Surin, begged him to order something in difficult Latin; and the Demon thereupon performed what was wanted.

A Jesuit wishing to try what so many people stated they had experienced, gave an inward order to a demon who had been exorcised; and then immediately another. In the space of a second he gave five or six orders, which he countermanded one after another; and thus tormented the Devil, who was ordered to obey his intentions. The Demon repeated his commands aloud, beginning by the first, and adding, "But you wont," and when he had come to the last he said, "Now let's see whether we can do this."

"When it rained," says Father Surin, "the Devil used to place the Mother Superior under the water spout. As I knew this to be a habit of his, I commanded him mentally to bring her to me; whereupon she used to come and ask me: 'What do you want.'"

Another thing which struck the Exorcists, was the instantaneous answers they gave to the most difficult questions of Theology, as to grace, the vision of God, Angels, the Incarnation and similar subjects, always in the very terms used in the schools.

The corporal effect of possession is a proof which strikes the coarsest minds. It has this other advantage, that an example convinces a whole assembly.

Now the nuns of Loudun gave these proofs daily. When the Exorcist gave some order to the Devil, the nuns suddenly passed from a state of quiet into the most terrible convulsions, and without the slightest increase of pulsation. They struck their chests and backs with their heads, as if they had had their neck broken, and with inconceivable rapidity; they twisted their arms at the joints of the shoulder, the elbow and the wrist two or three times round; lying on their stomachs they joined their palms of their hands to the soles of their feet; their faces became so frightful one could not bear to look at them; their eyes remained open without winking; their tongues issued suddenly from their mouths, horribly swollen, black, hard, and covered with pimples, and yet while in this state they spoke distinctly; they threw themselves back till their heads touched their feet, and walked in this position with wonderful rapidity, and for a long time. They uttered cries so horrible and so loud that nothing like it was ever heard before; they made use of expressions so indecent as to shame the most debauched of men, while their acts, both in exposing themselves and inviting lewd behavior from those present, would have astonished the inmates of the lowest brothel in the country; they uttered maledictions against the three Divine Persons of the Trinity, oaths and blasphemous expressions so execrable, so unheard of, that they could not have suggested themselves to the human mind. They used to watch without rest, and fast five or six days at a time, or be tortured twice a day as we have described during several hours, without their health suffering; on the contrary, those that were somewhat delicate, appeared healthier than before their possession.

The Devil sometimes made them fall suddenly asleep: they fell to the ground and became so heavy, that the strongest man had great trouble in even moving their heads. Françoise Filestreau having her mouth closed, one could hear within her body different voices speaking at the same time, quarreling, and discussing who should make her speak.

Lastly, one often saw Elizabeth Blanchard, in her convulsions, with her feet in the air and her head on the ground, leaning against a chair or a window sill without other support.

The Mother Superior from the beginning was carried off her feet and remained suspended in the air at the height of 24 inches. A report of this was drawn up and sent to the Sorbonne, signed by a great number of witnesses, ecclesiastics and doctors, and the judgement thereon of the Bishop of Poitiers who was also a witness. The doctors of the Sorbonne were of the same opinion as the Bishop, and declared that infernal possession was proved.

Both she and other nuns lying flat, without moving foot, hand, or body, were suddenly lifted to their feet like statues.

In another exorcism the Mother Superior was suspended in the air, only touching the ground with her elbow.

Others, when comatose, became supple like a thin piece of lead, so that their body could be bent in every direction, forward, backward, or sideways, till their head touched the ground; and they remained thus so long as their position was not altered by others.

At other times they passed the left foot over their shoulder to the cheek. They passed also their feet over their head till the big toe touched the tip of the nose.

Others again were able to stretch their legs so far to the right and left that they sat on the ground without any space being visible between their bodies and the floor, their bodies erect and their hands joined.

One, the Mother Superior, stretched her legs to such an extraordinary extent, that from toe to toe the distance was 7 feet, though she was herself but 4 feet high.

But sometime before the death of Grandier, this lady had a still stranger experience. In a few words this is what happened: In an exorcism the Devil promised Father Lactance as a sign of his exit, that he would make three wounds on the left side of the Mother Superior. He described their appearance and stated the day and hour when they would appear. He said he would come out from within, without affecting the nun's health, and forbade that any remedy should be applied, as the wounds would leave no mark.

On the day named, the exorcism took place; and as many doctors had come from the neighboring towns to be present at this event, M. de Laubardemont made them draw near, and permitted them to examine the clothes of the nun, to uncover her side in the presence of the assembly, to look into all the folds of her dress, of her stays which were of whalebone, and of her chemise, to make sure there was no weapon: she only had about her her scissors, which were given over to another. M. de Laubardemont asked the doctors to tie her; but they begged him to let them first see the convulsions they had heard spoken of. He granted this, and during the convulsions the Superior suddenly came to herself with a sigh, pressed her right hand to her left side and withdrew it covered with blood. She was again examined, and the doctors with the whole assembly saw three bloody wounds, of the size stated by the Devil; the chemise, the stays, and the dress were pierced in three places, the largest hole looking as if a pistol bullet had passed through. The nun was thereupon entirely stripped, but no instrument of any description was found upon her. A report was immediately drawn up, and Monsieur, brother of the King, who witnessed the facts, with all the nobles of his Court, attested the document.

SAMUEL WILLARD, "A BRIEFE ACCOUNT OF A STRANGE & UNUSUALL PROVIDENCE OF GOD BEFALLEN TO ELIZABETH KNAP OF GROTON"[1]

1673

In 1672, the Reverend Samuel Willard of Groton, Massachusetts, wrote an 8,000-word treatise to Increase Mather in Boston, describing the apparent possession of his servant girl, Elizabeth Knapp (as her name is commonly spelled today). Willard's treatise has had a disproportionate influence on how witchcraft was understood in New England and remembered today. Knapp is mentioned in Increase Mather's Remarkable Providences *as well as Cotton Mather's* Magnalia Christi Americana. *As authorities on witchcraft, both men influenced the Salem witch trials of 1692–1693. Knapp's story was also an influence cited by director Robert Eggers on his cult horror film* The Witch *(2015).*

Historian John Demos has produced one of the most thorough analyses of the case, including a genealogy of Knapp and her descendants.[2] Knapp was born April 21, 1655, and died between 1700 and 1706. She was sixteen when she began showing signs of possession on October 16, 1671. Willard's account ends abruptly on January 15, 1672, leaving it unclear how the situation was resolved. However, we know that Knapp married in 1674 and bore seven children. Knapp's symptoms included "fits" during which she would contort her body and exhibit seemingly unnatural strength. She described Satan urging her to suicide and homicide, and Willard reports encountering her on the stairs one night wielding a billhook—an agricultural tool similar to a machete—with which Satan had sent her to murder him. Strangely, the devil would speak through Knapp even when her fits rendered her mouth either permanently open or sealed shut. Willard was particularly confounded that she could produce "labial letters" (sounds that require pressing the lips together) while her mouth remained open.

In November, Knapp was examined by a medical doctor, who diagnosed her condition as at least mostly natural and prescribed medicine. However, as the possession wore on, supernatural explanations arose. In Willard's account, Knapp seems to vacillate on whether she made a pact with the devil. Demos suggests that Willard and other observers may have coached her in making this confession, not to prosecute her for witchcraft but to affirm that Knapp's problems were of her own making. In Willard's conclusion he expresses uncertainty whether Knapp actually made any such pact. He describes the entire affair as a "tragedye" and Knapp as an "object of pitye." This attitude of skeptical sympathy was not always the case in New England. In October 1692, Thomas Brattle wrote a letter condemning the Salem witch trials. Brattle challenged why Knapp's accusations of witchcraft were not taken seriously yet people in Salem were being imprisoned as witches based on the testimony of similarly disturbed people.

This poore & miserable object, about a fortnight before shee was taken, wee observed to carry herselfe in a strange & unwonted manner, sometimes shee would give sudden shriekes, & if wee enquired a Reason, would alwayes put it off with some excuse, & then would burst forth into imoderate & extravagant laughter, in such wise, as some times shee fell onto ye ground wth it: I my selfe observed oftentimes a strange change in here countenance, but could not suspect ye true reason, but conceived shee might bee ill, & y'fore divers times enquired how shee did, & shee alwayes answered well; wch made mee wonder: but the tragedye began to unfold itselfe upon Munday, Octob. 30. 71, after this maner (as I received by credible information, being that day my selfe gon from home). In the evening, a little before shee went to bed, sitting by ye fire, shee cryed out, oh my legs! & clapt her hand on ym, imediately oh my breast! & removed her hands thither; & forthwith, oh I am strangled, & put her hands on her throat: those y' observed her could not see what to make of it; whither shee was in earnest or dissembled, & in this maner they left her (excepting ye pson [person] yt lay with her) complaining of her breath being stopt: The next day shee was in a strange frame, (as was observed by divers) sometimes weeping, sometimes laughing, & many foolish & apish gestures. In ye evening, going into ye cellar, shee shrieked suddenly, & being enquired of ye cause, shee answered, yt shee saw 2 psons in ye cellar; whereupon some went downe with her to search, but found none; shee also looking with ym; at last shee turned her head, & looking one way stedfastly, used ye exp'ssion, wt cheere old man? which, they that were with her tooke for a fansye, & soe ceased; afterwards (ye same evening,) ye rest of ye family being in bed, shee was (as one lying in ye roome saw, & shee herselfe also afterwards related) suddenly throwne downe into ye midst of ye floore w't violence, & taken with a violent fit, whereupon ye whole family was raised, & with much adoe was shee kept out of ye fire fro destroying herselfe after wch time she was followed wth fits from thence till ye sabbath day; in which shee was violent in bodily motions, leapings, strainings & strange agitations, scarce to bee held in bounds by the strength of 3 or 4: violent alsoe in roarings & screamings, rep'senting a dark resemblance of hellish tormts & frequently using in these fits divers words, sometimes crying out money, money, sometimes, sin & misery with other words. On Wednesday, being in ye time of intermission questioned about ye case shee was in, w't reference to ye cause or occasion of it, shee seemed to impeach one of ye neighbors, a pson (I doubt not) of sincere uprightnesse before God, as though either shee, or ye devill in her likenesse & habit, pticularly her riding hood, had come downe ye chimney, stricken her that night shee was first taken violently, wch was ye occasion of her being cast into ye floore; whereupon those about her sent to request ye pson to come to her, who coming unwittingly, was at ye first assaulted by her stranglye, for though her eyes were (as it were) sealed up (as they were alwayes, or for ye most pt, in those fits, & soe continue in ym all to this day) shee yet knew her very touch from any other, though no voice were uttered, & discovered evidently by her gestures, soe powerfull were Satans suggestions in her, yet afterward God was pleased to vindicate ye case & justifye ye inocent, even to remove jealousyes fro ye spirits of ye pty [party] concerned, & satisfaction of ye by standers; for after shee had gon to prayer wth her, shee confessed that she beleeved Satan had deluded her, & hath never since complained of any such apparition or disturbance from ye pson. These fits continuing, (though wth intermission) divers, (when they had opportunity) p'ssed upon her to declare wt might bee ye true & real occasion of these amazing fits. Shee used many tergiversations & excuses, prtending shee would to ys & yt young pson, who coming, she put off to another, till at ye last, on thursday night, shee brake forth into a large confession in ye prsence of many, ye substance whereof amounted to thus much: That ye devill had oftentimes appeared to her, prsenting ye treaty of a Covenant, and offering largely to her: viz. such things as suted her youthfull fancye, money, silkes, fine cloaths, ease from labor to show her ye whole world, &c: that it had bin then 3 yeers since his first appearance, occasioned by her discontent: That at first his apparitions had bin more rare, but lately more frequent; yea those few weekes yt shee had dwelt with us almost constant, that shee seldome went out of one roome into another, but hee appeared to her urging of her: & yt hee had prsented her a booke written wth blood of covenants made by others wth him, & told her such & such (of some wherof we hope better things) had a name there; that hee urged upon her constant temptations to murder her pents [parents], her neighbors, our children, especially ye youngest, tempting her to throw it into ye fire, on ye hearth, into ye oven; & that once hee put a bill hooke into her hand, to murder my selfe, psuading her I was asleep, but coming about it, shee met me on ye staires at which shee was affrighted, the time I remember well, & observd a strange frame in her countenance & saw she endeavred to hide something, but I knew not what, neither did I at all suspect any such matter; and yt often he psuaded her to make away wth herselfe & once she was going to drowne herselfe in ye well, for, looking into it, shee saw such sights as allured her, & was gotten within ye curbe, & was by God's providence prevented, many other like things shee related, too tedious to recollect: but being prssed to declare whither she had not consented to a cov-ent wth ye Devill, shee with solemne assertions denyed it . . .

* * *

Fryday [December 8, 1671] was a sad day wth her, for shee was sorely handled wth fits, which some pceiving pressed that ye was something yet behind not discovered by her; & shee after a violent fit, holding her betweene two & 3 houres did first to one, & afterwards to many acknowledge that shee had given of her blood to ye Devill, & made a covenant wt him, whereupon I was sent for to her; & understanding how things had passed, I found that there was no roome for privacye, in another alredy made by her soe publicke, I therefore examined her concerning the matter; & found her not soe forward to confesse, as shee had bin to others, yet thus much I gathered fro her confession:

That after shee came to dwell wth us, one day as shee was alone in a lower roome, all ye rest of us being in ye chamber, she looked out at ye window, & saw ye devill in ye habit of an old man, coming over a great meadow lying neere the house; & suspecting his designe, shee had thoughts to have gon away, yet at length resolved to tarry it out, & heare wth hee had to say to her; when hee came hee demanded of her some of her blood, which shee forthwith consented to, & with a knife cut her finger, hee caught ye blood in his hand, & then told her she

must write her name in his booke, shee answered, shee could
not write, but hee told her he wld direct her hand, & then took
a little sharpened sticke, & dipt in the blood, & put it into her
hand, & guided it & shee wrote her name with his helpe: what
was the matter shee set her hand to, I could not learne from her;
but thus much shee confessed, that the terme of time agreed
upon with him was for 7 yeers; one yeere shee was to be faithfull in his service, & then ye other six hee would serve her, &
make her a witch: shee also related, yt ye ground of contest between her & ye devill which was ye occasion of this sad providence, was this, ye after her covenant made the devill showed
her hell & ye damed, & told her if shee were not faithfull to
him, shee should goe thither, & bee tormented there; shee desired of him to show her heaven, but hee told her heaven was
an ougly place, that none went thither but a company of base
roagues whom he hated; but if shee wld obey him, should be
well with her: but afterward shee considered with herselfe, that
the terme of her covent, was but short, & would soone bee at
an end, & shee doubted (for all ye devills pmises [promises])
shee must at last come to ye place hee had showne her, & withall, feared, if shee were a witch, shee should bee discovered, &
brought to a shamefull end; which was many times a trouble
on her spirits; this the Devill pceiving, urged upon her to give
him more of her blood, & set her hand agen to his booke, which
shee refused to doe, but ptly through promises, ptly by threat-
nings, hee brought her at last to a promise yt shee would sometime doe it: after which hee left not incessantly to urge her to
ye pformance of it, once hee met her on the staires & often
elsewhere pressing her with vehemencye, but shee still put it
off; till the first night shee was taken when ye devill came to
her, & told her he would not tarry any longer: shee told him
shee would not doe it hee Answered shee had done already, &
wt further damage would it bee to doe it agen, for shee was his
sure enough: she rejoyned shee had done it already, & if shee
were his sure enough, what need hee to desire any more of her:
whereupon he strucke her ye first night, agen more violently ye
2d as is above exprst . . .
　　[. . .]

On Fryday [January 12, 1672], in ye evening shee was taken wth a passion of weeping, & sighing, which held her till late in ye night, at length she sent for me; but ye unseasonablenesse of ye weather, & my owne bodily indisposednesse prvented: I went ye next morning, when shee strove to speake somthing but could not, but was taken wth her fits, which held her as long as I tarried, which was more yn an houre, & I left her in them: & thus she continues speechlesse to this instant, Jan. 15. & followed wth fits: concerning which state of hers I shall suspend my owne Judgment, & willingly leave it to ye censure of those ye are more learned, aged, & Judicious: only I shall leave my thoughts in resp. of 2 or 3 questions wch have risen about her: viz. 1. Whither her distemper be reale or counterfiet: I shall say no more to yt but this, the great strength appearing in ym, & great weaknesse after them, will disclaime ye contrary opinion: for tho a pson may counterfiet much, yet such a strength is beyond ye force of dissimulation: 2. Whither her distemp bee naturall or Diabolicall, I suppose ye prmises will strongly enough conclude ye latter, yet I will adde these 2 further argumts: 1. ye actings of convulsion, wch these come nearest to, are (as psons acquainted wth ym observe) in many, yea ye most essentiall pts of ym quite contrary to these actings: 2. Shee hath no wayes wasted in body, or strength by all these fits, though soe dreadfulle, but gathered flesh exceedinglye, & hath her naturall strength when her fits are off, for ye most pt: 3. Whither ye Devill did really speake in her: to yt point wch some have much doubted of, thus much I will say to countermand this apprhension: 1. The manner of exprssion I diligently observed, & could not pceive any organ, any instrument of speech (which ye philosopher makes mention of) to have any motion at all, yea her mouth was sometimes shut without opening sometimes open without shutting or moving, & then both I & others saw her tongue (as it used to bee when shee was in some fits, when speechlesse) turned up circularly to the roofe of her mouth. 2. ye labial letters, divers of which were used by her, viz. B. M. P. which canot bee naturally exprssed without motion of ye lips, which must needs come within or ken, if observed, were uttered wthot any such motion, if shee had used only Lingualls,

Gutturalls &c: ye matter might have bin more suspicious: 3. ye reviling termes yn used, were such as shee never used before nor since, in all this time of her being thus taken: yea, hath bin al- wayes observed to speake respectively concerning mee; 4. They were exprssions which ye devill (by her confession) aspersed mee, & others wthall, in ye houre of temptation, pticularly shee had freely acknowledged yt ye Devill was wont to appear to her in ye house of God & divert her mind, & charge her shee should not give eare to what yt Blacke coated roage spake: 5 wee observed when the voice spake, her throat was swelled formidably as big at least as ones fist: These argumts I shall leave to ye censure of ye Judicious: 4. whither shee have cove- nanted wth ye Devill or noe: I thinke this is a case unanswer- able, her declarations have been soe contradictorye, one to another, yt wee know not wt to make of ym, & her condition is such as administers many doubts; charity would hope ye best, love would alsoe feare ye worst, but thus much is cleare, shee is an object of pitye, & I desire yt all yt heare of her wld compassionate her forlorne state, Shee is (I question not) a sub- ject of hope, & therfore all meanes ought to bee used for her recoverye, Shee is a monumt of divine severitye, & the Lord grant yt all yt see or heare, may feare & tremble: Amen.

                                                                    s.w.

THE DIARY OF
JOSEPH PITKIN

1741

Relatively little is known about exorcism in North America during the eighteenth century. The Enlightenment was under way, and leading theologians seemed embarrassed to write about Satan, let alone demonic possession. However, the writings of religious elites are often not representative of the beliefs and practices of ordinary people. This is why the diary of Joseph Pitkin is significant. Pitkin (1696–1748) was a successful businessman, justice of the peace, sheriff, and judge of the Connecticut General Court. His unpublished diary, held at the Connecticut State library, describes a trip to Boston in 1741¹ during which he encountered a woman named Martha Roberson, who claimed she was possessed.

Central to this narrative is a debate over the revivals of the First Great Awakening. Roberson had attended revivals held by George Whitefield and Gilbert Tennent (whom Pitkin refers to as Tonant), both important figures in the Awakening. Revivals led by itinerant preachers frequently induced moaning, fainting, and other strong expressions of emotion. Opponents of the revivals, known as "Old Lights," regarded the revivals of the "New Lights" as overly emotional and potentially dangerous. Roberson's apparent possession was a talking point in this debate. While Pitkin regards the possession as genuine, he relates that it was "reproach-filled said" that Tennent had attempted to cast the demon out of Roberson, indicating that exorcism was regarded by some as evidence of New Light impropriety. Later Pitkin mentions accusations that

*Tennent "puts the devil in her," in other words, that Rob-
erson was being manipulated to heighten the drama of
the revivals. Notably, less than fifty years after the Salem
witch trials, there is no evidence that witchcraft was even
discussed in debating Roberson's possession.*

*Pitkin became a deacon following this encounter and
seems pleased that he could help Roberson. However,
historian Kenneth P. Minkema notes that when George
Whitefield visited Boston again in 1744, Colonel John
Phillips reported in his diary, "There were many cried
out, Robinson's [Roberson; spelling at this time was in-
consistent] daughter and others."² This suggests Roberson's possession did not end after her encounter with
Pitkin.*

*The text below is the complete description of the en-
counter based on Pitkin's original manuscript. The text is
not in perfect condition and some words have been lost.
Other words are visible but indecipherable. The author
has worked with librarians to produce the most faithful
copy possible.*

In Janry. 1740/4d my Buisness called me to Boston; and when
[. . .] then there I heard of a Young Woman which was supposed to be possessed [by] the Devile and it was Reproach
filled said that Mr Tonant (A minister Belonging to the Jerseys
who had lately been in Boston) had attempted to call him out;
again my Buisness with some of A Publick nature led me there
again in March following; I traveld in a Difficult labor yett was
Caryed Safe and it being a Wonderfull Time of the Exercise of
Religion there. I was Entertaind in Publick Worship; and in
Conversation in Private with so much of the Life and Power of
Religion that I found it Proffitable to my soul to be there; it
was the observations of Good men that Religion did not now
sneak into corners, but Triumphed openly, and Vice sought
where to hide its Head; I was well Informed that in the Biggest
part of the familyes in Town ther were more or Less under

Convictions and many To the Best Judgments Brot Saveing by Home; and in some Large familys the work almost Gone Through and almost all Rejoicing Together in Hope of Eternall Life; and on one evening Lecture at Dr Colmans; Mr Cooper vindicated the Reality of the work of Gods Spirits; he told us that everyday produced new Instances of An [word missing]; and almost every Day of Conversions; and the work was [evi]dently of God and his power and Goodness were to be ad[vancing?] lest the Pharisee and Publican stand and fleer and Lang[?] Divide it as they will; Yett Nevertheless it appears to be the [Won]derfull Work of God: But after I had accomplished Buisness according to my Desire, and was coming out of Town I mett with something so Remarkable that I think it my duty to Record it; and first I take notice how Providentially I was called into the way of it (it being a Conference with the young woman which I had heard in the winter was possessed with the Devil) I had not in my Being in Town this time heard a word mentioned about her; it was now on Fryday after noon Two Hours after the Time I Designed and Expected to have come out of Boston; and I sat writeing in Capt Sheldins House where I Lodged; Mrs Sheldin came to the Door and Beckened to me to come out; and Told me that her Little Daughter had been over to a near neighbours; and there was a Young Woman had a great Desire to speak with me (Haveing seen me and Heard Something about me). I asked her what her Case was; she told me she had been under Great Trouble in her mind and had strange kind of fitts; (but mentioned nothing of her Being the person which was supposed to be possessd). I told her I know nothing of ye person or her Case; and was just going on my Journey Home; However, not knowing what might be the Designe of Providence; I would Go over if she would Go with me and we went Together, and were Desired to Go up into a Chamber; where were two or three Women; and immediately after Came up the Young Woman who had sent for me; (whose name was Martha Roberson). She appeard something surprised. And partly out of Breath. But Desird me to sitt Down and told me she was Glad to see me; I waited till she had a little Recoverd her self. She asked me whence I came; I told her from Hartford; well said she I hear of Glorious Things there and with an uplifted Hand said Blessed be God for it: I asked her How she came to send for me, being wholy a Stranger: She replyd that some person had told her they saw a Stranger at Meeting on the Sabath and suposed him to be a minister; and observed that att noon he went to Govr Belchers [governor Jonathan Belcher]; and said she I was persuaded the more he was a good man Because he went to the Govournours; for the Devil is Inraged more against the Gouvernour Than any Body in the world, Because he is one that is so zealous in promoteing Religion; and said she they Describd Your Dress and I had observed that You went into Capt Sheldins: and had soon [Yonder?] [word missing] pass the street, and ~~was persuaded~~ told my freinds was persuaded You [were] one of the gracious servants of Christ; and I could not [word(s) missing (rest until?)] I spake with You and hope God will make our meeting to be for good. [She] replyd the Devill is Disturbed at Your coming, he knows You are a Good man and he hates all such and he will Roar in me anon. I then asked her want she meant by that; she Replyed it is now 15 weeks since the Devil Began to speak in me; I then asked her what was the occasion upon which she desired to speak with me; she then proceeded to Relate in the following maner; I was under Considerable Convictions by turns from a child; and then they would abate and wear off; and I Grew as Light and vain as ever again, or worse; but was under considerable convictions when Mr Whitefield came to town and prepard to go and hear him; but before I went I beggd Heartily of God that if ever he designd my Conversion this might be the time; and this man might be the Instrument by which I might be converted; and I found [a plain?] change in my soul before ever I heard him speak a Word; but I went to hear him and was peirsd by the Word and pressed Down by Conviction; and after service was over: gott as near him as I could; and let him know I was peirsd by the word: He turnd to me and said he prayed God to sett home my Conviction to haveing Conversion; and said little more to me. But my Conviction went on and continued; all my sins were Brot over in order before me; and I went to several Ministers for advise and assistance—But although my Convictions went very deep; yet I have never been Lost to Despair of the Mercy of God: and when Mr Tonant came to Town I went to hear him; I had att turns before some light, but hearing him I had considerable Light and Comfort; and went one evening to see him with 2 or three of my freinds and when I came found him sitting with 4 or 5 ministers: and when he understood that I wanted to speak with him he took me and my friends into another Room; and asked me whether I was willing my friends should hear what I had to say: I told him Yes—butt before he had said much to me or I to him; the Devil filld me with such Rage and spite against him that I could have torn him to [pieces] and should have torn his Cloaths off if my freinds had not held me. Mr Tonant then went out and told the other Ministers there was one pos-sessed with the Devill as he thought and desired them to come in and pray with me: and they Did by Turns four or five of them, but I had a Dismal night of it, was Tossd about the Room; and filld with Rage and Spite against all Good people; and from that time the Devil has spoken in me; and hath spo-ken me every thing that is Bad: he hath spoke Blasphemy in me; and then told me I had committed the unpardonable sin he has spoke in me all manner of Prophane Talk, all manner of Unclean Talk; all manner of follish songs; and made me Dance two Hours together, and I could by no means forbear [two words missing] was [a Dancer?] in my Life. He had spoke in me all such Tea Table Talk such foolish talk as is commonly there, [Hind-?]Times he hath bid me curse God and Dye: Ye, but before [I had] gone for in this Relation she said several times the Devil is Greatly Disturbed and he will Roar in me anon; and then a loud shreik as loud as her voice would cary it which was so surpriseing to me that I supose she saw it in my Countenance: and she recoverd the next Breath and said pray sir dont be surprised the Devil endeavors to scare every Body from me that is Good. But pray Dont you be surprised. But go on; I asked her whether that which I was saying was ofensive to her. She sd not at all but the Devil cant Bear it. I then went on further in asking questions or Remarking upon what she said: and profundly her countenance was changed in a moment into

the most Dismall form of Rage and Disdain (and as the ministers in Boston call it; as she and her mother both told me) the
Devill with her Toungue Broke forth in the most Hideous outcry Contradicting, Denying and Mocking as if he would spit
in my face; this was so extraordinary and Unexpected that it
seemd to give the Blood a stop in my veins for a Moment but
did not att all put me out of a presenes of mind; but Glory be
to God who had as I before related providentially called me to
Encounter Satan Speaking with a Tongue of flesh as though
fully oppened to me. I was by Divine Strength Raised to a
Double Degree of Courage and had Great presenes of mind
given; by the word of God to assist this poor soul in her Con-
flicts; and those shocks only made me move Back as into my
Tower where I then stood Undaunted; and when she had recovered her self she again Desired me to Go on in saying what
I was about and not to be stoppd I then askd her whether she
could hear what I said when she made such a noise; (and so I
did several times:) She told me Yes, and it Revives my soul
within me; but the Devil cant Bear it. She then said the Devil
would Roar Louder Yet, But what is this to the Hearing of him
Roar in Hell forever—this is nothing to that; Blessd be God
who has Deliverd my soul—as a pray from his Tooth; he now
Rages; Knowing he Hath but a short time: But I have need of
all this: and when the Devil speaks all of is Bad in me then he
would fain Impute it to me as my Sin; I can freely Justifie God
in all this: Yea I can freely Justifie him in my Damnation; we
were all overrun with pride here among us and I among the
Rest: but God is Righteous; and I cant Tell how I could have
Done without this. But Though he slay me yet [word missing]
I trust in him; if I perish I will perish at the [words missing]
and none ever perished there; here am I Lett him Do with me
as Seemeth him Good. By this Time it appeared to my sattis-
faction that Christ had Gott the Possession of her soul by his
Holy Spirit and had Dethroned Satan; but yet permitted him
to vent his Rage and Spite with her Tongue; and under this
view I aplyd my Discourse to her. And my Answer to Satan;
Takeing the Sword of the Spirit over the word of God: and
[Crouded?] that home against him and putt Christ above him

as one that Came [into] the world to Destroy the works of the Devil; and Rejoiced to see Satan fall as Lightning from Heaven; and as I Thus proceeded the Devils Rage Grew more feirce. Interupted her near half her time. Till she Rose up with such a Countenance of Rage and Disdain with her fist Double as if she would Come in my face: but my soul was soft so far above his Terror that I could Smile in my Heart and face to see Grace in her soul steadily oposeing all the attempts of the Devil and when he had used her Tongue a few Breaths in Contradicting and Revileing then the Spirit of God Guideing her Tongue in Repeating the Scriptures to Refute his fals hoods. And to Quench his firey Darts; and as I was unable [to] assiste her therein; and when I urged a [place] of Scripture close against where Satan endeavord to maintain her with Great Disdain in her Countenance said how Do you now this; I replyd. I Do know this to be True and so do You Lett the Devil say what he will; then she Recoverd and said So I Do. A man Blessed be God: and Generally after Satan had Taken his Turn with her Tongue: she would Recover into a Calm Giveing her Amen and Amen to the truths of Gods word Blessing and praiseing God. Trusting in him and submitting to his Will; and as she first urged me not to be Surprised; now it came to be my Turn when the Devil took his Turn to speak so often I said to her Don't be afraid of the evil Spirit he is in Chains and You find he is. She replyd- Yea he is so: Blessed be God; but he has many a Time bid me fall Down and Worship him; but I have Repelled him with this Thou Shall Worship the Lord thy God and him only shall thou Love——fear him who is able to Destroy Body and soul in Hell; thou shalt fear the Lord thy God let him be your fear and Lett him be your Dread. And much in this Maner we held Discourse I supose an hour or more; her Mother told me she Thought her Daughter would be Glad if I would pray- with her but ⊖ the Devil will not let her ask any Body to pray with her. The Young Woman Replyd: no the Devil hates prayer; I then Inquired whether [it was] common for Christians to pray with her: they Told me it was: and that the Minister of The Town had kept a Day of fasting and prayer for her. But she was not [profiants?]. They allso Told me that Satan after made a Great outcry in prayer time; I then Turnd to her and said Cant You ask me to pray with You; and Imediately the Devil [made?] a Mocking and Hissing at it. I told her I would have her Try and was persuaded she Could anon if she would Try; and the Devil would not always have such power over her; and after several attempts she Recoverd her self; and said Yes Sir I should be Heartily Glad if you would pray with me; I askd her if she Could Compose her self and keep from Making a noise; she said she Could not Tell; but the Devil had not Been so Clamorous and Disturbed this [indecipherable] she kneeld Down by ye side of a bed; and I prayd with her and was Assisted by the Holy Sprit to be fervent in pleading her Case with God; she Continued some time silent but when I Came to her Case the Devil began to Cry aloud with her Voice; Hold Your Tongue; Hold Your Tongue: as often and as Loud as she Could Speak for several Breaths; but by Dvine assistance it was no Interruption to me; But Rather an argument to more Divine Compassion; and then she would be Recoverd again and I could hear her softly say Amen; and then presently a Long outcry again. And so Continued through the [Duty?] and when prayer was ended she Rose up washed with Tears; and when she had Composed herself I asked her whether she Could hear and Join in prayer. She said Yea she could Give her amen to Every so at once though the Devil made such a Clamour; we then sat and Discoursed again a Considerable Time and then I took my leave intending to come out of Town that night. She professed her self much Refreshed in her soull and Blessed God for our meeting together and her friends Expresst a good Deal of Thankfullness; and as for my own soul it was brot so near to God and I was so assisted by him and had so sollid and direct Experience of Divine Assistance and more than a Recompense for my first Surprise; and so much Instruction given me in many points; That I had Rather missd of any Days Buisness of my own; than to have missed of that opportunity in Bearing Wittness for Christ, and assisting one of his thus opresed— But before this I inquired what effect these things Comonly had upon those who saw them; and they told me that some had said Mr Tonant puts the Devil into her and when he was

gone he would go out again; and that some who were [indeci-
pherable] were Throughly awakend by it; and had since said
they had Reason to Bless God they had seen her: She told me
that some Ministers had been almost frightened of their witts;
one Especially who dare not come near her nor suffer her to
come near him; but Did pray with her and said a few words
and went away, and never came to see her More; this justly
[word missing] upon a more Thankfull acknowledgement of
the assistance I had from above; that after the first to or three
shocks, all the mockery of Satan was no more Troublesome to
my soul than the Buzing of a fly: not unto me O Lord, but unto
thy name be the Glory: that I could thus smile at Satans Rage;
may I never want the Like assistance whenever I must encounter him within my soul or without: for Jesus sake Amen amen.

When I came out of ye House I found the day was gone and
concluded to tary that Night; and the Beginning of evening
Mrs Sheldin sent word to the Family that I was there and they
sent a Desire that by all Means I would go over again; (and
Col. Tim: Dwight of North Hampton was in ye House and
had been told by Mrs Sheldin of the things that had passed;
was very Desirous to go over with me and Did) when I came
again she was exceeding Glad to see me and told me as she had
told her freinds that she found her soul much Refreshed by my
Conversation and prayer: we sat Down and there were soon
a Considerable number of people there; I told her who Col.
Dwight was and whence he Came; and when he Began to
speak the Devils Rage seemd mostly Directed at him in the same
Maner as it had been against me: but went further in Contradicting plain Scripture Truths: when Col Dwight mentioned the
name of God, ye Devil Replyd there is no God: another Time
he Turnd to us Both and said with a most Disdainfull Countenance and Tone in her; Ay you Came from Hartford and he
came from North Hampton; they Tell of Conversion there Conversion, Conversion. Conversion; (in the Highest Degree of Derision) there is no such thing it is all a notion; and then with a
soft sly voice said, ay I know what they are about there. Once
or Twice she Rose up with her fist Doubled as if she would
have gone in Col Dwights face; But after The Devil had with

her Tongue Denyed the Being of God; and the work of Conversion; she satt weeping sometime and said now the Devil Reproaches me that I have Been so Impudent; But Except those
too Expressions of her Tongue was Interchangably filled by
two Different Spirits as it was when I was there before. After
considerable Discourse it was moved that one of us should pray
with Her and I then put it upon Col Dwight; and he prayed
with her; and ye Devil made A great Deal of noise again; and
after prayer we sat down and Discoursed her till near 1 o Clock.
She had some Longer Turns of Liberty to speak without Int-
eruption; once I Remember one of us were Remarking something that she had [mett?] with and the Devill said How do
You know this; she Told You a jade: she prefoessed Great Sat-
tisfaction and said she could Willingly sit and Hear all night:
Then I took my Leave of her Again and Left her Blessing God
and [word missing]-ing in his Mercy; when we came out Col
Dwight Told me he Never was so Surprised in all the Days of
his Life: nor [never] mett with any thing Like it; the Young
Woman told us she [was] in perfect Health and Generally
Rested well in the Night.; and that the Night before she and
her Aunt were Both awake [and] Heard a noise Like the Bleat-
ing of a Goat (and so said her Aunt) and something came out of
Capt Sheldins which Dragged the Goat away. And has he was
Driven away there came a violent Gust of Wind as if it would
have Taken the Topp of the House off (in this also her Aunt
whois wife to Mr S[?] the Barber at Hartford Agreed) they
Being both Throughly awake.

This being one of the Last things in which I was Concernd
in Boston; filld up my Meditation Great part of the way: I pittyed her Case as under Great affliction by the Power of the Devill seemd to have over her Tongue: but much more all Those to
be pittyed who are serene and at ease in a state of Unregener-
acy where Satan Reignes Quietly in their Hearts.

I That much on the maner of my Being Called in and the
view of Providence seeemd to be as if Christ should Say: Come
You whom I have Used and Treated from Your Birth with a
Peculiar Case: and for 29 years past as my Special friend and

favourite; I have now Brot You safe [herein?] a Dificult Season
and have Caryd You Through Your own Buisness according to
Your Hearts Desire; and You have now in Publick and private
mett with Soul [Rejoiceing?] Cordial in this Town; You have
found it Good to be here; But Before You Leave this place You
Must Stop in to the Help of the Lord Against the Mighty adversary of souls; to Bear Testimony for me in oposition to his
his vile sugestions. And to Lett a poor opressed soul Know how
faithfull and Good I have Been to You and to strengthen her
Hands in God—who is Caled to Wrestle with Principalitys and
powers. The Ruler of the Darkness of this World; Bee not
afraidof him tho' he Reproach you with A to Tongue of flesh: I
will Give you a Mouth to Speak; and Courage to Assist a poor
Soul to Triumph over him; then fear not: have not A comand:
Your help and strength from above: Thanks be to God. that I
have found it so:

I meditated much allso what should be the Designe of providence in permitting Satan thus to have the Comand of the
Tongue of the person whose soul seemed to me [word missing]
the Habitation of Christ by the Indwelling of the Spirit—and
here I would be very Cautious; and only Mention what I Do;
as appeared to me- which was Thus it seemd Very Confident
[unto?] the Divine Wisdome That Sattan should be permitted
to show openly what are his words and what his Language is,
in Clear Distinction from what the Spirit and Word of God
Speaks; and that it might be the more Clearly Discernd; Both
the Spirit of Christ; and Satan should by Turns Speak with the
same Tongue and what Satan spake was abhored by her soul at
the same Time her Tongue [uttered] the Words; so that for the
future I shall Remember when I hear any Deny the Being of
God; or Blaspheme his Sacred Name; or utter Ph Prophane, or
Unclean Words or Deride and Scorn the Servants of God; or
make a mock of prayer or say of Conversion there is no such
Thing I shall Remember that these were the Expressions which
the Devil Uttered with her Tongue.

About After this I was Inquisitive what Became of this Person and was Informed by credible Persons where she had dwelt

that she was Gradually Deliverd out of that Difficulty and walked very Humbly and Circumspectly and was very Inquisitive to find out what Provocation she was Guilty of that God should lay this sore affliction upon her—and the same way [Confirmed] by others of the Best Character—near Two Years after I was in Boston with some men who were Present at my Going to see her in the Evening and we Agreed to Go and see her and found her at her Fathers House. She Told me she was Glad to see me and behaved very very Decently. I Inquired whether she knew me she said yes she Remembered that she saw me when she was Under that Great [Dis?] I asked her whether she Remembered what Passed then she said she Rememberd it very well. And Thankfully acknowledged her obligation to me for That Kindness. I asked her how she was Deliverd she told me God had Gradually Deliverd her from that Distress I then Particularly Inquird whether she could now say as she then Did that the Evil words which were utterd with her Tongue were the abhorrence of her Soul as She answered it was Generally So. But Sometimes I was almost all Devil: Quest. could you not Help your Ton Uttering those words with your Tongue. Answ. No if might have had thew whole World. Q: Could you now be Provoked [with] to speak such words A[.] no if I might have the world for it. Q: How Did you feel when You say you were forced to Utter such words. A: I was Pressd as if my soul would be pressd out of my Body. She Told me she was Considerably in the Dark. And had Great Cause to be Humble in absence of that sore affliction.

Upon the Testimony of others with the Conversation I had with her I had no Reason to Think of her state otherwise than I Did at first. And now my Hearty Desire is that all who see this Narrative may be Excited to Draft their souls and Tongues to the Service and Glory of God: that by his grace they may be deliverd from the Power of the Devil and from being his volluntary slaves and [vassals?] Especially to Beware how they utter those Expressions which were Uttered by her Tongue which I have Recitd.

FRAY JUAN JOSÉ TOLEDO, AN EXORCISM IN THE NEW MEXICO COLONY[1]

1764

This letter was written by Juan Toledo, a Spanish missionary, to the governor of New Mexico—then a Spanish colony—from the small settlement of Abiquiu. It describes exorcisms performed by Toledo over five women, and eventually a man. Toledo's letters to the governor first raised concerns of witchcraft in 1760, when a mysterious illness spread through the settlement. It was rumored that Indian sorcerers in league with the Devil were spreading the plague by poisoning food. Toledo himself became ill and attributes his cure to visiting a curandera or folk healer.

The two women discussed most in the letter are "genizaros." These were Indians who had been taken from the Pueblo and other tribes and were now culturally Hispanic. They occupied a low social status within the Spanish colonies and were sometimes forced to work as servants. The letter suggests a blending of Spanish ideas of witchcraft with indigenous beliefs. For example, a possessed woman makes a sound like an owl. Owls were associated with shape-shifting witches among certain Pueblo communities in the Spanish colonies. In contemporary Mexican folklore, owls are still associated with witchcraft.

Unlike similar witch panics, no one accused of sorcery in Abiquiu was executed. Toledo had declared an Edict of Grace, stating that anyone who confessed to sorcery would not be punished. Although Toledo describes flogging a woman after a disruption in church, he does not

act on the accusations of sorcery made by the possessed,
noting, "They lie about whom they desire. It is not my
motivation or intention to place the blame on them."

Fray Juan José Toledo to Carlos Fernández,
Abiquiu, 22 January 1764, C.

Lord don Carlos Fernández: retired lieutenant of the royal pre-
sidio, alcalde mayor and war captain of the Villa nueva de la
Santa Cruz and its pertaining pueblos, commissary judge in the
proceedings regarding the discovery of genízaro Indian sorcerers at the Pueblo of Santo Tomás Apóstol de Abiquiu.

My Lordship,
   Arma virumque cano ["I sing of arms and the man
(Aeneas)"] said the poet Virgil to commence a profane
account of a certain bloody battle. Although I cannot say,
nor do I know how to move my pen to begin to explain
what has been presented before me, this uproar and battle
with the devil that, as a priest of God, I cannot ignore, as
it is within my jurisdiction, in my home and habitation. I
recognize, with humility, my moral weakness, and I confess
myself to be depraved and a bad priest, yet of a lively and
indubitable faith and confidence in God and our savior
Jesus Christ. Because He knows of my shortcomings, the
finger of God must cast out the devil and subdue that
roaring lion, the dragon that comes from hell.
   On the seventeenth day of December of the past year [1763],
I started to exorcise María Trujillo in the Holy Church, who is
the wife of José Valdez, resident of this jurisdiction, who for
the love of God pleaded with me to exorcise María, who, since
the month of June and for nine consecutive days after mass
and inside the church, would faint at the moment of the prayer
of exorcism. We have witnessed that she would become
covered with purple blemishes on the right shoulder, the
elbow, the palm of the hand, and the knee.

She appeared to be free of this illness until the eleventh day of November, when, having arrived at the hour of childbirth close to daybreak, she experienced a great fainting spell and, coming to, she followed through in the delivery with great ease. When the sun arose, she had given birth to a child that was well and healthy.

On the fourteenth day, she felt a great headache, and there appeared a weight in her stomach and a blockage in her intestines. After all this, apparently she was given to great sadness of an extreme nature. On the day of the allegiance to Our Lady [either the Feast of Immaculate Conception or the feast of Our Lady of Guadalupe], it happened that while in the church, she would get very sleepy during the mass and sermon and could not be amused by the diversions of the fiesta.

She remained in her state of melancholy until the fourteenth day of December, when she fainted after the prayer in her house and, instead of awaking, she went into a fury and began to exhaust herself with unnatural strength. For this reason and because of the continued evil which continued at all hours, I resorted to the spiritual remedy and as such I proceeded exorcising on the eighteenth day of the month of December, which was Sunday.

Francisca Barela, also a resident of this place, a young maiden, poor and cloistered, eighteen years old more or less, left her home about four in the afternoon with an earthen jar to supply the house with water. Upon reaching a small spring which is located between two rocky and rugged hills close to the chapel in order to take some water, she felt a certain motion in her body. With great dread and fear and without knowing from where this originated, she returned to her home. She then heard the sound of a pig, which lived in those places as well as in domestication. She could not see what had scared her. Having got her water, she arrived at her house and, having placed corn in her mill to crush it for supper, she was suddenly stunned by a tingling sensation that she felt over her body. She returned a second time before it got too late to get some more water to finish the task. She filled the

earthen jar at the small spring and once again heard the same
noise as before. Having seen nothing, she felt a major shudder
and fear until she arrived at her home, and her anxiety
increased. She was further afflicted and the sensations caused
her to fall into a seizure. Her brother noticed the movements
she had in her body and, upon seeing her on the floor,
attempted to lift her, and when she felt this movement, she
began to give furious and frightful shouts which the people
heard. When asked what was wrong, she responded that she
did not see anything nor was she afflicted by any pain. By
common agreement and in view of the astonishing
occurrence, they brought the woman to this mission with
difficulty, as she was resistant to my presence. As soon as she
arrived and saw me, there were imponderable shouts which
issued forth from her mouth and the clamor of the members
of her body and the movement of her eyes. Her coloring had
changed to a faded grey. The fury that she was in at each
instant fatigued the people who held her. They held her so
that she would not get loose from those hands, which she
tried to do, becoming livid in her attempt to break loose,
throwing punches and trying to bite and grab the hair of
those around her. Given the tumult she made, it took a
lot of work to undo the seizure. I tried to observe her for a
while and seeing how realistically she mimicked the sound
of pigs, cows, horned and spotted owls, and other animals,
I got the stole, cross, and holy water and said the gospel
of Saint John and other petitions over her head in order to
finish discovering if this was the will of our Lord or
something else.

At the words of the Holy Gospel, her body made wild
movements, she shouted and shrieked, which ceased
immediately once I grabbed the book of exorcisms. She began
to make insolent remarks to me: that I was a kid goat
mulatto, and that she did not fear me nor what I intended to
accomplish. When I began the exorcism, she cursed me and
tried to interrupt and impede the exorcism with great shouts,
disgraces, and extreme shaking. By the time she appeared to
be secured, the four men who held her were exhausted. She

wanted to escape from their hands, arching her body upward, then to one side, and at an instant of the men's weakness, she kicked off one of her shoes with such violence that those who had her secured were unable to avoid the shoe. She continued in this manner during the night of the same day until daybreak. As she rested, she was thrown onto the floor, howling in a very loud voice like the Indians of this land are accustomed to do.

On Monday the nineteenth, while it was dark, a young maiden of twelve years was discovered whose name is María de Chávez, who had a pain in her right side. This caused her to sob and she began to tremble without stopping her sobbing, shaking with more violence and other demonstrations which were strange. Because of this, it was necessary for me to bring it to the attention of the lieutenant in order to show the girl to the discoverer Joaquín. There were two other witnesses from this place, men who were more than fifty years old. They were Pedro Cisneros and Gerónimo Martín, who in my presence, and in the house of the discoverer, having thought about and observed the illness, declared to the lieutenant that on Friday the sixteenth of the same month, Indian bread makers had made the priest bread and given María a piece and that the spirit was discovered on the same day. Immediately at that point, it had been given to her by the older bread maker named Jacinta, daughter of the Indian woman who is called by the bad name Atole Caliente, a great sorcerer who Joaquín did not dare confront. Under no circumstance was he a disciple of hers, but his brother Juan Largo and Janisco had learned the art from the woman so that the Lord Governor would know the strength of the pact.

At this time, this same girl, being in the hands of those who held her in the presence of the lieutenant and witnesses, said it was true that Jacinta had given her the piece of bread. From here they took her peacefully until the arrival of the hour of the mass, when she situated herself at the foot of the steps in order to receive the exorcism and hear the mass. At the start of the *Introit,* the afflicted women fell to the floor at the same time, beginning to exasperate and exhaust themselves so that people went to their aid to hold them and, upon realizing they had been seized, they let out Indian war howls of the type which the Indians are accustomed to giving when they grind corn. After making motions with their hands of that exercise, and when they finished with the manic behavior, they sang like an owl, a fox, a pig, a cow, etc. They then were raised up high and fell without being assisted by those who held them. The disturbance in the temple was so great that one was unable to hear the chorus of the singers, nor the minister at the altar. The other energumens, having quieted for a while, began the uproar once more. Francisca Barela continued in her insolence and loud shouts when she was seated. It became necessary to order her to be removed from the church, which caused the others who remained in the church to scream and move about as they had done at the start of the mass, though they were tolerable, as this happened every once in a while, and they did not disturb the congregation. When the mass was over, I performed the exorcism of the evil spirit which the devil felt a great deal, as he was inside of the bodies of the sick women. This was not only a bewitching, but also the devil who is behind such things. Removed from the church, after the exorcism, the possessed women were more furious, remaining in such a state of suffering that there is not a pen that can adequately explain it.

All of this went on the same night and day in full view of many people, and it became necessary to contain the sick women so they would not injure themselves with the major afflictions of this sickness, I mean sick woman. During the exorcisms, María shouted in an intelligible voice that the Indian Jacinta and her mother, the old woman called Atole Caliente, were suffocating her. This was apparent by the anxieties and demonstrations she made with her body and hands. She also said that they commanded her the other day, which was a Holy Day of Obligation and festival, not to attend Mass. I said she should be taken by force. She responded that I did not govern her, that she was subject to the two Indians referred to, who controlled her. Their motive was that she should not go to the church and report what she talked about, and she declared they would suffocate her more.

At daybreak, María had a short rest. On that same day, the sick women entered the church and, because people were there, I went to the altar and began to examine the missal before putting on the vestments. All the sick women fell to the floor, the first being María de Chávez. I turned my face to see her while some men held her down. The Indian Atole Caliente was above her head, holding the sick woman by the throat with one hand, and with the other, gesturing to suffocate her by inserting the point of a blanket into her mouth in the manner that an executioner does with a gag used for hanging. I heard someone try to quiet her by saying, "Mariquita, Mariquita," [a diminutive of Maria, possibly meant as a taunt] which was the reason it was necessary for me to turn around and, leaving the altar, put myself in the middle of the disturbance in order to remove the Indian Atole Caliente, whose insolence caused me great indisposition. I was not so incapacitated that I could not celebrate the Mass. It was the Mass of Our Lady. Nevertheless, I should have done what Our Lord did when he whipped those who profaned the temple, by leaving part of the deserved penalty for this sort of boldness in full view of so much of the congregation. Instead I did it afterward outside of the church in the presence of the lieutenant and many people, charging that the punishment was given for such irreverence committed in such a place and questioning Atole about her motives for committing such an act. Atole Caliente did not respond beyond saying she did it charitably to remove the evil. Immediately, she was prepared for the legal proceeding and entrusted to her daughter Jacinta. The Indian Joaquín went to the Lord Governor (whom he was referred to), so that he might participate in the situation he started, which was the exposure of the sorcery. This woman did not rest, nor did the others during the day or night until close to daybreak.

On the twenty first day of the same month, all these women were in place below the altar steps for the Mass and exorcisms. They were calm until I began to sing the first phrases of the gospel, which is when they let loose, one after the other, with grimaces, shaking, trembling, fainting, violent acts and other controversies. Because they exhibited so much cackling, annoyances, etc., which were horrifying, I had the good sense to perform the exorcism with the exposition of the sacrament and with the recital of *"quomodo caecidisti Lucifer qui manè orievaris"* [How art thou fallen from heaven, O Lucifer, who didst rise in the morning?]. One of the possessed women responded "by way of insolence and arrogance," and in the same instance her body fell to the floor and she remained exhausted until the exorcism entered her mind so that she could get up and then the exorcism was finished.

This same day, another young maiden furiously let loose inside of the church exhibiting a certain spirit of illness discovered in the month of September of 1763 with such a powerful evil that four to six men were overcome by her. In this bad state, her tongue let loose and they, the energumens, all began to chatter. By their responses, it was evident they understood Latin, which is a most certain sign of possession, and on the words of the major mysteries, they laughed, giving shouts, and making idle conversation. When I said *in nomine Patri* etc., they made demonstrations with their heads that the doctrine of the Trinity was not true. When I said *"al verbum caro factum est"* [the Word became flesh], they did the same. Continuing in this manner, I questioned Francisca Barela in Latin, "Why do the spirits injure this creature?" She responded that what was happening came from above. At this point, she exited the church. On the same day outside of the church, the women spent the whole day talking, wanting to exhaust themselves. One after the other they began to reveal various people. On different days, they identified the people according to their names, signs, homes and places of residence. As is evident in the attached document, the possessed affirmed that all the men and women named were evil sorcerers who murder with their arts. The women gave the reason that the principal foundation of the declaration was so the sorcery would be discovered, along with all of the

wickedness, even beyond this particular situation, that was in
this land. They also said that the Lord Governor wanted to
make an example and leave this land clean. On the same day,
they ended their fantastic demonstrations, howls, and
extreme chants, opening their eyes. They loudly declared
some other imaginings with their eyes closed very tightly.

At some point, not one of the ill women, but all of them,
left the hands of those who held them. They did not fear
stepping on the snow, or the cold air, or darkness of the
night. Following behind them were the people who observed
the times the women stopped, the plants and sticks they
gathered, and the many stones that at the end of a great while
they gave to me. They did not do this right away, but when
God determined. For, although they insisted on giving me the
stones, they did not do it until the hour had come to pass.
The women explained how each stone, plant, or stick
represented the art of this person, that person, etc. They also
described the method with which the sorcerers bewitched
people. This persuaded me that these deliveries, which have
been many, were the effect of those words of the exorcism
*precipio vobis ub obs incantatconibus facisnationibus signos
tuis Ligaturis et omnes vestras pactiones novis*s etc.
[Martinez translates, "I adjure you by incantation to reveal to
us your ligatures and all of your pacts."] In these comings
and goings, those who followed the possessed women have
seen many novelties, as when crows rested upon their heads
or behind their bodies. They have also seen how, while
indoors, corn husks, cheese, stones of all sizes, pieces of
wool, horses' hair, and many other forms of filth appeared,
much in the same manner as when elves throw things, but
cannot be seen. That is how it was when we were present.
When these women stretched out their empty hands, we went
and found that what they had removed was burning in the
holy fire as is prepared by a Roman priest. What is prepared
in the mouth they swallow, and, in less than twenty-four
hours, they remove it, such that much has been burned in
order to remove the evil. They appear to be very tormented
inside of the church as well as outside of it. This is manifested

through natural vomiting. They have been provoked on other occasions when they have been given sulphur, holy oil, and the smoke of the incense. They were overcome by this, and this is approved by the Church. After the vomiting, some of the women remained calm for the rest of the day. María de Chávez was the only one not to vomit.

The other day, which was the twenty-second, I proceeded with the spiritual remedy inside of the church. At the start of the Mass, they made the already referred to demonstrations with many more additions, such that there is no mind or judgment that can explain this. On this same day in the church, in the middle of the incantation, another young maiden of about twenty years of age fell down, exhausting herself in a fit, biting herself with more force than the others. She was the sister of Francisca Barela [María Agueda], the one named here and also the one who, last year in the month of June, I exorcised in the Holy Church. Although she was not in the same state of fury as the one I now mention, her condition ran parallel in all aspects to the four women mentioned. During all the days and those that followed, until the twenty-fourth, the women did not calm down, continuing to such an extent that the greater part of the people moved. Without ignoring this charity, the lieutenant assisted two days and nights without leaving, and also on other days.

After the first day of Easter, the possessed proceeded in the same manner. I proceeded with the holy repetition of the exorcism because I know the evil spirits are being defeated, because they have publicly declared it so in the church in a formidable shedding of tears and in an intelligible voice. The possessed shouted that they do not wish to be mistreated and then they rendered themselves at my feet, which is what I sought to accomplish. I knew I should take care and follow the insights of other priests. I should do what Saint Anthony Abbot did in his life. The terror of the devils took him to a woman who had a very powerful devil inside her, and he sent it away through his disciple Paul by saying "in the name of [Saint] Anthony Abbot." For me, these are the incomprehensible justices of God.

On the twenty-second day of this illness with the women of the church, a spirit left Francisca Barela, who said through her mouth that it had been there in order to treat her badly and that it was there in order to enter José Valdez, so that he might murder his wife, induced by two of his sisters-in-law. It wanted to enter him and said that their wills should be reconciled, that the worst of sins were of the tongue, and the other spirits would leave those who they were punishing.

On the twenty-eighth day of the exorcism, Lucifer left, bringing a sign during the fainting spell of María Trujillo inside the church. He caused a great deal of anxieties and movements, having expelled through her mouth the tooth of a horse with such effort that it became necessary to repeatedly place the stole on her back. Finally, forced by the dominion of the Word of God, she spit it out and remained at my feet. Her body was not injured. The spirit also said that it had entered her in the summer on the plains close to her house and at that place and home there were a legion of spirits. Another spirit remained inside of the body of this sick woman [María Trujillo] and it declared that it had entered this town on the occasion that they, the energumens, forced the spirit up from the crows and brought and delivered the plants. This spirit said it was called Satanus. The third day after Lucifer's departure, Satanus left and brought the same signs as the first. In order to be certain that it had left, I made her make a solemn incantation to God our Lord. If she did not comply, I would know that Lucifer was lying, and I would punish him. This woman was successfully delivered of the evil spirit.

Within two days of its leaving this sick woman at this place there was a continuing pathetic lament outside of the church and during the whole Mass and exorcism. So that she would not forget, María Trujillo also said that all those named, at all times and occasions, while in their evil and depraved state, spit on the Cross, the *Agnus Dei,* relics, holy water, and on the rosary. They seized the rosary and broke it to pieces, and those same women also removed the relic, etc. The third sick woman, the sister of Francisca Barela named María Agueda, was left by the spirit on another day than that of María Trujillo's and it said its name was the devil Cojuelo. She said it entered her the previous year at Chimayo in order to abuse her, and although it was leaving, there remained another three spirits in all.

This same day, there was not much rest. Immediately after the sun went down, one of the possessed women began to stretch out her hands and catch stones. When she took nourishment, she warned that what they put on the plate of food and the supper was blessed with a special benediction. We removed from that plate splinters, stones, pieces of adobe, etc. María de Chávez and María Rosalía, since the fifteenth of January, have been calm, without giving signs as to when the spirit would leave, which is why I continued with the exorcism, returning to María Trujillo, who, as I said has remained well two days. On the third day, over what displeasure with her husband I did not know, in a house of the Pueblo, she was found standing for the benefit of the exorcism. She invoked the devil for a long time while enraged and deranged, as the devil, who was not made deaf, came, bringing as signs the shaking of the house. This was declared by those who were present.

María Trujillo's face and body started to make various grimaces and forceful gestures, as she wanted to break free from the hands of those who held her. She blasphemed and apostatized verbally, and her lips were black like coal. This lasted more than two and a half hours. Many people who went and saw this remarkable occurrence came to call me. I, considering that the woman had invoked him, ignored all of the calls and did not want to go, considering that I could be disabled to say the Mass and exorcise the others. It was best that I finished preparing. Giving all of myself to God, I asked at the moment of the Mass not to remember my offenses, rather His infinite clemency. This action pained this same child, and the spirit said that it was present and the other energumens were the cause of María's affliction. My greatest sins were consoled, and it all came together at the same instant of the *Memento*s. With myself in the church and the ill woman at her home with many people, she shouted "that friar is avoiding this attack; call him to me!" When I finished, I expressed what had happened during the sacrifice of the Mass. The people who were with her excused me, yet they still came to me, and gave me the message so that I had to yield to the supplication. I did this with some reservation, because of the cunning of the devil. I had to go help the possessed woman, so I protected myself with the prayer of exorcism. After I had succeeded in the execution of the exorcism, María proved to me the spirit was not inside her body by reciting the divine oath. As I was over her head, she advised me of the danger of certain people, so as to publicly announce the goodness of their souls, etc. She revealed things of a personal nature about many who were present. Because so many people saw these signs, they were reconciled through the sacrament of penance by me, asking for pardon. Finally, the spirit withdrew, leaving María's sanity in good condition, and her coloring returned. However, she was very maimed.

The next day, María Trujillo returned at the same hour and declared herself to be ecstatic. She gave helpful advice for souls. On the third day, she returned. With the alcalde mayor present, she advised him as to what he should do to cleanse this land of so much impurity. She did this by giving signs, from place to place, and by advising the Indian discoverer not to fail or cover up a thing, because it was the will of the Creator that so much adoration of the devil should stop and, instead, such actions should be given to our Creator. She finished, referring to me what she had said to the alcalde mayor.

There is not a mind that can comprehend this situation, for as in a battle, where the leader cannot lose faith, I am assisting without getting caught up again. Hence, I am in great danger and the target of this battle. It seems I will never stop recounting for being incapable for so many bad days and nights. I am certain that, although I have jurisdiction, am healthy, and I have He who is Our Lord Jesus Christ, and while I am a very sinful man, I have nevertheless struggled with the idea that these women are tormented by the devil.

Through the exorcism I performed and by the signs the authors of the manuals of exorcism present, it is evident there are very few signs of possession these creatures are lacking. The possessed have had frightful experiences in their dreams, as well as outside of them, in their judgment a tingling sensation issued forth through their bodies. With the exorcism, they became deaf, they understood Latin, and their coloring changed at the hour of these bad events. When the spirit withdrew, their good coloring came back, they declared that which was within their soul, and their major goal was to make sins public.

These they have not carried out, for they admit that they are subjects of the Minister of the Church and the Lord, who has ordered them not to reveal the sins of others. They have chanted in the Tewa language, chants they do not know in the Taos language. In her evil state, one declared to have been taken to Sandia, Isleta, and Belen. Another said the spirits take her to Chimayo, while another said she was taken to Pojoaque, Nambe, and Tesuque. Besides all this, the most significant sign, which is when they are free and using their own judgment, they do not remember the things that they have said. Being violent when they were ordered to be silent, they did not obey many times. This was outside of the exorcism. If devout prayers were said for them, or some prayed, those who were prayed for would get furious. Many other times, whoever would enter, they would call by their name, even though they did not know that person. To all those present, including myself, they say "son of a whore" and other disgraceful words.

On the twenty-ninth day of December, I began to exorcise, along with the sick women, Santiago Martín, resident of this jurisdiction, who, since the time he went with the chief magistrate to the Cerro del Pedernal, has felt an obstacle to arriving at that place and, since that time, reverted to the medicine with which he has not been able to find comfort. On the first day of the exorcism, he felt rising to his head a perturbation of the mind and a great deal of churning in his belly, accompanied by a shaking of the limbs of his body.

When the exorcism was over, his body was very limp. Because of his appearance, I asked that he be removed from the church, taking him by the shoulders and other parts of the body. He was maintained for nine days in the village for the exorcism. On the feast day of the Holy Kings, he was taken to his home, where he was in little comfort.

On the eleventh day of January of this year, since his illness was even more alleviated, he spoke to the sick women about his alleviation and improvement. At three in the afternoon on Wednesday, these three sick maidens, while in their evil state, said "Sunday the fifteenth was the soul of Purgatory," a thing deserving of mention. Even though what is happening is tragic, I feel it is merciful that God informs us with such happenings. Our benefit and good are exhibited in what we see. We are able to glimpse the torments that take place in the other life if we do not repent.

On the same day, God called on Santiago Martín with a beautiful disposition and good signs of his leaving. He was buried on Monday. How can I explain my simplicity so that your Lordship will be satisfied and the Lord Governor will participate so that in his high understanding he will consider and destroy the many lies of the populace, who always want novelties? They add and remove facts because they are ignorant. It is not my intention to prosecute any crime, for I have such confidence in God and I do not doubt He communicates in light. I therefore send my auxiliaries to the Superior, in order to certify the truth, honor, glory, and exaltation of His Holy Name and Law.

I am also remitting the list of those who have been accused of sorcery without being questioned. All this has been done before the public, since there has been no shortage of people to help. They lie about whom they desire. It is not my motivation or intention to place the blame on them because I know, through the practice of exorcism, that it is not licit for me to discover this crime, when it is only to the exorcist that the devil will reveal it. It has not been revealed only to me, nor questioned by me alone. Rather, other people have voluntarily given this information. Nevertheless, I do not ignore that the devil, the father of lies, has attempted to excuse all of this information. But I am not ashamed, nor afraid to use all the means necessary to remove all obstacles and give adoration to the Highest. This is advised for the alcalde mayor, the Indian discoverer, and myself. As I told the alcalde mayor, so I say to the Governor vocally: May the majesty of all powerful God illuminate our senses and hearts. May Your Lordship be granted much health and may God protect you many years. From this Pueblo of Abiquiu, 22 of January 1764

Your assured servant and chaplain kisses the hand of Your Lordship

fray Juan José Toledo

GEORGE LUKINS, THE YATTON DEMONIAC

1788

*George Lukins (1744–1805) of Somerset, England, be-
came infamous as "The Yatton Demoniac" when a war
of pamphlets ensued following his exorcism in 1788
by ministers allied with the recently created Methodist
movement. The pamphlets point to a clash between the
supernaturalism of the Methodist revival and the Enlightenment values of skepticism and reason. Lukins's
troubles began after performing in a Christmas "mum-
mering play" through the neighborhood during the winter
of 1769–1770. After performing for one Mr. Love, Lukins
fell down on Love's porch—either because a demonic
force was punishing him for performing in a Christmas
pageant, as Lukins claimed, or because he was drunk
from strong beer that Love had offered the performers, as
skeptics claimed. Following this incident, Lukins began
suffering fits. The fits were bad enough that he was unable to continue his work as a tailor and required financial support from the parish. In 1775, the parish sent him
to St. George's Hospital, but he was declared incurable
and sent home. Lukins believed he was bewitched. He
turned to "cunning women" in search of folk remedies.
He also accused various senior citizens of bewitching
him, at one point assaulting an elderly woman.*

*For a time he became better and could work again, but
in 1787 his fits returned and the parish refused to give
further financial relief. It was around this time that his
diagnosis shifted from bewitchment to possession. Like
Mary Magdalene, Lukins claimed he was possessed by
seven devils and could be cured if seven ministers prayed*

over him at once. He requested two guineas to go to Bristol to find seven clergymen, but was given only ten shillings and sixpence. He arrived in Bristol on June 7, 1788, and found Reverend Joseph Easterbrook, vicar of Temple Church.

Easterbrook asked Anglican clergy for assistance but they declined. Instead, he found six Wesleyan Methodists who agreed to help. The exorcism was performed on Friday, June 13, and lasted about two hours. The Methodists did not use a ritual, but prayed, sang hymns, and ordered the demons out in the name of God, Jesus, and the Holy Spirit. Afterward Lukins was reportedly cured of his fits.

That summer, a series of articles appeared in The Bristol Gazette debating Lukins's possession. Samuel Norman, a surgeon who at one point lodged with Lukins in Yatton, wrote a letter alleging Lukins simply faked all of his symptoms. He also chided the Methodists for reverting to "Popish" superstitions. Norman's account reveals that Lukins's possession was to some extent contagious, as similar symptoms began manifesting in other people. He also admits to using deliberately cruel medical techniques to discourage people from exhibiting signs of possession.

Norman's skepticism offended some, who responded with more letters to the paper. This escalated, and writers weighing in on the issue began to use pseudonyms such as "Justiae Vindex" and "Antifanatic." These letters were eventually collected into pamphlets that, unfortunately, spend more words expressing outrage at the opposition than presenting evidence concerning Lukins's condition. Historian Owen Davies reports that inside a copy of Rev. Easterbrook's pamphlet, a handwritten poem was found on a slip of paper dated 1794:

Lo Lukins comes, and with him comes a train,
of parsons famous for a lack of brain,
With vol-like faces and with raven coats;

Their solemn stile their solemn task denotes;
By exercisings, prayer, and pluckings,
To drive some sturdy devils out of Lukins[1]

Letter of William Robert Wake to *The Bristol Gazette*[2]

Sir,

When you can spare room in your Gazette, I think you will not be able to present your readers with any account so extrardinary and surprizing as the following. It is the most singular case of perverted reason and bodily suffering that I ever heard of; nor have the most learned and ingenious persons been able to solve the phenomenon, much less to administer relief to the afflicted object. You may depend on the authenticity of every part of the relation, a member of my family having been near thirty years Minister of the place where the person resides, many of my friends fill inhabiting it, and myself having been frequently a witness to the facts I shall mention.

About eighteen years ago the unfortunate subject of this epistle, going about the neighbourhood with other young fellows, acting Christmas plays or mummeries, suddenly fell down senseless, and was with great difficulty recovered. When he came to himself, the account he gave was, that he seemed at the moment of his fall to have received a violent blow from the hand of some person, who, as he thought, was allowed thus to punish him for acting a part in the play. From that moment, he has been subject, at uncertain and different periods, to fits of a most singular and dreadful nature. The first symptom is a powerful agitation of the right hand, to which succeed terrible distortions of the countenance. The influence of the fit has then commenced. He declares in a roaring voice that he is the devil, who with many horrid execrations summons about him certain persons devoted to his will, and commands them to torture this unhappy patient with all the diabolical means in their power. The supposed demon then directs his servants to sing. Accordingly the patient sings in a different voice a jovial hunting song, which, having received the approbation of *the foul fiend*, is succeeded by a song in a female voice, very delicately expressed; and this is followed, at the particular injunction of the demon, by a pastoral song in the form of a dialogue, sung by, and in the real character of the patient himself. After a pause and more violent distortions, he again personates the demon, and sings in a hoarse, frightful voice another hunting song. But in all these songs, whenever any expression of goodness, benevolence, or innocence, occurs in the original, it is regularly changed to another of its opposite meaning; neither can the patient bear to hear any good words whatever, nor any expression relating to the church, during the influence of his fit, but is exasperated by them into the most shocking degree of blasphemy and outrage. Neither can he speak or write any expressions of this tendency, whilst the subsequent weakness of his fits is upon him; but is driven to madness by their mention. Having performed the songs, he continues to personate the demon, and derides the attempts which the patient has been making to get out of his power, that he will persecute and torment him more and more to the end of his life, and that all the efforts of parsons and physicians shall prove fruitless. An *inverted Te Deum* is then sung in the alternate voices of a man and woman, who with much profaneness thank the demon for having given them power over the patient, which they will continue to exercise as long as he lives. The demon then concludes the ceremony, by declaring his unalterable resolution to punish him for ever; and after barking fiercely, and interspersing many assertions of his own diabolical dignity, the fit subsides into the same strong agitation of the hand that introduced it, and the patient recovers from its influence, utterly weakened and exhausted. At certain periods of the fit, he is so violent, that an assistant is always obliged to be at hand, to restrain him from committing some injury on himself; though to the spectators he is perfectly harmless. He understands all that is said and done during his fits, and will even reply sometimes to questions asked him. He is under the influence of these paroxisms generally near an hour, during which time his eyes are fast closed.—Sometimes he fancies himself changed into the form of an animal, when he assumes all the motions and sounds that are peculiar to it. From the execrations he utters it may be presumed that he is or was of an abandoned and profligate character, but the reverse is the truth; he was ever of a remarkable innocent and inoffensive disposition. Every method that the variety of persons who have come to see him have suggested, every effort of some very ingenious gentlemen of the faculty who applied their serious attention to his case, has been long ago and recently exerted without success; and some years ago he was sent to St. George's Hospital, where he remained about twenty weeks, and was pronounced incurable. Of late, he has every day at least three and sometimes nine of these fits, which have reduced him to great weakness and almost to despair; for he cannot hear any virtuous or religious expression used without pain and horror. The emaciated and exhausted figure that he presents, the number of years that he has been subject to this malady, and the prospect of want and distress that lies before him, through being thus disabled from following his business; all preclude the suspicion of imposture. His life is become a series of intense and anxiety.

Should any of your readers question the authenticity of this relation, or conceive themselves able to administer relief or even mitigation to this afflicted object, you know your correspondent, and have my free consent to refer them to me.

I remain,

Your very humble servant,

Wrington, June 5, 1788.   W. R. W.

*Joseph Easterbrook, Short Account of the singular De-
liverance of George Lukins, of the parish of Yatton, in*

the county of Somerset, aged forty-four, and by trade a taylor.[3]

Some persons, who had been acquainted with his unhappy situation for many years, had heard him repeatedly say that he was possessed with seven devils, and if seven ministers could be got to pray with him in faith, they would be cast out. But this declaration being treated as a visionary matter, he remained in his former state, notwithstanding every means made use of for his cure. However, a person who felt much for his deplorable case had him brought to Bristol last week, to see if any thing could be done for him, and to meet the subject on his own ground of an expected cure.

After he had been here a few days, and was seen by many persons in his fits of spasms, (who observed that the particular circumstances attending them fully coincided with the foregoing letter) several Ministers were prevailed upon to meet on the occasion. They accordingly met in the Vestry-room of Temple church, on Friday the 13th instant, at eleven o'clock in the forenoon, attended by the poor man, and several other persons to assist in managing of him in his fits: and the following is a relation of some of the particulars on the above awful occasion.

1. They began singing an hymn, on which the man was immediately thrown into strange agitations, (very different from his usual seizures) his face was variously distorted, and his whole body strongly convulsed. His right hand and arm then began to shake with violence, and after some violent throes, he spake in a deep, hoarse, hollow voice, *personating an invisible agent*, calling the man to an account, and upbraiding him as a fool for bringing that silly company together: said it was to no purpose, and swore "by his infernal den," that he would never quit his hold of him, but would torment him a thousand times worse for making this vain attempt.

2. He then began to sing in his usual manner, (*still person-ating some invisible agent*) horribly blaspheming, boasted of his power, and vowed eternal vengeance on the miser-able object, and on those present for daring to oppose him; and commanded his "faithful and obedient servants" to appear, and take their stations.

3. He then spake in a female voice, very expressive of scorn and derision, and demanded to know why the fool had brought such a company there? And swore "by the devil" that he would not quit his hold of him, and bid de-fiance to and cursed all, who should attempt to rescue the miserable object from them. He then sung, in the same fe-male voice, a kind of love song, at the conclusion of which he was violently tortured, and repeated most horrible im-precations.

4. Another invisible agent came forth, assuming a differ-ent voice, but his manner much the same as the preceding one. A kind of dialogue was then sung in a hoarse and soft voice alternately; at the conclusion of which, as be-fore, the man was thrown into violent agonies, and blas-phemed in a manner too dreadful to be expressed.

5. He then personated, and said, "I am the great Devil;" and after much boasting of his power, and bidding defi-ance to all his opposers, sung a kind of hunting song; at the conclusion of which he was most violently tortured, so that it was with difficulty that two strong men could hold him (though he is but a small man, and very weak in constitution); sometimes he would set up a hideous laugh, and at other times bark in a manner indescribably horrid.

6. After this he summoned all the infernals to appear, and drive the company away. And while the ministers were engaged in fervent prayer, he sung a Te Deum to the devil,

in different voices, saying, "We praise thee, O devil; we acknowledge thee to be the supreme governor," &c. &c.

7. When the noise was so great as to obstruct the company proceeding in prayer, they sang together an hymn suitable to the occasion. Whilst they were in prayer, the voice which personated the great Devil bid them defiance, curling and vowing dreadful vengeance on all present. One in the company commanded him in the name of the great Jehovah to declare his name? To which he replied, "I am the Devil." The same person then charged him in the name of Jehovah to declare why he tormented the man? To which he made answer, "That I may shew my power amongst men."

8. The poor man still remained in great agonies and torture, and prayer was continued for his deliverance. A clergyman present desired him to endeavor to speak the name of "Jesus," and several times repeated it to him, at all of which he replied "Devil." —During this attempt a small faint voice was heard saying, "Why don't you adjure?" On which the clergy man commanded, in the name of Jesus, and in the name of the Father, the Son and the Holy Ghost, the evil spirit to depart from the man; which he repeated several times: —when a voice was heard to say, "Must I give up my power?" and this was followed by dreadful howlings. Soon after another voice, as with astonishment, said, "Our master has deceived us."—The clergyman still continuing to repeat the adjuration, a voice was heard to say, "Where shall we go?" and the reply was, "To hell, thine own infernal den, and return no more to torment this man." —On this the man's agitations and distortions were stronger than ever, attended with the most dreadful howling that can be conceived. But as soon as this conflict was over, he said, in his own natural voice, "Blessed Jesus!" —became quite serene, immediately praised God for his deliverance, and kneeling down said the Lord's prayer and returned his most devout thanks to all who were present.

* * *

The meeting broke up a little before one o'clock, having lasted near two hours, and the man went away entirely delivered, and has had no return of the disorder since.

Letter of Samuel Norman to *The Bristol Gazette*[4]

Sir,

Few things could surprise me more than the narrative of George Lukins's case, published in your paper of the 19th instant by W. R. W. of Wrington, and that too as introductory to the cure of the pretended daemoniac.

I doubt not but that many pious people will give implicit belief to the whole story; and it is with the sincerest regret that I find myself obliged from a love to plain truth, to give a brief and faithful relation of that case. I know too well the narrow limits of my abilities as a writer, not to tremble at even the thought of a literary discussion, with so able an opponent; but trusting to that generosity and candour which an enlightened public will ever extend to the cause of truth, though exhibited in the poor garb of simplicity only, I inlist myself its votary. Indeed without this persuasion I should not venture thus to address myself to you.

In the latter end of the year 1769, or beginning of 1770, G. Lukins of Yatton, the person whose case I have been speaking of, with some young people, went to the house of the late Mr. Love, to perform Christmas plays. Mr. Love being of a generous disposition, gave them so much liquor as to intoxicate them. G. Lukins was greatly overloaded, and in endeavouring to walk out, fell down at the door, where he remained till assistance was given him. The next day, and for a considerable time after, he pretended he was hurted by Mr. Love's dog. Soon after this incident, his fits commenced. In some few weeks he pretended he was bewitched. At certain intervals his fits would return, or he would be speechless during a determinate space of time, always foretold by himself.—Sometimes he attempted to run into a pond or shallow river. At other times he would leap, howl, &c. and distort himself violently. Several times he danced in a large chimney corner, upon burning coals; and lay down on a box near a large fire, covered with many cloaths, and sweated profusely. During all his pretended paroxisms he has fully retained his different senses and understanding, from the first of his performances to the termination of them. But his curses, execrations, and expressions during his fits have notwithstanding been most truly horrible.

All these oddities were attributed to the power of witchcraft, or influence of an evil spirit. In June 1770, I settled at Yatton, and for some time lodged in the same house with this man; so that I had frequent opportunities to see him in his fits; in every one of which except in singing, he performed not more than most active young people can easily do. I except singing for this reason, because many have neither an ear for music nor knowledge of notes; but from his youth this man was, as it were, bred to singing. Convinced that all his complaints were feigned, or occasioned by hypocondriacism, I directed the people to permit him to trample on the fire, or run into the river or the pool, which were very shallow, and observed to them, that no ill consequences could follow, as in case of necessity they could instantly save him.—From that time he left off those attempts, and the fears of his friends on that head were dissipated. To prove himself bewitched, he gave me and others many relations of the power of witches, their iniquitous practices and punishments for them. When he would be thought speechless, he could thrust his tongue out of his mouth towards his nose or chin, make use of it in every manner necessary for speech; modify his voice to almost all sounds; and being perfectly sensible at those times, singing many agreeable tunes, swallowing and doing every act and thing with understanding and precision, and having the free and proper use of every part and organ subservient to speech; no good reason can possibly be aligned for his obstinate taciturnity, but his predetermination. Soon after I saw him, he thought, or pretended that his fingers were contracted, and kept his fist clinched: but I easily put his fingers out strait, and kept them so upon a handboard, without occasioning swelling, pain or spasm, which could not have been the case had there been a contraction of the muscular and tendonous parts. His next subterfuge was a pretended contraction of his thumb, which he would pertinaciously keep close to the palm of his hand. I had previously given up the care of him, being disgusted at his ridiculous pretences: but to convince the family where he lodged of the impropriety of this trick also, I desired a discreet man with whom he slept, to observe his hand in the morning before he awoke; so watchful was the patient, that it was several mornings before this could be done; at length, however, Mr. P. instantly recollecting himself when he awoke, gently turned down the bedcloaths, and found his thumb fully extended, and at rest upon his breast. Mr. P. then pretended to awake disturbed, and George Lukins awaking, instantly contracted his thumb as before. I need not draw any inference; the intelligent reader must discern the cause of this complaint: but the principles of compassion operated too powerfully upon many for them to allow themselves even to reason upon his case. About that time a person of credit reading in the bible, designedly pronounced father improperly; our patient was at that time as speechless as at different other times: but he endeavoured as she thought to tell her: she as often repeated that word wrongly, till at last our speechless actor hastily gave her the proper pronunciation, and then appeared as recollecting himself and greatly distressed.

He continued in the same way a long time, till by means of a petition he had collected something considerable; soon after which his complaints left him, or he them. It must be admitted, that wrong apprehensions produce various influences upon the body, which people of weak understanding may greatly suffer from. The cases of a young man and a young woman, who went to see George Lukins in his paroxisms, if I may so call them, fully prove this.

The first was a servant man of Mr. John Young, of this parish. Soon after seeing George Lukins, he fancied himself bewitched, and appeared greatly affrighted, distorted his face and limbs, bellowing, leaping, falling down, acting, and singing with, as it were, different voices, very much like him. His master hasted to my house, and desired me to go with him. It was agreed between us, that if I found it prudent, I should be allowed to threaten either himself, Mrs. Young, or any of the family. The fellow on my arrival appeared all distraction. I treated him roughly; threatened his master, &c. for hearkening to the fool; insisted instantly upon bleeding him, vomited him, and on the next morning purged him briskly. The fellow, expecting a daily repetition of the same treatment, assumed by the morning his proper understanding, and followed his business as before. The other was a poor girl of Chelvey. This girl was affected in the same manner, and from the same cause as Mr. Young's man-servant. She was supposed to be lunatic or hysteric, by her neighbours. I was employed for her, and gave her, at the request of the overseer, large quantities of antispasmodic or nervous medicines, during the space of five or six days, without the least benefit; when pursuing my own inclination, I exhibited two surly emetics a little while before the appointed times for the return of her fits; leaving her wholly at other times, to herself during her performances, and in two or three days she left them off, and was fully restored to a due sense of her folly.

But to return to the case of George Lukins. He remained a considerable time free from his pretended fits, and followed his business as a Taylor, or some other employment. But the same disposition returning, his old tricks were renewed. The attention of most people was again attracted to him, and many schemes to rescue him from the hands of the witches were devised and employed; even pretended conjurors were sought out & applied to; but their directions and exorcisms were practiced in vain. But shameful to think of, several very indigent and infirm old people were again cruelly censured for bewitching him. At length he was sent to St. George's Hospital in London, where he remained many weeks. Some of the faculty there desired to be sent for whenever his fits returned; but this never happened, after he was duly admitted as a patient in that hospital, notwithstanding the punctuality with which his fits ever have returned, according to his own prognostications, before and since his return thence. We must not suppose that an intimation from the nurse of the beneficial effects, in such cases, of the laced waistcoat could operate so powerfully as to drive the witches or devils, whether *he or she or small or great*, out of him; but it seems an undoubted fact, that he never had a fit after he went before the board of governors in that hospital. After his return to his brother's at Yatton, be played off the same feats. His brother grew tired of him, and Richard Beacham of this parish was desired to lodge him. He consulted me on the occasion. I advised both him and his wife to take him in, and gave it as my opinion, that they would not suffer the least inconvenience from his lodging with them; being fully persuaded that he would not have any fits, if he was not suffered to see, or be seen by, any persons at their house, during the times he may be desirous of exhibiting his feats. For the space of several months he stayed with them, and the event justified my opinion. After he left R. Beacham's house, a very long interval elapsed before he again commenced his old performances, which happened in the course of last year. He was not, however, so forgetful of his interest, as not to have recourse to another petition. All his former mockeries or performances were sometimes attributed to the power of the devil; but since this last renewal of them, after pretending to wound a poor inoffensive old woman because she bewitched him, he has now fully and generally attributed all his absurdities and abominable performances to the invisible influence of satan only. In his performances the commencement and duration of which have always been foretold by him, if any well informed person, under pretense of holding him, would not support him so as to enable him to play off his tricks, without suffering him to fall or injure himself, he has constantly left off that part of his antics, and substituted another in its stead; and unusual and horrible as his tricks have been through the whole continuance of them, he has taken due care at all times not materially to injure himself or any person. So that he appears to have been possessed with the act of volition, fully and perfectly at all times, enjoying also his powers of observation, recollection, and reasoning, as completely during his abominable antics and horrible blasphemies, as at any other time. I am surprised to see him represented as in a meagre and emaciated state; this is by no means the case allowing for his increase of years. I have not known him look better than at the present time; and if walking between twenty and thirty miles in seven or eight hours is not a full proof of his strength which he has done very lately, I wish to know what will or can be deemed such. With equal truth is the assertion made, of his keeping his eyes fast during his fits for he takes care frequently to peep, or slyly to squint at his wise visitors. The late pious Mr. Wake, our vicar, soon looked upon his pretences with due contempt. And I hope this plain account of the subject will prevent the honest and well meaning from being deceived by groundless pretences.

S. N.
Yatton, June 21, 1788.

JEWISH TRADITIONS
OF EXORCISM

FLAVIUS JOSEPHUS, ANTIQUITIES OF THE JEWS[1]

94 CE

Titus Flavius Josephus was a Jew born in Jerusalem in 37 CE. He initially participated in the Jewish revolt against Roman rule that led to the destruction of the Temple in Jerusalem; however, he surrendered to Vespasian, becoming his slave and interpreter. He served as an adviser to the Romans and was granted citizenship. Josephus became a historian, explaining Jewish history and traditions to a Greek and Roman audience. His accounts of first-century Judaism are invaluable to modern classicists and religion scholars. Antiquities of the Jews *is a twenty-volume work, completed in either 93 or 94 CE.*

A passage describing Jewish exorcism attributes the knowledge of casting out demons to King Solomon. Josephus then describes witnessing a Jew named Eleazar performing an exorcism by using an enchanted ring. Josephus's account emphasizes empirical evidence, noting that the exorcism was witnessed by not only him but also the emperor Vespasian and his army. He describes cups of water that were inexplicably knocked over and cited as evidence that a spirit had departed. He also frames exorcism as a gift from the Jews to the rest of the world, including the Romans.

Over time, King Solomon became an increasingly important figure in demonological lore. The Testament of Solomon, most likely composed during the Middle Ages, describes in detail how Solomon used a magical ring not only to bind various demons but also to use them as slave labor to construct his temple.

* * *

Now the sagacity and wisdom which God had bestowed on Solomon was so great, that he exceeded the ancients: insomuch that he was no way inferior to the Egyptians, who are said to have been beyond all men in understanding; nay, indeed, it is evident that their sagacity was very much inferior to that of the king's. He also excelled and distinguished himself in wisdom above those who were most eminent among the Hebrews at that time for shrewdness; those I mean were Ethan, and Heman, and Chalcol, and Darda, the sons of Mahol. He also composed books of odes and songs, a thousand and five; of parables and similitudes three thousand; for he spake a parable upon every sort of tree, from the hyssop to the cedar; and in like manner also about beasts, about all sorts of living creatures, whether upon the earth, or in the seas, or in the air; for he was not unacquainted with any of their nature, nor omitted inquiries about them, but described them all like a philosopher, and demonstrated his exquisite knowledge of their several properties. God also enabled him to learn that skill which expels demons, which is a science useful and sanative to men. He composed such incantations also by which distempers are alleviated. And he left behind him the manner of using exorcisms, by which they drive away demons, so that they never return; and this method of cure is of great force unto this day: for I have seen a certain man of my own country, whose name was Eleazar, releasing people that were demoniacal in the presence of Vespasian, and his sons, and his captains, and the whole multitude of his soldiers. The manner of the cure was this; he put a ring that had a root of one of those sorts mentioned by Solomon to the nostrils of the demoniac, after which he drew out the demon through his nostrils: and when the man fell down immediately, he abjured him to return into him no more, making still mention of Solomon, and reciting the incantations which he composed. And when Eleazar would persuade and demonstrate to the spectators that he had such a power, he set a little way off a cup or basin full of water, and commanded the demon, as he went out of the man, to overturn it, and thereby to let the spectators know that he had left the man: and when this was done, the skill and wisdom of Solomon was showed very manifestly; for which reason it is that all men may know the vastness of Solomon's abilities, and how he was beloved of God, and that the extraordinary virtues of every kind with which this King was endowed, may not be unknown to any people under the sun; for this reason, I say, it is that we have proceeded to speak so largely of these matters.

THE SPIRIT IN THE
WIDOW OF SAFED[1]

1571

The Jewish tradition of exorcism concerns an entity known as the dybbuk *(plural* dybbukim), *generally believed to be a spirit of the dead. The term* dybbuk *appears for the first time in a Yiddish pamphlet from Volhyna, Ukraine, in the seventeenth century. However, the tradition of exorcising spirits of the dead was defined by a series of accounts dating back to the Galilean town of Safed in the sixteenth century. This was the same period when demonic possession and accusations of witchcraft were sweeping Christian Europe. Sixteenth-century Safed was a cultural center of Jewish mysticism known as kabbalah. It was the home of Rabbi Isaac Luria (1534–1572), perhaps the most famous kabbalist who ever lived. The idea of the* dybbuk *is closely related to the kabbalistic idea of* gilgul, *or the transmigration of the dead.*[2]

The exorcism below is a classic tale recorded in several sources. However, the exorcist, Luria's protégé Rabbi Hayyim Vital (1542–1620), recorded the encounter in his diary from 1571. At the opening of the story, the widow is already a celebrity in Safed, as the possessing spirit exhibits a form of clairvoyance. A visiting sage identifies the spirit as that of his former rabbinical student. The widow's relatives seek out Isaac Luria, who sends Hayyim Vital in his stead. Luria transmits some of his spiritual "intentions" (kavvanot) to Vital and gives him holy names that can be used to expel the spirit.

Once the exorcism begins, the narrator describes the widow as a "him," indicating the spirit, not the possessed. The spirit is unable to even look at Vital, as he can see divine glory (shekhina) emitting from the rabbi's face. Vital then compels the spirit to tell its tale. This is a pathetic story that reveals much of the cosmology surrounding the idea of dybbuk possession. The spirit was unable to enter spiritual paradise (Gan Eden) because of his sexual transgressions, a common trope in dybbuk stories. He was sentenced to twelve months in Gehinnom— a Jewish analogue to the Catholic idea of purgatory—a place where souls are purified. But the spirit was driven away from the gates of Gehinnom by a crowd of other spirits, also awaiting purification. Vengeful angels and other antagonists pursued him, causing him to seek a body to inhabit.

The spirit traveled to the city of Ormuz, only to find the Jews there were uninhabitable because they too engaged in sexual transgression by fornicating with gentiles. He briefly inhabited a doe and then a Jew of the priestly class in Shekhem, before being expelled by Muslim exorcists. The spirit explains that Muslim exorcisms do work, but only by filling the host body with even more impurities so that spirits may no longer inhabit it. The spirit was finally able to enter the widow of Safed because she doubted the miracles of the Exodus story. The spirit's story is a morality tale, demonstrating by example how Jews ought to act and believe. This is common in many forms of exorcism, where possessing spirits give confessions that affirm the religious worldview of the exorcist. Vital banishes the spirit through the widow's left foot, suggesting a rather physical model of spirit possession. It is prevented from returning by ensuring the widow's home has a proper mezuza—a ritual ornament containing verses of the Torah that is traditionally fixed to doorways.

There occurred an event at the time that the holy and pure Rav [teacher], the divine kabbalist Isaac Luria Ashkenazi, his memory for a blessing, was in Safed. A spirit entered one woman, a widow, and made her suffer very great and enormous suffering. Many people assembled about her, and spoke with her and the spirit replied to each and every one, making known the wounds of his heart and all of his needs for that which he lacked. And among those who came one sage entered his midst, and his name was our teacher, the rabbi R. J. I., may the memory of the righteous be a blessing. Immediately the spirit said to him, "Blessed is he who comes, my master, my teacher and my rabbi! I recall my master, for I was his student in Egypt for a long time, and my name is so and so, and my father's name is so and so.

Now, when the relatives of the woman saw her suffering and her pain, that it was very great, they went to the Holy Rav, Isaac Luria, to beg him to go with them to the woman and to remove this spirit from the woman. Being that the Rav was not free to go himself, he sent his student, Hayyim Calabrese, and laid his hands upon him and transmitted to him *kavvanot* [intentions] with Names. He also commanded him to decree upon him bans and excommunications and to remove him against his will.

As soon our teacher Hayyim Vital entered her midst, the woman immediately turned her face away to the wall. The Rav said to her, "Evildoer, why did you turn your face away from me?" The spirit replied to him and said, "I am unable to gaze upon your face, for the wicked are unable to gaze upon the face of the *Shekhina!*" Immediately our teacher the Hayyim decreed upon him that he turn his face, and he then immediately turned his face. He said to him, "What is your sin and your transgression for which they have punished you with this severe punishment?" The spirit replied to him and said, "I sinned with a married woman and fathered bastards. It has now been twenty-five years since I began wandering in the land, and they have given me no respite, neither for an hour nor for a minute. For three angels of destruction go with me to all the places to which I go, and punish me and beat me with exceedingly hard blows, and declare before me, 'Such will be done to one who multiplied bastards among Israel.' And these three angels of destruction are alluded to in the verse: Appoint

over him a wicked man, and may Satan stand at his right'
(Psalms 109:7-8)." And the spirit also said to the Rav, "Do you
not see one angel of the angels who stands on my right, and
one on my left, and they decree, and the third strikes me death
blows?" The Rav asked him and said to him, "Did our sages
not say, "The sentence of the wicked in Gehinnom is twelve
months'? (*Eduyot* 2:10)." The spirit responded to him and said
to him,

> My master was not precise in this statement, for when our sages
> said that "the sentence of the wicked in Gehinnom is twelve
> months," it was after they have suffered the punishments out-
> side of Gehinnom, in reincarnations and through other hard
> judgments. Then they are admitted to Gehinnom, and there they
> spend twelve months. They whiten and wash them in order to
> remove from them the stains of their souls, in order for them to
> be summoned and prepared to enter *Gan Eden*. This is like an
> expert doctor who first administers stinging substances upon
> the wound, which consume the living flesh, and afterward he
> administers good salves and bandages in order to cool and re-
> store the flesh to its former state. So is the matter of Gehinnom,
> for the suffering of Gehinnom is not one fiftieth part that the
> soul endures before it enters Gehinnom.

The Rav then asked him, "How did you die?" He responded
and said to him, "My death was by choking, for although the
four manners of death of the *Bet Din* (Supreme Rabbinical
Court) have been abrogated, the four types of death have not
been abrogated. When I left from Alexandria in a boat to go to
Egypt, my boat was sunk in the Nile delta region, where the
Nile enters the sea. We drowned, other Jews who were with
me on the boat and I." Hayyim then asked him, "Why did you
not say the confession at the hour of the departure of your soul
from your body; perhaps it would have helped you." The spirit
responded to him, "I did not manage to confess, for immediately the water choked me in my throat. Also immediately in
the drowning in the sea my mind became confused, and I was
not in my right mind to confess."

The Rav then asked him, "Tell me what happened to you after you drowned in the sea and after the departure of your soul from your body." The spirit responded and said,

Know that when the matter of the sunken boat became known in Egypt, immediately the Jews of Egypt went into the sea and took all of us out of the sea and buried us. Immediately thereafter, when the Jews left the cemetery, a cruel angel came, with a staff of fire in his hand, and he struck my grave roughly with that staff. Immediately the grave split in two from the strike, which was so very great and strong. That angel said to me, "Evil one, evil one, arise in judgment!" Immediately he took me and put me in the hollow of the sling and slung me in one shot from Egypt to before the opening of Gehinnom in the wilderness. And as I fell there before the opening of Gehinnom, immediately 1,000,000 souls of evildoers who are being judged there came out of Gehinnom, all of them shouting against me and saying to me, "Depart, depart, man of blood, depart from here evildoer, tormentor of Israel!" And they cursed me with vehement curses and said to me, "You are still unworthy of entering here, and you still have no permission to enter Gehinnom." Then they cast me from mountain to mountain and from hill to hill, those three angels of destruction ever with me, decreeing before me and striking me always. And at each and every moment other angels of destruction, evil spirits, demons, and she-devils injure me. And upon hearing the decree that they decree before me, they beat me with great and difficult blows as well. These pull me here, and that one pulls me there, until all the knots of my soul are unwound.

In this way, I went wandering to and fro in the land, until reaching the city of Ormuz, a large city close to the land of India. My intention was to enter into the body of some Jew, perhaps to be saved from those blows, sufferings, and torments. Now, since those Jews are evil and sinning to the Lord exceedingly, fornicating with Gentile women and committing other transgressions, I was unable to enter even one of them due to the many spirits of impurity that dwell in them and around them. Had I entered the body of one of them, I would have added defilement to my defilement and injury to my own injury. For that reason I returned, and went from mountain to hill and from hill to mountain, until I came to the wilderness of Gaza. There I found a pregnant doe; due to my great suffering and pain I entered her body. This was after seven years during which I went through many terrible troubles. When I entered the body of this doe, it was tremendously painful for me, for the soul of a human being and the soul of a beast are not equal, for one walks upright and the other bent. Also, the soul of the beast is full of filth and is repulsive, its smell foul before the soul of a human being. And its food is not human food. I also had great pain from the fetus in her belly. The doe also had great pain because of me; her belly swelled, and she ran in the mountains and in the rocks until her abdomen split and she died. From there I left and I came to the city of Shekhem, where I entered the body of a Jew, a *Kohen* [a Jew of the priestly caste]. And that *Kohen* immediately sent after the holy men and clerics of the Ishmaelites [Muslims], and from the number of their incantations and adjurations of impure names, and also the amulets of unholy names that they hung from his neck, I was unable to bear it and to remain in his body. I immediately left there and fled.

Immediately the Rav said to him, "Is it really the case that there is something to the forces of impurity to injure and to ameliorate by themselves?" He said to him, "No, but because the clerics, through their adjurations, infused so many spirits of impurity into the body of that *Kohen*-Jew, I saw that if I continued to stay there all those spirits would cling to me. Thus I was unable to stay with them.

"I then came to Safed, and I entered the body of this woman. For me, as of today it has been twenty-five years that my suffering persists." The Rav said to him, "For how long will you have this suffering, for have you no recovery forever?" The spirit responded to him, "Not until all the bastards whom I fathered have died. For as long as they live and exist, I have no reparation." Then all those who were there, a very great multitude, all of them cried many cries, for fear of judgment fell upon them. A great awakening took place throughout the region from that very occurrence. The Rav then asked him, "Who gave you permission to enter the body of this woman?" The spirit responded, "I spent one night in her house; at dawn this woman arose from her bed and wanted to light a fire from the stone and iron, but the burnt rag did not catch the sparks. She persisted stubbornly, but did not succeed. She then became intensely angry and cast the iron and the stone and the burnt rag—everything—from her hand to the ground and angrily said, 'To Satan with you!' Immediately I was given permission to enter her body." The Rav asked him and said, "And for a minor transgression such as this they gave you permission to enter her body?" The spirit responded and said, "Know, my master the sage, that this woman's inside is not like her outside, for she does not believe in the miracles that the Holy One, blessed be He, did for Israel, and in particular in the Exodus from Egypt. Every Passover night, when all of Israel is rejoicing and good hearted, saying the great Hallel and telling of the Exodus from Egypt, it is vanity in her eyes, a mockery and a farce. And she thinks in her heart that there was never a miracle such as this."

Immediately the Rav said to the woman so-and-so, "Do you believe with perfect belief that the Holy One, blessed be He, is One and Unique, and that He created the heavens and the earth, and that He has the power and capacity to do anything that He desires, and that there is no one who can tell him what to do?" She responded to him and said, "Yes, I believe in it all in perfect faith." The Rav further said to her, "Do you believe in perfect faith that the Holy One, blessed be He, took us out of Egypt from the house of slavery, and split the sea for us, and accomplished many miracles for us?" She responded, "Yes, master, I believe in it all with perfect faith, and if I had at times a different view, I regret it." And she began to cry.

Immediately the Rav decreed a ban on the spirit to depart, and he decreed upon him that he not depart by way of any limb other than via the little toe of the left foot, because the reason is that from the limb that it departs, that limb is ruined and destroyed utterly. And the Rav intended the Names that his teacher had transmitted to him, and immediately the little toe swelled and became like a turnip, and [the spirit] left by that way. After that, on a number of nights the spirit came to the windows of the house and to the entryway and terrorized the woman [threatening] to return and to enter her body. The relatives of the woman returned to the Kabbalist [Isaac Luria]. The Rav sent his student Hayyim to check the mezuzah, and he found the entryway without any mezuzah. Immediately the Rav commanded that a kosher mezuzah be affixed to the entryway, and so they did. And from them on, the spirit did not return.

EXORCISMS OF
THE BAAL SHEM TOV[1]

1814

*Rabbi Israel ben Eliezer (c. 1700–1760), better known as
Baal Shem Tov (Master of the Good Name), is regarded
as the founder of modern Hasidism, a Jewish revivalist
movement that began in the Ukraine in the eighteenth
century. Baal Shem Tov is frequently shortened to the ac-
ronym BeShT or simply "the Besht." There are numerous
legends about miracles performed by the Besht, including
stories of exorcism. Rabbi Dov Ber (also known as Dob
Baer ben Samuel) collected more than two hundred tales
and anecdotes about the Besht into a book called* Shivḥei
ha-Besht (In Praise of the Besht). *Dov Ber was the son-in-
law of Rabbi Alexander the Shoḥet, who had been the
Baal Shem Tov's scribe for eight years. Manuscripts of
this collection circulated in Jewish communities, the first
of which was printed in Hebrew in 1814. In 1970, Dan
Ben-Amos and Jerome R. Mintz produced the first English translation of this volume, from which the two stories below have been excerpted.*

*In the Jewish tradition, exorcism may be used to expel
demons (*shedim)*, but more often concerns an entity
known as a* dybbuk, *which is typically understood to be
a spirit of the dead. (On the* dybbuk, *see the previous
chapter, "The Spirit in the Widow of Safed.") The first
tale is a classic* dybbuk *story in that the entity reveals its
identity and the sin that caused it to become a spirit. The
Besht is expected to expel the spirit using the power of
holy names that can be wielded only by the most advanced practitioners. But he elects to reason with the
spirit, learning its name so that a prayer and study ses-*

sion can be held for the redemption of his soul. Signifi-
cantly, the spirit recognizes the Besht's power immediately,
a trope the translators note also occurs in accounts of Je-
sus's exorcisms (Mark 1:23-28).

  In the second story, the demons were clearly never
human, having been born of lustful thoughts. In both
these stories, the Besht uses exorcism to restore harmony
rather than to destroy evil forces. Spirits are helped to
pass on, while demons are sent to places where they are
unlikely to trouble humans (an attic, a remote well, etc.).

THE BESHT EXORCISES A MADWOMAN

Once the Besht came to a town where there was a madwoman
who revealed to everyone his virtues and vices. When the Besht,
God bless his holy memory, came to the town, Rabbi Gershon
asked the righteous rabbi, the head of the court of the holy community of Kuty, the righteous rabbi, the great light, our master
and teacher, Moses, to take the Besht to this woman. Perhaps
he would take to heart her reproaches and return to the proper
path. And all of them went to her.

  When the rabbi of the holy community of Kuty entered, she
said: "Welcome to you who are holy and pure." She greeted
each one according to his merits. The Besht came in last and
when she saw him she said: "Welcome, Rabbi Israel," although
he was still a young man. "Do you suppose that I am afraid of
you?" she said to him. "Not in the least, since I know that you
have been warned from heaven not to practice with holy names
until you are thirty-six years old."

  The Besht was very modest.[2] And the people asked her:
"What did you say?"

  She repeated her words to them until the Besht chided her
and said: "Be quiet. If not, I will appoint a court to release me
from my vow of secrecy, and I shall exorcise you from this
woman." She began to implore him, "I will be quiet." The Hasidim who accompanied him said that they would permit him
to break his vow and urged him to exorcise the spirit from the

woman. The Besht asked them not to grant him permission since the spirit was very dangerous, but they insisted. Then the Besht said to the spirit: "Look what you have done. My advice to you is to leave this woman without causing any difficulty and all of us will study on your behalf." And he asked the spirit for his name.

He answered: "I cannot reveal it before the others. Let the people leave here and I will reveal it to you." Otherwise, it would have shamed his children who were living in the town. When the people left, he revealed his name to the Besht. My father-in-law, blessed be his memory, also knew him. He had become a spirit only because he had mocked the Hasidim of the community of Kuty. Then the spirit released himself from that woman without causing any trouble.

From that time on they did not let the Besht stay in that village. A certain *arrendator* [lease holder] hired him as a melamed [a teacher of children] for his children. My father-in-law, God bless his memory, told me that the *arrendator* who accepted him as a melamed told him that he had only one house for him, but it was thought to be inhabited by impure spirits. The Besht said that he would live in it. The Besht assigned the attic to the demons, God forbid, and when they laughed he scolded them and they became silent.

THE BESHT BANISHES DEMONS

I heard from the rabbi of our community and also from the rabbi of the holy community of Polonnoye that in the holy community of Zbarazh two demons were seen in the women's section of the synagogue. The women were so frightened that they had to leave the synagogue.

Rabbi Hayyim, the maggid [preacher] of our community, went to sit in the synagogue. The demons appeared while he was studying and he banished them. So they went and entered into his two children. Rabbi Hayyim sent for the Besht.

The Besht went to sleep in his house of seclusion with *Mar* Tsevi, the scribe. He told them to bring the children to his sleeping quarters. And they did. When they went to bed, the Besht's couch was placed at the head of the table, and the scribe slept next to the Besht's head. They were not yet asleep when the demons came to the house. They stood at the door and mocked the Besht's way of singing "Come my beloved."³ The Besht rose and sat on his bed. He said to the scribe: "Have you seen them?"

The scribe saw them also, but he tucked his head under the Besht's pillow and said: "Leave me alone."

When the demons finished mocking him they went toward the children. The Besht jumped from his couch and scolded them, saying, "Where are you going?"

They were not afraid and they said: "It is none of your business." They began to mock him again and to sing the Besht's melody "Come my beloved."

The Besht did whatever he did, and the two demons fell down and could not get up. They began to appeal to him, and he said: "See to it that the children recover immediately."

One of them said: "What is done is done, since their internal organs are injured. We came to finish them off. It's their luck that you, sir, were here."

He asked them: "How and why did you go to the synagogue?"

They answered: "Because the cantor who used to sing in the synagogue, the one with the bass voice, was a great adulterer. He purposely attracted the women with his singing. He thought about them and they thought about him, and from these thoughts we were created, two demons, a male and a female. We live in the synagogue."

The Besht gave them a place at a certain well where human beings did not go.

THE ISLAMIC
TRADITION

"THE PROPHET MUHAMMAD CASTS AN ENEMY OF GOD OUT OF A YOUNG BOY: A TRADITION FROM AHMAD B. HANBAL'S *MUSNAD*"[1]

855 CE

Like all world religions, Islam contains many different traditions and practices, including forms of exorcism. The Quran describes spirits known as jinn *(singular* jinni*), who were part of Arab folklore long before Muhammad. The* jinn *can take many forms but are normally invisible, as God made them from "smokeless fire." Like humans,* jinn *have free will and may be either good or evil. Evil* jinn *can cause a variety of problems for humans, including possession. In addition to the* jinn*, Islamic exorcism traditions have also been used to rid people of the influence of the evil eye* (ayn) *and sorcery* (sihr).[2]

Exorcism remains a controversial practice within Islam. As with Christianity, there is debate about how exorcism should be done. Many Muslims reject exorcism as either incompatible with a modern, scientific understanding of Islam, or a superstitious practice that was added to Islamic tradition centuries after Muhammad. The most common form of exorcism involves incantation of Quranic verses known as ruqya*. Quranic verses may also be adapted into amulets or other applications. In some parts of the Islamic world, individuals suspected of possession may be taken to the tomb of a saint in the hopes that the holiness of the place will drive out the spirit. In parts of*

*Africa, certain charismatic exorcists may claim to have
their own jinn, who can expel evil jinn from others. (See
the next chapter, "The Trial of Husain Suliman Karrar.")
More conservative Muslims may reject these methods as
shirk (idolatry), arguing that resorting to tombs or spirits
does not show sufficient faith in God.*

*Fueling this debate is the fact that the Quran clearly ac-
knowledges the existence of jinn, but says little about possession or exorcism. However, there are accounts in the
hadith of Muhammad performing exorcisms. The hadith—
often described as the "sayings" of the prophet—are words
and actions of Muhammad recorded by his companions.
Muslims do not regard all hadith as equally reliable, but
they are a key source of Islamic law, second in authority
to the Quran.*

*The hadith below comes from the Musnad of Ahmad ibn
Hanbal. Ibn Hanbal (780–855) was the founder of the
Hanbali legal school of Sunni Islam. The Musnad contains more than five thousand distinct hadith along with
more than twenty-seven thousand variations. The text
below begins with a chain of transmission called an isnad
that establishes the provenance of this story.³ Muhammad's
exorcism is extremely simple, involving little more than
calling on God and blowing into the patient's mouth. The
end of the story has interesting implications for whether
Muslims should accept payment for casting out spirits.*

It was related to us from 'Abd Allah b. Numayr from 'Uthman
b. Hakim from 'Abd al-Rahman b. 'Abd al- 'Aziz from Ya'la b.
Murra, he said: "Verily, I have just seen the Messenger of God
do three things that no one witnessed before me and no one
will witness after me.

I set out on a trip with him and along the way we passed by
a woman sitting with a young boy, and she called out: 'Oh,
Messenger of God, this boy has been struck by an evil afflic-

tion and through him we have likewise been struck. I don't even know how many times per day he is seized [by the affliction].' The Prophet Muhammad replied, 'Give him to me!' So she lifted the boy up to the Prophet and put him between the Prophet and the middle of the camel saddle. Then the Prophet opened the boy's mouth and blew into it three times, and he said, 'In the name of God—I am the servant of God—Go away, O enemy of God!' After this he gave the boy back to the woman and said to her, 'Meet us again at this place on our return and update us as to how he has fared.'

So we set off and upon our return we found the woman in this exact place and she had three sheep with her. The Prophet Muhammad asked her, 'How has the boy fared?' And she responded, 'Lo, by the One who sent you with the truth, we have not noticed a trace of the affliction in him until now. Take these sheep.' And the Prophet said [to Ya'la], 'Dismount, take one of the sheep and return the rest.'"

THE TRIAL OF HUSAIN
SULIMAN KARRAR

1920[1]

*Muslim populations across east and north Africa as well
as the Middle East and parts of Iran have a tradition of
spirit possession known as* zar. Zar *spirits are often assumed to be a species of* jinni, *although their exact nature
is unclear.* Zar *resemble spirits of the dead, in that they
are said to have particular religions, occupations, and na-
tionalities. They possess only women, and most often
married women. They torment their hosts and typically
promise to leave if they are propitiated with music, animal
sacrifices, or fine gifts (which are given to the possessed
woman). Many countries are home to female-dominated
"zar cults," which hold long ceremonies to expel the* zar
*with music and dancing. Some modern people take the
existence of* zar *quite seriously, while others regard pro-
pitiating the* zar *as an excuse for socially deprived women
to enjoy a party.[2] Although the* zar *cult is largely a Muslim phenomenon, it has been condemned by conservative
Muslim clerics.*

    *The court record below is from a murder trial held in
El Obeid, Sudan, in 1913, when Sudan was under British
control. The exorcist is accused of beating a girl for three
days before strangling her to death in an attempt to drive
out a spirit. There is no legal counsel, and the accused represents himself. The British judge, E. N. Corbyn, struggles to establish what happened and also to understand
Sudanese practices related to spirit possession.*

    It is clear that this is not a typical case of zar *posses-
sion. Zar rarely possess girls as young as sixteen. While
beating is not unheard of as a method of* zar *expulsion, it*

is rare. The nature of the entity is also unclear. It is referred to as a zar *only in the defendant's final appeal. More often it is described as a* dastur *(plural* dasatir*), a word used in colloquial Sudanese Arabic to refer to* zar. *There is also discussion about whether it is a* jinni *or a devil. The exorcist claims the entity is both Christian and English, saying that this makes it particularly difficult to work with.*

Before sentencing, the exorcist admits that he spent time in an Egyptian mental asylum before relating how the jinni *appeared to him and called him to be a "sanjak." "Sanjak" was an officer's title used by the Ottoman Empire. Within the Sudanese* zar *cult, it signifies a male leader often with shamanistic powers.[3] The strangulation, he claims, was actually a battle between the* jinni *that possesses him and that which possessed his victim: "She was* majnūn *and I was* majnūn." *The Arabic term* majnūn *can indicate either clinical insanity or* jinn *possession.*

The prisoner, Husain Suliman Karrar, was charged with "having committed murder by whipping and strangling the woman 'Aisha bint 'Agab till she died."

The first witness was the father of the girl, a Sereihi from a village near Rahad. He stated as follows:—

"The girl 'Aisha was my daughter and newly grown up (about 16 years old). She was taken about Fatr last (September) with illness which she said was dasātir, possession by devils. I went to 'Aisha Um Barūd at Rahad who has a reputation for casting out devils. She played the tambura [a stringed instrument] for my daughter to cast them out, but my daughter only nodded her head and the devil refused to speak from her lips and say what he wanted given him to leave her. Then Um Barūd said he was too strong for her to cast out. So I took her and left her with her mother outside Um Barūd's house, and I went to look for some one else to undertake it. This was at sunset. Early in the night I returned having found no one.

When I arrived I heard my wife, the girl's mother, shouting. I asked what was the matter. She said accused, who was there, had beaten our daughter. I asked him why. He said he was a 'Sheikh el dasātir' one with power over the devils to cast them out."

Court: "Who brought him in your absence?"

Answer: "I don't know. He arrived himself. When he offered to cast out the devils, I said I must return to my village, where I had my animals. He said he would come too and cure my daughter, and if he failed to do so he would not ask for so much as a millieme [1/1000th of an Egyptian pound].

When we arrived at my home he started beating her with a medium-sized kurbag [whip] which had a piece of tin fastened round it a good way up the lash, but so that the tin would reach the body also when a blow was struck. When I saw that this beating was severe I asked him to stop it. He said those blows are not on her: they are blows on the devil. I have learned the language of the devils in Egypt, and I can bring him out be he jinn or devil. On the third day, the Monday, I had had enough of it, and I told him to stop. He used to use foreign words, as he struck her, which he said were English, and others. When I said it must stop, he refused. He said he could make her well in seven days, and even if the Mamur [a local government official] came now he should not stop him. Already she was able to walk, and he would cure her. If she died he was responsible. I made the people of the village witness to what he said.

On Tuesday, the fourth day, I went out in the morning, leaving my daughter sleeping there and leaving accused there also sitting doing nothing. When I came back she had been brought dead to the house from outside. Basilr Lāzim and 'Awad El Nūr told me accused had taken my daughter out to the Wadi [a dry riverbed or valley] and strangled her there."

Court: "On the Monday was she very ill from the beating?"

Answer: "She was extraordinarily strong. She would run and fight with accused and tore his clothes, and he would say they were Christian devils that were in her, and talk strange language to them. She had cuts from the whip over her back and round to her breast, and her cheeks were swollen from his cuffing her. She did not speak until the Sunday at night, and then she said 'That is my father' and 'that is my mother' of me and her mother, and when he asked her who the 'devils' were, she said 'Sidna Hasan and Husain.' Whereupon he said those two were not devils, but the devils be Christians or obstinate English."

Court: "Was she sleeping with you and her mother?"

Answer: "Her mother and I were in one tukl [thatched hut], and she in another just by."

Court: "Why did you not stop this cruel treatment?"

Answer: "He told me it would effect a cure, and I believed him."

Accused: "Did you not come to me yourself to my house with a woman from your village to invite me to undertake the cure?—"

Answer: "No: I don't know your house at all."

Evidence read over.

Accused does not examine further.

Witness withdraws.

The second witness, Medina bint 'Alī, Sereihia of El-Inderāba, mother of dead girl, sworn, states as follows:—

"My daughter 'Aisha got ill three months ago. We took her to Um Barūd in Rahad to make her well, but Um Barūd failed, and said she could do no more. We took the girl outside Um Barūd's house. A man came and told us he knew of another woman who could make a cure and would go to get her. My husband and this man went off to the woman he mentioned, leaving me and my daughter outside Um Barūd's house. My husband on reaching the woman was told by her that she would not come, but he could bring our daughter to her. Just as he was coming back to me, the accused came up and began beating my daughter with a kurbag. I began screaming out. My husband arrived and asked why I was screaming. I said this man has just beaten the girl. He asked him why he had done so. He said 'Because she has got a foreign devil, a Christian one, who won't come out except by beating.' My husband asked him, 'do you know how to cast them out.' He said he did. My husband took a piece of P.T. 10 [a silver coin] from me and gave it to accused. He took him to the Suk [marketplace],

and bought some 'libān' and 'fitna beida' (perfumes), and said
this is what the devils want. Then to our village, the girl walking with us because he beat her till she did. There he first
smoked her with the smoke from the perfumes we had bought,
and then that failed. He then said they were not ordinary devils but jinns. I said then we would look for someone else to
treat her. He then said he could cure her. And then he started
to go on beating her. Finally we told him he must not beat her
any more. He agreed to stop it, and said indeed that the beating was evidently no use; this was on the last morning. That
morning he started to take her out of the village into the open
country. I followed them. He then started squeezing her throat
with his hands, and striking the front of her throat, (about the
Adam's apple) with the side of his hand. I protested, 'You will
kill her.' Her feet were kicking spasmodically by then and this
shifted her clothes off her, and left her naked. I went and tried
to pull her clothes back over her. He struck at me with his kurbag and said 'Woman, are you trying to prevent me from curing her? I swear by Wad El Hindi she will be alright now. The
devils have left her.' Just then from the distance my husband,
who had gone out before, shouted to me to come and fill the
waterskins with water, and I went. I was anxious and ill at
ease though and did so hastily to go back to my daughter. As I
went back I met accused coming in carrying her. He said, 'She
will be all right now,' and carried her into the house, and sat
down by her side and began rubbing her hands and feet and
saying 'the devils have left her: she will be well now.' The people said to him she is dead, but he said no. It was not till about
midnight that he admitted she was dead. He had put her on an
'angarīb [a wooden bedstead] about sunset, and he sat on the
'angarīb himself, till he finally admitted she was dead."

Court: "Was the beating very severe?"

Answer: "Yes, her body was all cut about with it, and the
new strokes on the old would bring out matter from the wounds.
One day when I was away she was tied by the hands to a tree-
stump for beating. She had black marks afterwards at the side
of the throat made by the throttling."

Court: "When you saw the throttling why did you not scream for other people?"

Answer: "He struck me with the kurbag and said 'Don't let the devils get the better of us: let us show them that we are stronger than they: so I believed in him."

Accused: "Did not your husband tie her up, for the beating, not I?"

Answer: "The only time I saw her tied, it was you who had her: whether her father tied her up another time, I don't know."

Accused: "Was she not violent?"

Answer: "I heard that when she had her senses a bit she asked you why you had beaten her so and ran after you to strike you, but whether with a stick or an axe or what I don't know, and someone, I don't know who, interposed and she struck him on the arm instead."

Accused: "Did she not strike one on the head and one on the arm, with an axe, and chase the whole village with a spear?"

Accused does not examine further.

The third witness, Mohammed Abu Rāsein, Tereifi, Hillet Inderāba, sworn, states:—

"I was in my cultivation on the Monday. I came back and found people in the village crying out about something. I went and found 'Agab's daughter tied up by her wrists to a shei'ba [a forked tree limb] outside their house with her back covered with whip cuts, and accused there with a new kurbag in his hand bound round with a piece of tin in the middle, and the girl's cheeks and side of face under the jaw also all swollen with hitting. I asked him what he was doing: he said he was a doctor, and could drive out devils. I said there was the way of writing holy passages to cure them and the way of smoking the person who was ill, but there was no other way, unless he was a genuine doctor and authorised by the Government. He said he had been beating her for three days and that four more days would cure her. I told him to stop it. He said as there were four more days of his treatment he would not stop even though the Mamur came and I said, what if she dies or you throttle her? He said he was responsible. I left him.

On Tuesday I went out to my cultivation. When I came back I found the girl had been brought in dead from the Wadi. We sent to the Markaz [headquarters]. A policeman and the Sanitary Barber arrived that night and the Sub-Mamur early next morning. They saw the marks of the beating and the throttling"

Court: "When you found her tied up, was she conscious?"

Answer: "She had her head lolling at first, but when we stopped the beating, she wept and cried."

Court: "Was the girl violent and did she fight with the people?"

Answer: "I never saw or heard it. I only know she was said to be be possessed by devils."

Accused does not examine.

Another witness, El 'Awad El Nūr, aged about 33, a distant relative of deceased girl, Sereihi of Um Heglig, sworn, states:—

"I and Bashīr Lāzim were together when we heard the girls' mother Medina screaming. We went up, and found accused throttling the girl. We told him to stop. He said it is no business of yours; I am throttling the devils. We believed him and left him. We watched. We came up again and found her finished, dead. We had stood watching. We told him to carry her to the house; he did."

Court: "How could you stand there and see a girl throttled?"

Answer: "It was our ignorance; he said, 'Don't say anything: the more you object the more you encourage devils and handicap me.' We believed him."

Court: "Did her mother stop protesting?"

Answer: "The girl's legs kicked spasmodically and kicked her clothes off. I told accused to put them on again. Her mother put them on. Her mother then looked on crying. We all believed he was throttling the devils only as he said."

Court: "Do you think you played a proper part in standing by to see a girl killed?"

Answer: "We are ignorant and he deceived us: he said he was only throttling the devils."

Accused: "Did you not see my shirt torn?"

Answer: "No: I found you with your shirt taken round your middle, your body bare from the waist upwards."

Accused: "Did you not come out with me from the village together?"

Answer: "No."

Accused: "On the Monday did she not attack us all with a spear?"

Answer: "She hit Ahmed with a stick on that day after accused had beaten her, asking why they had brought a man to torture her like this. I saw her bound after this."

Accused: "Did you not bind her?"

Answer: "No."

Accused does not examine further.

The first witness for the defence, 'Aisha Um Barūd, Bedeirīa, of Rahad, sworn states as follows:—

"Agab and Medina brought me their daughter and stayed two nights. Then I told them I could not put her right. They were no ordinary devils (dasātir) in her but malicious jinns who had made her make water on my bed clothes. They took her outside. Her father rode off to look for a Fiki [a type of Islamic healer who can perform exorcisms], as I had advised. The mother and daughter sat near my door. Then accused appeared with a bamboo cane in his hand. He started beating the girl. I stopped him and asked him why. The girl having been beaten got up and seized the man. Her father then came up. Accused said to him 'I can cure her.' Her father agreed. I said to her father, there is no medicine for jinns: if you are going to have treatment of this kind, take her away from my zariba [an enclosure of thorn bushes surrounding a home]. He took her away and I know no more."

Court: "Was the beating with a stick only?"

Answer: "He beat her with the stick, and when I interfered he beat me and her and broke the stick over us, and then went on punching her with his fist. He was calling the devil a foreign Christian one and telling me I did not know that kind."

Accused: "Was it a light bamboo?"

Answer: "Yes, thicker than a finger."

Accused: "When they brought her to you, was she not on a donkey, and when I took her off was she not on her feet, the beating treatment was already effective?"

Answer: "They brought her on a donkey, and took her away walking: accused was walking with them with a handful of sticks he had brought, driving her with hard words."

Accused: "Is not beating a proper treatment to cast out devils?"

Answer: "Never."

Accused: "Does not a devil, if its requests are refused, break the neck of the afflicted person?"

Answer: "No, the dasātir do not do so; if their original request is more than people can afford, they (the latter) plead with them and they agree to reduce it."

Court: "And the jinns?"

Answer: "The difference in their case is that they never request anything."

Accused: "Do they not break necks?"

Answer: "No: the Fikis treat the patient for them."

Accused does not examine further.

Witness withdraws.

The accused makes the following statement:—

"I was imprisoned in Egypt once on a charge of theft. I was born at Sayyāla near Aswan. I was about 15 years old when I was imprisoned. There I became rather mad for a time and they transferred me to the Asylum in Cairo, where I stayed about seven months, and was then let out about 22 years ago. I then went all over Egypt. I was servant to Fathi Bey, an officer, then at Korosko, and went with his regiment to Haifa (1896). I was then a donkey boy there and I married there. I was then in Atbara and Suakin. I worked there on the Port Sudan-Atbara Railway when it was made: then on Khartoum Bridge: then on the El Obeid extension to Kosti, and then went to Um Ruaba; then to Semeiha, and Rahad.

A year after I came out of the Asylum the jinn Abu El Kabbas came to me in a dream, and appointed me a Sanjak of the dasātir. The meaning of this is that I am empowered to use the tambura (a musical instrument, mandoline style) to drive out the dasātir. Each devil has its special note. When it is struck the devil speaks and makes his demands for what he wants, which has to be provided by the friends of the patient, when he is satisfied and leaves the patient. Sidi El Geili is my destūr and he comes to me at times in the kharīf [autumn or the monsoon season], and orders me to produce his demands. He sends me a dream first in which he makes his demands. I ask him for a few days grace: if I have not then brought them he catches me by the throat and I lie as though half throttled until he leaves me. This is not continuous but happens off and on for two or three days, and if a friend lights a match and holds it to my throat, that drives him away at once. He may ask for clothes or dura [sorghum] or whatever it may be. If clothes, it is I who have to put them on, but other things I have to give as a gift to other people in his name. His time comes in the kharīf and then he comes on a Friday, and then on a Friday a month later, and again a month later, four times.

As to this matter, I was invited to undertake it by the girl's father and mother. I told them I could try for seven days and if I failed I would take nothing. We all went together to their village, her father riding. There I played the tambura, and the father and the mother brought pepper to smoke her with. I said that was no good, and said I would go. There was a Halabī [a "gypsy" or member of a nomadic tribal group] there and he said he would cure her with branding and heated a nail and branded her on the head and back of her neck. She remained without speaking, but got up and took me by the hand into a gottīa (hut). She made as though she wanted to drink, I told her mother to fetch water. She did so and she drank. Then she took me by the hand, and began walking back and down for a long time, from midday to evening. I got tired and sat down. Then she took a tōb [a traditional dress that covers the hair and resembles a robe] and filled it with sand and carried it and went on walking up and down. Then she said to me, 'I want two large amber necklaces (mansus) and a gold ring and a gallabia [a traditional Middle-Eastern dress] and a nose ornament. If these are not brought I shall die.' They refused to bring these things. That is all I have to say."

Court: "What did you do? That is not the end of your action."

Accused: "No, that's true. I am forgetting."

"I told them the devil demanded these things. They said they would bring them. They did not.

By Monday the devils got angry because nothing came and oppressed her terribly. I smoked her with perfumes on the Tuesday and then she said that she and I and her mother and those two men should go out with her. She stripped the upper part of her body and girded herself and went out. I had on a shirt and drawers and waist-coat. We all went out to a little distance. I had my kurbag. She caught me by the throat. Then I struck her with the whip. She fought with me. The whole village was looking on. She tore my clothes off me. Then I girded myself up also with my shirt off. She fought with me and the people looked on as at a spectacle. Finally we were both on the ground each catching at the other's throat kneeling: then she made the noise she used to make when thirsty and her mother brought water and she drank: she signalled to me to drink pushing the water over to me. Then she became unconscious. Her mother and her cousin each took her by a leg and we carried her in. As she lay there in the house she asked for water. After she drank she was as though panting. I left her for an hour. I came back and put my hand on her and said 'In the name of God etc.' She then died, and her mother and father raised the cry of mourning. The Sheikh of the village came and took me by the wrist and drew me out of the house. He said: 'Give me £E.10 [Egyptian pounds] and I will settle this so that you can go.' I said I had not got it. Then he brought a rope and they bound me, and the Sheikh went off to the Markaz."

Court: "Did you not beat her?"

Answer: "I stopped the beating."

Court: "Did you not then adopt the throttling as a method of treatment?"

Answer: "My jinn and her jinn entered on a struggle for mastery. Mine in me was throttling hers in her and vice versa. She was majnūn and I was majnūn. Her jinn overcame my jinn."

Court: "If she lay dead and you alive did not yours win?"

Answer: "Hers killed her because its demands were refused. Mine would do the same with me if I refused its demands."

The Court finds that the accused is guilty of Murder under Section 230 Sudan Penal Code.

A footnote adds that the condemned made the following appeal: "The death of the girl 'Aisha was caused by the disease of dasātir (Zar) and not by stabbing or wounding or beating inflicted by me. I am innocent of her blood. I only treated her by means of the tambura, just as is done by others in the Sudan who are learned in this craft. Some employ the tambura and others drum on a tisht (basin) or other implements. Usually the Zar demands certain things of the patient, and if these are not produced serious trouble to the patient results, until he either dies or is cured."

SOUTH AND
EAST ASIA

A HYMN TO DRIVE AWAY *GANDHARVAS* AND *APSARAS*[1]

ELEVENTH TO THIRTEENTH CENTURIES BCE

The Vedas are the most ancient text of Hinduism. Before they were ever written down, they were passed down for centuries by Brahman priests who committed them entirely to memory. The Artharva-Veda is a collection of 730 hymns, many of which concern ways to heal various ailments. Hymns banishing spirit entities from the patient are often combined with herbs, amulets, and other remedies.

*The hymn below involves driving away spirits using an herb called ajasringi or arataki. This appears to be a reference to the Indian ash tree (*Lannea coromandelica*), which is used in traditional Indian medicine. Some research suggests this plant has natural antibacterial and antifungal properties.*[2] *The plant is described as having "horns," which are compared to "spears" of the god Indra, a Vedic warrior god who slays demons.*

This hymn demonstrates the wide variety of spirit entities present in Vedic cosmology. The primary focus are apsaras *and* gandharvas, *spirit beings associated with dance and music, respectively. The* apsaras *are celestial nymphlike creatures, typically portrayed as beautiful female dancers in South Asian art. While normally benevolent, there are tales of* apsaras *seducing Hindu holy men who have retired to the forest.*

The gandharvas *are typically described as celestial musicians and husbands of the* apsaras. *Here, they are de-*

scribed as being hairy and monkeylike, yet handsome, not unlike the Greek satyr. They are also said to eat Blyxa (water reeds). Both entities are described as residing in sacred fig trees and are encouraged to return there rather than meddle with mortals. Five of the apsaras are named, and it is implied that knowing the name of a spirit gives the sage power over it.

The plant is also said to repel rakshas (or rakshasas), evil shape-shifting demons who appear throughout Hindu mythology. In some tales rakshasas may enter human beings through the mouth or other orifices, causing insanity. Finally, ajasringi is effective against pisachas. These are goblinlike entities said to live in cremation grounds and feed on the remains of corpses or even feces. According to some traditions, pisachas can also enter the body if mourners do not take proper precautions while visiting cremation grounds.

The opening lines of the hymn describe how great Hindu sages (rishis) have used this plant to repel spirit beings since time immemorial. Atharvan is one of the legendary authors of the Atharva-Veda, and his disciples, the Atharvans, were said to have been the first fire priests. Kasyapa, Kanva, and Agastya were likewise legendary sages believed to have authored the Vedas. Thus the remedy is proven to work.

1 With thee, O Plant, in olden time Atharvans smote
   and slew the fiends [rakshas].
Kasyapa smote with thee, with thee did Kanva and
   Agastya smite.
2 With thee we scare and drive away Gandharvas and
   Apsarases.
O Ajasringi, chase the fiends. Cause all to vanish
   with thy smell.
3 Let the Apsarases, puffed away, go to the river,
   to the ford,—
Guggulu, Pila, Naladi, Aukshagandhi, Pramandini.

Ye have become attentive since the Apsarases have
    past away.

4 Where great trees are, Asvatthas [holy fig tree] and
    Nyagrodhas [Indian fig tree] with their leafy crests,

There where your swings are green and bright, and
    lutes and cymbals sound in tune,

Ye have become attentive since the Apsarases have past
    away.

5 Hither hath come this one, the most effectual of herbs
    and plants.

6 Let Ajasringi penetrate, Arataki with sharpened horn.

7 From the Gandharva, dancing near, the lord of the
    Apsarases,

Wearing the tuft of hair, I take all manhood and
    virility.

8 With those dread hundred iron spears, the darts of
    Indra, let it pierce

The Blyxa-fed Gandharvas, those who bring no sacrificial
    gift.

9 With those dread hundred golden spears, the darts
    of Indra, let it pierce the Blyxa-fed Gandharvas, those
    who bring no sacrificial gift.

10 O Plant, be thou victorious, crush the Pisachas,
    one and all,

Blyxa-fed, shining in the floods, illumining the
    selfish ones.

11 Youthful, completely decked with hair, one monkey-
    like, one like a dog,—

So the Gandharva, putting on a lovely look, pursues
    a dame.

Him with an efficacious charm we scare and cause to
    vanish hence.

12 Your wives are the Apsarases, and ye, Gandharvas,
    are their lords.

Run ye, immortal ones, away: forbear to interfere with
    men!

CHANG TU,
"EXORCISING FOX-SPIRITS"

853 CE[1]

Chih-kuai *(describing anomalies) is a genre of Chinese literature cataloging legends of strange creatures and events. Possessing spirits are a common theme of this literature. Fox-spirits (hu mei, hu tsing, or hu kwai) are a particular type of possessing entity. These creatures are shape-shifters who often impersonate humans. They are also thought to cause illness and madness. In Chinese literature, they are sometimes described as residing in empty graves. Variations of the fox spirit can be found in Japan and Korea as well.*

The story below is from the Hsuan-shih chih *(Record of a Palace Chamber), recorded by Chang Tu around 853. Although it is presented as a legend, it gives an insight into the culture of exorcism that existed in Tang-dynasty China. The story suggests that exorcists were sought only when conventional medicine failed. While the protagonist seeks out a Daoist (Taoist) practitioner, there would also have been Buddhist monks and mediums, known as "wu," who could perform exorcisms. Daoism scholar Judith Boltz notes that this is one of the earliest narrative accounts to reference a Daoist exorcism technique called k'ao-chao (interrogating and calling the demon).[2] The purpose of this story is most likely entertainment. However, there also seems to be an element of social criticism in mocking the competing claims of rival exorcists and the paranoia that often accompanies claims of demonic possession.*

* * *

In the Ching yuen period of the Tang dynasty (A.D. 785–805),
Mr. P'ei of Kiang-ling (in the south of Hupeh province), a sub-
intendant of the palace, whose personal name is lost, had a
son over ten years of age, very clever and intelligent, studious,
brisk, and accomplished both in manners and appearance,
whom he therefore deeply loved. This boy was attacked by a
disease, which grew worse and worse for ten days. Medicines
took no effect, and P'ei was on the point of fetching a doctor
of Taoist arts who might reprimand and thwart (the demon
of the disease), in the hope of effecting a cure, when a man
knocked at his door, announcing himself as one of the surname Kao, whose profession was to work with charms. P'ei
forthwith invited him to walk in and look at his son. "This
boy suffers only from a sickness which is caused by a demon-
ish fox," said the doctor; "I possess an art of curing this." The
father thanked him and implored his help; the other set to work
to interrogate and call (the demon) by means of his charms,
and in the next moment the boy suddenly rose with the words:
"I am cured." The delighted father called Kao a real and true
master of arts, and having regaled him with food and drink,
paid him a liberal reward in money and silk, and thankfully
saw him off at the door. The doctor departed with the words:
"Henceforth I will call every day."

But though the boy was cured of that disease, still he lacked
a sufficient quantity of soul (*shen-hwun*), wherefore he uttered
every now and then insane talk, and had fits of laughter and
wailing, which they could not suppress. At each call of Kao,
P'ei requested him to attend to this matter too, but the other
said: "This boy's vital spirits are kept bound by a spectre, and
are as yet not restored to him; but in less than ten days he will
become quite calm; there is, I am happy to say, no reason to
feel concerned about him." And P'ei believed it.

A few days later, a doctor bearing the surname Wang called
on P'ei, announcing himself as an owner of charms with divine
power, and able to reprimand, thwart and expel therewith

diseases caused by demons. While discoursing with P'ei, he said: "I have been told that your darling son has been rendered ill, and is not yet cured; I should much like to see him." P'ei let him see the boy, when the doctor exclaimed with terror: "The young gentleman has fox-disease; if he be not forthwith placed under treatment, his condition will become grave." P'ei then told him of the doctor Kao, on which the other smiled and said, "How do you know this gentleman is no fox?" They sat down, and had just arranged a meal and begun the work of reprimanding and thwarting (the demon), when colleague Kao dropped in.

No sooner had he entered than he loudly upbraided P'ei: "How is that! This boy is cured, and you take a fox into his room? It is just this animal that caused his sickness!" Wang in his turn, on seeing Kao, cried out: "Verily, here we have the wicked fox; of surety, here he is; how could his arts serve to reprimand and summon the spectre!" In this way the two men went on reviling each other confusedly, and P'ei's family stood stupefied with fright and amazement, when unexpectedly a Taoist doctor appeared at the gate. "I hear," said he to the domestic, that Mr. P'ei has a son suffering of fox-disease; I am a ghost-seer; tell this to your master, and beg permission for me to enter and interview him." The servant hastened with this message to P'ei, who came forth and told the Taoist what was going on. With the words: "This matter is easy to arrange" he entered, in order to see the two; but at once they cried out against him: "This too is a fox; how has he managed to delude people here under the guise of a Taoist doctor?" He however returned their abuse: "You foxes, go back to the graves in the wilds beyond the town," he shouted, "Why do you harry these people?" With that he shut the door, and the trio continued for some moments to quarrel and fight, the fright of P'ei still increasing and his servants being too perturbed to devise a good means to get rid of them. But at nightfall all noise ceased. They then opened the door, and saw three foxes stretched on the ground, panting and motionless. P'ei scourged them soundly till they were dead, and in the next ten days the boy recovered.

A FOX TALE FROM THE
KONJAKU MONOGATRISHŪ[1]

EIGHTH TO TWELFTH CENTURIES CE

Japan has a rich culture of spirit possession. Following the 2011 tsunami that killed more than sixteen thousand people, numerous survivors reported being possessed by spirits of drowned people and animals, requiring Christian, Shinto, and Buddhist religious leaders to perform exorcisms for those affected.[2] *Of the many types of possessing entities in Japanese folklore, one of the most common is the fox or* kitsune. *As in China, fox spirits are believed to have the ability to possess people or take on human form. They are not necessarily malevolent, and some are associated with the popular Shinto fox deity, Inari, god of the harvest. Possession by fox spirits is known as* kitsune-tsuki. Kitsune *may possess people to avenge some slight, such as killing one of the fox's cubs or waking it from a nap, to acquire certain foods they crave (foxes are said to love tofu and rice boiled with red beans), or because they were sent by a human sorcerer called a* kitsune-tsukai *(fox-employer). One the first steps of exorcising* kitsune *is for the exorcist to hold a* mondō *(dialogue) with the spirit to determine why it has come.*[3] *The story below is from the* Konjaku Monogatrishū, *a collection of legends from the late Heian period (794–1185). It may be one of the first written stories of* kitsune-tsuki.[4] *It demonstrates the dual nature of* kitsune *as both troublesome and helpful.*

A spirit, which possessed a person and made him (or her) ill, was transferred to a *monotsuki no onna* ["possession-woman";

a woman called for the purpose of placing within her a bad spirit] and it spoke through her mouth to the following effect: "I am a fox. I have not come to do evil, but only to have a look round, because I thought that there was plenty of food at such places as this; the result was that I (that is the patient) was kept indoors." After these words she took from her bosom a white gem of the size of a small mandarin-orange (mikan), threw it up and caught it again. People who saw this said: "That is a strange gem. Probably the 'possession-woman' had that gem already in her pocket in order to delude mankind." Then a young man caught the gem, when the woman threw it up, and put it in his pocket. The fox which possessed the woman, begged him to give back the gem, but he refused, whereupon the fox wept and said: "To you the ball is valueless, for you do not know how to use it. Therefore, if you do not give back to me, I will be your enemy for ever, but if you give back, I will help and protect you as a god." The young man made the woman repeat the promise and then returned the gem. Afterwards, when an exorcist had driven out the fox, the gem was no longer to be found in the woman's pocket. This was a proof that it had really been the property of the being (that is, of the fox) which had possessed her. The fox kept his promise. Once when the young man was going home in a dark night, he became quite anxious and called the fox to his aid. Immediately the animal appeared and led him forward cautiously and stealing along a narrow lane instead of the main road. From a distance he could see the reason of this strange behaviour, for there were a great number of thieves, armed with bows and sticks, on the road where he would have passed if the fox had not led him elsewhere. At the end of the lane the fox disappeared and the man went on safely to his home. Many times he was helped and protected by the animal, proof, says the author, of how much more grateful animals are than men.

HARRIET M. BROWNE'S ACCOUNT OF *KITSUNE-TSUKI*[1]

1900

Kitsune-tsuki *is still reported in Japan in modern times, especially in rural areas.*[2] *In 1892, Dr. Shunichi Shimamura conducted a study of the* kitsune-tsuki *phenomenon in Shimane Prefecture. He found thirty-four people suffering from fox-possession: thirteen men and twenty-one women. Most were farmers. Shimamura attributed the alleged fox-possession to a misdiagnosis of various ailments including hysteria, alcoholism, and ovarian cysts. Some aspects of the phenomenon are more difficult to explain, however, such as an allegedly illiterate eighteenth-century man who was somehow able to produce calligraphy praising the god Inari while in a state of* kitsune-tsuki.[3]

The account below comes from Harriet M. Browne, a Baptist missionary who worked for an orphanage in Chofu, Japan, which is now part of Tokyo. Browne described how one of her charges, Nishiyama Tsugi, or "O Tsugi," began experiencing fox possession as well as possession by the spirit of her dead mother. Tsugi was never violent and merely demanded offerings of food, as is common in Shinto spirit possession. Browne, however, regarded the possession as satanic. She reported that after a Protestant exorcism that involved reading from the Gospels, Tsugi's strange behavior stopped. Several details of this account are consistent with the lore of kitsune-tsuki. *Tsugi is described as demanding food for the spirits, despite having already eaten. Browne also reports that her*

face physically changed "into a resemblance to foxes,"
suggesting a mild form of shape-shifting.

The "Japan Evangelist," May, 1900, furnishes a curious account of a case of this disease, taken by the reciter of the occurrences, Miss Harriet M. Browne, to be a case of actual
demoniacal possession. The patient, Nishiyama Tsugi, fifteen
years old, adopted in infancy by a man and his wife named
Nishiyama. At the age of nine years she ran away from home,
desiring something more exciting than the lonely country;
after a year she returned, only to steal and once more take her
flight; after this, according to her own account, she was servant and nurse girl in a prostitute house, and, leaving this,
took to the life of the lowest beggars, sleeping in the mountains, in graveyards, or in beggars' huts, a companion of thieves
and pickpockets as well as vagrants, and associating herself
with a young man in the commission of a burglary. She then
came to the orphanage, from which she had been kept by popular belief that the blood of the children was taken from them
while alive, and here manifested tokens of epilepsy and dangerous mania. The sequel may be told in the words of Miss
Browne:—

"We found that she greatly feared the well god and the rice
god, Inari, and his messengers, the foxes. She told us that, the
first year after she ran away, a kind landlady told her that she
had inquired of the oracle temple to tell her what was the matter with O Tsugi, and that it had said that O Tsugi's mother's
spirit had possessed her child because the blind woman she
was with had treated her cruelly.

"On the afternoon of the fifth of January she had a much
worse attack than before. We tried to bind her, but could not,
as she showed such strength, and it took several to manage
her. She would not pay the least attention to what was going
on around her, nor could she be roused, nor would she turn
her face toward any one. During the two former attacks she
had acted in dumb pantomime, but during this one she talked

incessantly. At first the words and actions were those of an in-
fant just learning to walk. Then after a time she changed and
said, as if it were a third person addressing herself, 'Your father has come on an errand from your mother;' and she replied
angrily, 'What do I want with my father?' with other abusive
words. Then, changing again, after further talk she said, personating the patron god of Chofu, 'You stole offerings from
me, you did! I saw you steal food from Inari in Bakan, and I
kept still, but now you have come to Chofu and stolen three
eggs that were offered up to me. You return them at once, I tell
you!' 'I haven't any eggs. Please forgive me.' 'Return them, I tell
you, or I will do something dreadful to you.' 'Well, forgive me,
and I will work hard and replace them.' 'Mind that you present them as offerings. Just bringing them to me won't answer.
If you don't, I'll pinch you,' suiting the (invisible) action to the
words; at which she cried out, '*Aa itai!* [O, it hurts!] Do forgive
me! I'll replace them.' 'Well, I'll forgive you if you make me the
offering, but if you don't, I'll pinch you well.' Saying this, she fell
as before and waked as usual in a few minutes. During this attack also, as soon as the members of the household recovered
from the fright, and collected their thoughts to kneel and pray,
she soon became quiet, and the demons left her. It may sound
only amusing written down; but I assure you to see the evil face
and actions, and hear the evil spirits as they in turn use a human
being to say and do what they will, the face and voice changing with the speaker—to have indisputable, visible, and audible
evidence before one that demons are in one's house, tormenting
and using at their will one of us, who but a half hour ago was
laughing and talking with the rest, is a fearful experience that
is apt to shake even pretty strong nerves.

"The next attack was on the evening of the eighth, when suddenly, while happily engaged with knitting, she began laughing
a fearful laugh, and her features changed, becoming distorted
into a resemblance to foxes. She called out and beckoned as to
someone at a distance with great delight, saying, 'Oh, come I'm
so glad you've come!' 'Yes, I've come' breathlessly, as if she had
been running; and then the evil spirits who personated foxes
had a fine time together, laughing and talking and joking. One

said: 'I know where there are some nice offerings in Bakan, eggs and fish and rice. Let's go and get them,' and off they went apparently. 'Don't talk so loud; they'll hear us.' 'Oh, here they are. Put them in your sleeve.' 'We must cook them. You go and buy some *oshitaji* [soy] and I'll make the fire. Put on your hat and go through the graveyard, and hide it under your hat.' 'How well it burns! Now it's boiling. Ah, you've come back, and now it will soon be done.' 'Yes, oh how good it tastes! How jolly this is!' . . . "Well, let's go home and we'll come again.' Saying which, she bounded out of the room as if about to leave the house. We brought her back to the dark room, and then she became possessed by a demon personating her dead mother's spirit. First she said several times '*Gomen nasai!*' as if a visitor at the door; then, 'I am the mother of the girl you call O Kane. Her name is O Tsugi. I have come 100 *ri* from Amakusa. She was treated so badly that I entered into her, and went with her to Kumamoto and to Hiroshima and back again; but now she is so well cared for here I will leave never to possess her again. But you must give me an offering of a bunch of rice-balls—enough to last for three days on the journey back. It will take a good many, for I have many maid-servants (*koshimoto*) for whom I find it hard to provide food. Then you must put them in a bundle on my back. It will not do just to give them to me.' No one replying to her repeated request, she angrily exclaimed: 'The master of this house is deaf in his ears; he won't listen. I tell you I shall not leave unless you give me a rice-ball. Do you hear? If you do that, I will leave never to come again.' The girl could hardly be hungry, for she had just eaten a hearty supper. It must have been a half hour that she kept repeating this demand, at last pounding the floor, and shouting it out in a voice that we heard clear out on the street. At this time I returned from prayer meeting. God had been preparing my heart for months, showing me the personality and presence of evil spirits about us and impressing deeply on my mind his promise to his disciples that He has given us *authority* over all the power of Satan. In the strength of this I spoke to the evil spirits in his name. We had been unable to quiet her before, but she listened while I said: 'This house and all in it belongs to our God Jehovah. We will never give so much as one rice grain to such as you. Go and get offerings from those who worship you.' I commanded the evil spirits in the name of Jesus to come out of her and never come again."

D. H. GORDON, D.S.O., "SOME NOTES ON POSSESSION BY BHŪTS IN THE PUNJAB"[1]

1912

The Bhūt or Bhoot *is a type of possessing ghost. Although the* Bhūt *likely originates in Hindu tradition, people throughout the Indian subcontinent tell stories of* Bhūt *possession, including Muslims and Sikhs. The report below is from Donald Hamilton Gordon, a British officer who served in the Punjab with the 11th Sikh regiment.*[2] *After retiring, he became an archaeologist and wrote several books on Indian culture and history. Gordon describes witnessing* Bhūt *possession, and although he is skeptical, investigated the possession as a real medical phenomenon. Gordon reports that* Bhūts *were assumed to be in decline as more wilderness was being cultivated, however modern people continue to believe in* Bhūts *in the Indian subcontinent.*

The simplest method of expelling Bhūts *involves exposing the possessed to unclean objects such as shoes and dog feces. Paradoxically, the* Bhūt *are frequently believed to reside in filthy places such as latrines and privys, or outhouses. In a footnote to the report below, Gordon adds, "I have heard recently of an Englishman who became so obsessed by the idea of the 'privy* Bhūt' *that he kept the lid of his privy padlocked."*

Other methods of Bhūt *exorcism involve religious specialists reading either Muslim or Hindu religious texts. Gordon describes the use of "mantars" (mantras) as well as "kalam," in the case of Muslim exorcisms. Kalam normally means "speech" or "discourse," but Gordon uses this term to describe Quranic verses used for exorcism. A footnote explains: "Among Mahomedans the usual Kalam employed is the reading of, or the swallowing of water in which have been soaked, the two preventative Suras of the Koran, namely, 'I betake me for refuge to the Lord of the DAYBREAK, against the mischiefs of his creation; and against the mischief of the night when it overtaketh me,' etc. And, 'I betake me for refuge to the Lord of MEN, The King of men, The God of men, against the mischief of the stealthily withdrawing whisperer (Satan).'"*

The belief in "possession by bhūts" is common to all the less educated people of the Punjab. The occurrence of "possession" is indeed so common that very little notice is taken of it. The man may become "possessed" in a number of different ways, according to various special and personal beliefs on the subject, but the three generally recognised forms are the following. One, the fortuitous encountering of a wandering Bhūt, which will seize upon a man in order that it may inhabit his body when inclined. Secondly, the entering in of a spirit of a great friend, who is either dead or who has power to transport his spirit. Lastly, possession as a result of a jādūgar [wizard] or any other person who is learned in Mantar or who is a Kalām parhne-wālā [a type of Muslim exorcist], having despatched the Bhūt as a "sending."

The first class is the most common. Wandering Bhūts may be met with in waste and desert places, among tombs and ruins, and on the banks of small ponds. These Bhūts are normally invisible, the only occasional manifestation of their presence being small flickering flames, which are supposed to be seen wandering in waste places. Impurity is one of the usual opportunities which a Bhūt can seize of entering a man. A man goes out into a waste place to relieve nature and neglects to cleanse his hands. The Bhūt, who is lying in wait, takes his opportunity and the man will soon show the symptoms of possession.

I recently heard a tale relating to this matter from a Sikh Indian Officer, who said that, when a child, he went down to a small pond to bathe and on leaving the pond he found a red cap alongside his own sāfā (turban). He had seen no one come to leave the cap there and could find no one about, so he went home wearing the cap. That evening he fell into the trance that is the usual symptom of possession. The Bhūt was exorcised, but this man maintains that evil effects have been present off and on ever since.

With regard to the Bhūt as a "sending," the belief is that, when a jādūgar sends a Bhūt, if the man he sends it against, or any friend of his, has more powerful spells than the sender, then the Bhūt may be returned. A returned Bhūt is considered to be much more dangerous than when first sent out, and is believed to vent its energies on the original sender, who will die. The ordinary symptoms that I have personally observed in this lesser possession are not very severe. The possessed falls into a trance, the muscles of the body and limbs become tense, the face is somewhat distorted from the tensing of the muscles, the eyes open but without intelligence or recognition, the breathing very laboured and heavy, the head is moved from side to side at intervals, the whole of the muscles twitch incessantly, the pulse is normal and the chest, when sounded with a stethoscope, gives no indication of any disorder. I have no observations of temperature.

The brief duration of the fit and the relatively small effect sustained is shown by an instance of a servant who fell in a trance at 7.25 p.m. After being examined, exorcism was used, the subject fell into a natural sleep, and by 8.00 p.m. was up and waiting at table.

The usual method of temporary exorcism is to shame the Bhūt into departing. This is done either by holding a shoe over the man's mouth, or, occasionally, some dog's droppings specially prepared by burning or, more properly, toasting.

During exorcism the subject has to be held, as he fights with actually supernatural strength. That is, a slightly built, weedy man, as I have myself seen, will tax the strength of two strong and well-built men while trying to keep him held.

The Bhūt will try and persuade the exorcists to leave it alone as it does not intend to do the man any harm; if, however, the shoe is kept menacing the Bhūt, the possessed firmly held down, and the bystanders help matters by telling the Bhūt to go, then it will leave the man, whose breathing at once becomes natural and who falls into a normal sleep. The subject on waking recalls nothing of what he has said, or rather what it is believed the Bhūt has said through him. Nothing but the reading of a Kalām or Mantar, by one skilled in these matters, is supposed to effect a permanent exorcism. The Bhūt fears the reading of a spell, and I have heard a possessed man say, "You are my enemy, don't mutter spells in my presence," clearly showing the fear of the Bhūt for the Kalām reader; but on this occasion there was no one versed in spells obtainable, and no one will attempt exorcism by Kalām unless he feels sure that his spell is powerful enough. Satisfactory temporary exorcism, after a struggle and loud pleas on the part of the Bhūt to be allowed to remain, was effected by a slipper.

This form of Bhūt is quite different to a Jinn, about which I have heard many tales, but have no personal experience.

In all cases of exorcism the Bhūt is requested to give some sign that he has departed. Usually a pair of shoes are inverted on the threshold and the Bhūt is asked to set them right side up. The fact is, that in the confusion of the exorcism, someone obligingly assists the Bhūt by turning the shoes over or by so setting the shoes that they are bound to topple over of their own accord.

GEORGES DE ROERICH, "THE CEREMONY OF BREAKING THE STONE"[1]

1931

The Tibetan cultural landscape is filled with numerous gods, demons, and other spirits, and Tibetan folklore and literature is replete with stories of Buddhist masters with the power to banish demons or, in some cases, transform them into "dharma protectors," who use their wrathful abilities to protect Buddhist institutions. The ritual sometimes called Breaking the Stone is one of the more spectacular forms of public exorcism in Tibetan tradition. The ritual is still practiced in the Spiti Valley, in the Himalayan borderlands between India and Tibet. It is performed by ritual specialists called lo-chen (lo chen, in Tibetan) or bu-chen (bu chen).[2] "Bu-chen" has been variously translated as "magician," "traveling lama-actor," "strolling monk," or "friar."[3] Their performances are simultaneously acts of Buddhist piety, feats of athleticism, and magical operations. The central act of the ritual is placing a stone on a man's chest and shattering it, symbolizing the destruction of the demon. One story about this ritual attributes its origins to a fourteenth-century master named Thang-stong rgyal-po. Thang-stong rgyal-po was said to have been an architect and is credited with building suspension bridges, ferries, and other structures throughout Tibet. However, he is also said to have been a yogic master with supernatural powers, who could banish demons and rode on a giant eagle. In this origin story for the ritual, the stone houses the spirit of a demon that is spreading plague throughout Lhasa, the capital of

Tibet. (Trapping entities within an animal or object and then slaughtering, destroying, or burying it is a common feature of exorcism in many cultures.) However, in the breaking the stone ceremony, the demon is not specifically associated with disease or any other misfortune: it simply stands for negative forces destroyed by the ritual to ensure prosperity. It is performed annually in some communities, and sometimes on special occasions such as weddings.[4]

The account below comes from Russian Tibetologist Georges de Roerich, whose father founded the Nicholas Roerich Museum in New York City. The full ceremony is actually an assemblage of seemingly unconnected martial feats, singing, dancing, and other performances. The songs have been excised for the sake of brevity. Roerich predicted that the ceremony was dying out. However, Tibetologist Pascale Dollfus traveled to the Spiti Valley between 1999 and 2000 and observed the ceremony twice. Dollfus records that the entire performance lasts about three hours.

Among the many popular plays of a religious character in Tibet, there exists one that enjoys special veneration, and whose performers are considered to possess supernatural powers that enable them to carry out the play. Such a ceremony is the "breaking of stone" known under the Tibetan name of pho-bar rdo-gčog (pronounced pʻo-war do-čok). Nowadays it is only seldom performed, and the ancient art of rdo-gčog or stonebreaking is rapidly vanishing. The purpose of the ceremony is to destroy an evil spirit which takes its abode in a stone. The ceremony of "breaking the stone" is said to have been first performed by the great mahāsiddha Thaṅ-stoṅ rgyal-po, a Tibetan wizard of the XIV–XVth centuries (born in 1385), and the famous builder of the Čhu-bo ri bridge on the Yaru tsang-po, some 32 miles South-West of Lhasa. During my stay in Lahul, North-West Himalayas, I was fortunate to witness twice this ceremony performed by a troupe of traveling lama-actors from Spiti. After the ceremony, the chief lama-actor or lo-čhen (lo-tsā-ba čhen-po), who is usually the preceptor and trainer of the rest of the troupe, was good enough to recite the songs accompanying the ceremony, and to give me a brief historical outline on the origin of the ceremony. The Tibetan text of the story as told by the lama māni-pa (actor) has been revised by Lama Lobzang Mingyur Dorje, and is here given . . . in translation.

[. . .]

Translation:—
"At the time when Pha-grub-čhen Thaṅ-stoṅ rgyal-po (Pha-grub-čhen is an honorary title given to a great seer; the word "pha" is used here in the sense of our "father, elder, reverend") was erecting the monastery of Čuṅ Ri-bo-čhe, evil omens made their appearance. Whatever was built by men during the day, was destroyed by demons during the night.[5] After performing the ceremony of breaking the stone for the first time, they were able to resume work on the monastery. At the time of building the iron bridge of Čhu-bo-ri, the demon dBaṅ-rgyal caused the water to rise, and thus hindered the construction of the bridge. After performing the ceremony of breaking the stone there for the second time, the iron bridge was built.

In Lhasa the demon Hala rta-brgyad and a "planetary demon" (gza'-bdud often stands for Rāhula) caused a great many diseases, especially the disease of the bowels and pains in the intestines. Doctors administered their medicines, magicians their charms, but these were of no avail. Some died while collecting wood in the mountains, others while partaking of food. Some died while dressing, others while enjoying themselves. The Precious Lord of Lhasa (rJe-rin-po-čhe Tsoṅ-kha-pa, 1357–1419) pondered over the matter, and said: "The people of Lhasa are mostly dying out! If the great mahāsiddha[6] Thaṅ-stoṅ rgyal-po of the Čuṅ Ri-bo-čhe Monastery possesses no means to control the disease, no one else can do anything." The Precious

Lord despatched messengers to the Čuṅ Ri-bo-čhe Monastery with the message: "My people of Lhasa are mostly dying out! You are the only one who can subdue this disease, others can do nothing. Come at once!"

The great mahāsiddha Thaṅ-stoṅ rgyal-po after reflecting on the matters said: "This being a command of the Precious Lord, I must go!" Pointing his fore-finger to heaven, he perceived a mighty white-tailed eagle flying high in the sky. The great mahāsiddha Thaṅ-stoṅ rgyal-po having assumed the form of an "iron Asgara" (none was able to explain to me the meaning of the word lčags "iron" in this sentence. It may mean "iron-coloured," or according to others it may mean "well-protected," that is, Thaṅ-stoṅ rgyal-po going to fight the spirit of the epidemic, assumed a well-protected magic form) mounted the mighty white-tailed eagle, and proceeded to Lhasa.

The Precious Lord ordered to his seven door-keepers: "I am expecting to-morrow an important guest to arrive. Let him come upstairs without hindrance!"

The great mahāsiddha Thaṅ-stoṅ rgyal-po having arrived, the door-keepers did not recognize him, and detained him for a while. The Precious Lord perceived this in his mind, and said to the door-keepers: "My guest did not arrive as yet?" The door-keepers replied: "There is no other guest, except one At-sara who came riding on a mighty white-tailed eagle. Is this the one?" The Precious Lord exclaimed: "Why did you not let him in at once?," and having pulled out a sword from beneath his leg, he was ready to strike the door-keepers. The door-keepers opened the gate and led the guest into the presence of the Precious Lord. The Precious Lord said: "Nowadays my people of Lhasa are mostly dying out! If you are unable to help in this, no one else can do anything."

The mahāsiddha Thaṅ-stoṅ rgyal-po then requested the Precious Lord: "Where resides the spirit of the present epidemic?" To this the Precious Lord answered: "At present he is found under the threshold of my door, and has the shape of a stomach." Then the mahāsiddha Thaṅ-stoṅ rgyal-po having caused the spirit of the epidemic to enter inside this brownish stone, which had the shape of a stomach, invited the stone to the

market place of Lhasa. From the five fingers of the mahāsiddha
five flames sprang up. One assumed the form of Avalokiteçvara,
and acted as preacher of the Doctrine; another assumed the
form of Vajrapāṇi, and acted as his assistant; a third one assumed the form of a goddess possessing a melodious voice.[7]

Having placed the stone in a yard, all the elderly people of
Lhasa gathered to see the ceremony, saying: "To-day a mad
mahāsiddha will perform some crazy things!" And there in
the presence of the assembled elderly people of Lhasa, who
came to the ceremony riding on sticks, he (Thaṅ-stoṅ rgyal-po)
broke this stone, which was just the size of a stomach, with another stone similar to a magic dagger.

In the present evil kalpa [aeon], one has to use a bigger stone
to break it,[8] for the purpose of subduing demons, ogresses and
evil spirits. If one breaks the stone with the first stroke it signifies dharmakāya. If one breaks the stone with the second
stroke it signifies saṁbhogakāya. If one breaks it with the
third stroke it signifies nirmāṇakāya.[9] If one breaks it with the
fourth stroke it signifies the Lords of the Four Quarters. If one
breaks it with the fifth stroke it signifies the five dhyāni-
buddhas. If one breaks it with the sixth stroke it signifies the
manifestation of Buddha in the six state of existence. If one
breaks it with the seventh stroke it signifies the seven groups of
Buddhas. If one breaks it with the eighth stroke it signifies the
eight Sugatas.[10] If one breaks the stone with the ninth stroke it
signifies the nine stages of the Vehicle (Doctrine). If one breaks
it with the tenth stroke it signifies the ten forms of the Teacher.
If one breaks it with the eleventh stroke it signifies the eleven-
headed Avalokiteçvara. If one breaks the stone with the twelfth
stroke it signifies the twelve manifestations of the Earth-goddess.
If one breaks it with the thirteenth stroke it signifies the sphere
of Vajradhara. If one is unable to break the stone, one should
not proceed with the ceremony, this being an evil omen. If the
stone is found under the threshold of a monastery, a great lama
should subdue it; again if it is found under the threshold of a
castle, a great king should subdue it. If one is unable to break
it in a region where there are no castles or monasteries, one
should place it at the meeting place of three highways, and there

it should be broken either by a hundred blacksmiths striking it with their hammers, or by a hundred boys attacking it with loud cries, or by eight strong young men smashing it."

Such is the story of the origin of this ceremony. It will be noticed from the above story that each stroke with which the stone is broken corresponds to a divine manifestation. At the beginning of the ceremony the lama-actors or lama-māṇi-pas arrange a traveling altar or mčhod-bçams with the image of Thaṅ-stoṅ rgyal-po placed on it. Thaṅ-stoṅ rgyal-po is usually represented as an old man, sitting naked and cross-legged, his white hair arranged in a kind of knot on the crown of his head. In his hands, which are placed on his lap, the sage holds the tshe-bum or amrta vase. Behind the image of Thaṅ-stoṅ rgyal-po two painted images or thaṅ-sku are placed: one representing the four-armed manifestation of the Bodhisattva Avalokiteçvara, and the other representing the life-story or rnam-thar of Dri-med kun-ldan. The head lama-actor or lo-čhen wears the usual monastic attire. On his head he wears the five-colored hat of an actor (Tibetan: phod-ka) adorned with multicolored ribbons. During the initial prayer before the ceremony, the lo-čhen or chief lama-actor holds in his left hand the rosary ('phreṅ-ba), and in his right hand the prayer wheel (māṇi 'khor-lo).

He opens the ceremony by blowing the conch and reciting [a] prayer. . . .

A large stone, which is obtained from the neighborhood by the lo-čhen and his assistants, is placed in front of the traveling altar. Frequently these stones are extremely heavy and can hardly be lifted by one man. After placing the stone in front of the altar, one of the lama-actors draws on its surface a human figure, representing the nad-bdag or spirit of the epidemic who is to be destroyed through the ceremony. The initial prayer and burning of incenses over the stone is followed by a dance. The head lama-dancer leads the dance, and rhythmically strikes the cymbals. Two of his assistants follow him in a frantic dance. With each ringing sound of the cymbals the dance doubles its pace, and at the end of the dance the performers whirl past the onlookers, their dancing skirts tracing large circles in the air.

When the dance is over, the performers rest, while the lo-
čhen turns his prayer-wheel in a silent prayer. The silence is interrupted by shrill sounds similar to those used by Tibetan
herdsmen in driving yaks. There appears one of the performers attired as a shepherd in a grey homespun coat, and wearing
a black sheep-skin cap. His face is smeared with tsam-pa or
parched barley flour. He is holding a sling (Tibetan: 'ur-rdo)
and a bag with tsam-pa. He makes the round of the place on
which the ceremony is held, and jeers at the crowd of onlookers, swinging his sling. During this part of the dance the lo-čhen
or head lama-actor represents the dharmarāja [Dharma-king]
Nor-bzaṅ, the destroyer of evil ones (the dharmarāja Nor-bzaṅ
and Thaṅ-stoṅ rgyal-po are both considered to be destroyers
of evil forces; there seems to be no inner connection between
the Čhos-rgyal Nor-bzan-gi rnam-thar, and the ceremony of
"breaking the stone"). The lo-čhen representing the king Nor-
bzaṅ questions the shepherd, and notwithstanding the latter's
evasive answers, discovers in the shepherd the Wild King of
the North (byaṅ mi-rgod rgyal-po), his deadly enemy.[11] "Who
are you, and what is the purpose of your coming here?"—is
the question put by the king Nor-bzaṅ to the shepherd, who
sits down before the altar and plays with a tsam-pa ball. King
Nor-bzaṅ then challenges the disguised Wild King of the North.
A fight takes place during which the Wild King of the North
rolls several times on the floor. Mortally wounded by king Nor-
bzaṅ, the Wild King of the North sings [a] song.

[. . .]

This brings the second part of the ceremony to an end.
While one of the lama-actors recites the mani-prayer over the
stone, the lo čhen prepares himself for the sword-dance. The
upper part of his body is stripped naked, and a light shawl is
fixed to his naked shoulders with two long pins. A large pin is
introduced through his left cheek. These gruesome preparations take a considerable time, and cause great excitement
among the crowd of onlookers. Then the lo-čhen takes two
swords and begins a slow dance, with each step swinging the
swords in front of himself. Several times during the dance, he
points the two swords towards his belly, and jumps on them

resting his body on the swords' points. Then pointing the swords towards his armpits he makes several similar jumps resting his body on the sword-points. A tense moment during which the onlookers draw nearer to the dancing man; one false step on his part and the sharp points of the two swords would pierce his body, causing fatal injury. . . .

. . . On finishing the sword-dance, the head lama-actor attires himself in his monastic garment, and begins the preparations of the final and culminating part of the ceremony—the breaking of the stone and the driving away of the evil spirit. The mantle belonging to one of the lama-actors, on whose body the stone is to be broken, is held over the stone, and the head lama-actor passes his sword over it, reciting the māni-prayer and sounding his bell. The dancer, on whose body the stone is to be broken, then lies down in front of the stone, covers his head with the mantle, and for some time remains in this posture, inhaling some burning incense which he is holding in his clasped hands in front of him. The rest of the lama-actors continue to recite prayers over him. The blue smoke of the incense envelops the body of the lying man. His fellow dancers with a grave and concentrated look continue to murmur prayers. The cadence of the prayer becomes quicker and quicker, and then suddenly comes to a stop, as if interrupted. The actor is then declared to be ready for the final ceremony. He lies down on his back, a piece of thin cloth is placed on his stomach, and the heavy stone is lifted by two dancers and slowly placed on his body. The head lama-actor then lifts the second stone and drops it twice on the stone which is on the dancer's body. With the second stroke, a crash is heard and the huge stone breaks asunder. The dancer gets up, a bit pale, but none the worse for his experience. Immunity from fatal injury while performing the ceremony is attained by long years of special training. The dancer who underwent the ceremony in my presence had an unusually developed chest and powerful build.

The breaking of the stone is followed by a dance accompanied by music on a string instrument or pi-wang, played during the dance by the lo-čhen or head lama-actor. . . .

The singers improvise their own tunes, and vary them according to their desire. If you ask them to repeat the same song several times, the tunes will be different each time.

The different parts of the ceremony have apparently no inner connection between themselves, and serve merely to draw away the attention of the onlookers from the secret part of the ceremony which precedes the "breaking of the stone," and is performed by the lo-čhen or head of the troupe.

These ceremonies represent a vanishing art, closely interwoven with religious beliefs and magic practices. A few decades more, and the Land of Snows will see the last of its religious actors.

MODERN
EXORCISMS

AN EXORCISM PERFORMED BY JOSEPH SMITH

1830

The Church of Jesus Christ of Latter-day Saints (LDS) has no prescribed ritual of exorcism. Despite this, historian Stephen Taysom has recorded numerous cases of LDS priests casting out spirits, as recently as 1977.[1] Founder Joseph Smith described casting out a demon by calling on the name of Jesus, describing this as the first miracle that ever occurred within the new church.

In LDS theology, Satan and his demons were denied bodies as punishment for their rebellion. They are jealous that human beings possess bodies to shelter their spirits and they seek to temporarily obtain bodies through demonic possession. Smith described this in a sermon delivered May 21, 1843:

"When Lucifer was hurled from Heaven the decree was that he Should not obtain a tabernacle [body] nor those that were with him, but go abroad upon the earth exposed to the anger of the elements naked & bare, but ofttimes he lays hold upon men binds up their Spirits enters their habitations laughs at the decree of God and rejoices in that he hath a house to dwell in, by & by he is expelled by Authority and goes abroad mourning naked upon the earth like a man without a house exposed to the tempest & the storm."[2]

The demonic craving for bodies, according to Smith, explains the story of the Gerasene demoniac in Mark 5:1-20, in which the banished demons beg Jesus to be sent into pigs: Even the form of a pig is a comfort to spirits with no bodies.

In the account below, Smith recounts a miracle that

*took place on April 30, 1830, in Colesville, New York.
The possessed person, Newel Knight, is described as suffering contortions and levitation due to demonic attack.
Knight was a close friend of Smith's and became an early
LDS leader. In his autobiography, Knight described how
he eventually gained the ability to cast out demons as
well, identifying and banishing one from his aunt.*

JOSEPH SMITH,
"HISTORY OF JOSEPH SMITH CONT."
IN *THE TIMES AND SEASONS*,
VOL. 4, NO. 1 (NOVEMBER 15, 1842)

During this month of April I went on a visit to the residence of
Mr. Joseph Knight, of Colesville, Broom co. N. Y., with whom
and his family I had been previously acquainted, and of whose
name I have above mentioned as having been so kind and
thoughtful towards us, while translating the Book of Mormon. Mr. Knight and his family were Universalists, but were
willing to reason with me upon my religious views, and were
as usual friendly and hospitable. We held several meetings in
the neighborhood, we had many friends, and some enemies.
Our meetings were well attended, and many began to pray fer-
vently to Almighty God, that he would give them wisdom to
understand the truth. Amongst those who attended our meetings regularly, was Newel Knight son to Joseph Knight. He
and I had many serious conversations on the important subject
of man's eternal salvation: we had got into the habit of praying
much at our meetings and Newel had said that he would try
and take up his cross, and pray vocally during meeting; but
when we again met together he rather excused himself; I tried
to prevail upon him making use of the figure, supposing that
he should get into a mudhole would he not try to help himself
out? and that we were willing now to help him out of the mudhole, he replied that provided he had got into a mudhole
through carelessness, he would rather wait and get out himself
than have others to help him, and so he would wait until he

should get into the woods by himself, and there he would pray. Accordingly he deferred praying until next morning, when he retired into the woods; where (according to his own account afterwards) he made several attempts to pray but could scarcely do so, feeling that he had not done his duty, but that he should have prayed in the presence of others. He began to feel uneasy, and continued to feel worse both in mind and body, until upon reaching his own house, his appearance was such as to alarm his wife very much. He requested her to go and bring me to him. I went and found him suffering very much in his mind, and his body acted upon in a very strange manner. His visage and limbs distorted and twisted in every shape and appearance possible to imagine; and finally he was caught up off the floor of the apartment and tossed about most fearfully. His situation was soon made known to his neighbors and relatives, and in a short time as many as eight or nine grown persons had got together to witness the scene. After he had thus suffered for a time, I succeeded in getting hold of him by the hand, when almost immediately he spoke to me, and with great earnestness requested of me, that I should cast the devil out of him, saying that he knew he was in him, and that he also knew that I could cast him out. I replied "if you know that I can it shall be done," and then almost unconsciously I rebuked the devil; and commanded him in the name of Jesus Christ to depart from him; when immediately Newel spoke out and said that he saw the devil leave him and vanish from his sight.

This was the first miracle which was done in this church or by any member of it, and it was done not by man nor by the powor [sic] of man, but it was done by God, and by the power of godliness: therefore let the honor and the praise, the dominion and the glory be ascribed to the Father, Son, and Holy Spirit for ever and ever Amen.

Joseph Smith's attempts to found a new church were met with derision and scorn. Smith's critics assumed he was inventing stories of visions and miracles for personal gain. The excerpt below from The Reflector *provides a mocking account of the demon being expelled from Newel Knight. Smith is derisively referred to as "Jo." Ironically, this attack confirms that Knight really had described an exorcism in 1830 and that Smith's 1842 account was not invented later. This account also has similar details to Smith's, noting that the primary symptom of possession was painful bodily contortions.*

OBADIAH DOGBERRY, ESQ.
"A HUNGRY LEAN-FACED VILLAIN."
THE REFLECTOR (PALMYRA, NEW YORK)
(30 JUNE 1830): 53–54.

Jo's greatest as well as latest miracle, as narrated by St. Martin, is his "casting out of a devil," of an uncommon size from a miserable man in the neighborhood of the "great bend" of the Susquehanna. The whole family of *spirits*, who are said to have possessed the fair Magdalene, were mere children, when compared to the *imp* in question. Such was his malignant disposition that before Jo took him in hand, he had nigh demolished the frail tenement which had for a long time afforded him a comfortable shelter—the flesh was "about to cleave from the bones"—the muscles, tendons, &c. could no longer perform their different functions—the habitation of Satan, was about to be laid open to the light of day, when the prophet interfered—went to prayer—the demoniac had faith—the devil was routed, and nature resumed her accustomed order.

W. S. LACH-SZYRMA,
EXORCISING A RUSALKA[1]

1881

A rusalka *is a water spirit found in Slavic folklore. Although different cultures attribute different forms to the* rusulki, *they are most frequently described as beautiful women. While they are not invariably evil, the* rusulki *are typically said to lure peasants to a watery death. Although they resemble nature spirits like the Greek naiad, it is often claimed that* rusulki *are the souls of either drowned women or unbaptized or stillborn babies. (One legend even claims they are the souls of pharaoh's army, drowned pursuing the Israelites across the Red Sea.) Although the word "rusalka" cannot be traced back further than the seventeenth century, it seems likely that the rusalka has its origins in Slavic paganism. "Rusul'naiia week" was an agricultural festival held in Russia in late spring, when it was said the* rusulki *were free to leave their waters and roam the land, and when various folk practices were used to appease or protect against the* rusulki. *Christian documents condemn demonic dancing and games of the "Rusalii," hinting that these were more ambiguous spirits before they underwent a process of Christian demonization.[2]*

The legend below was recorded by Wladislaw Somerville Lach-Szyrma on a visit to Poland. Lach-Szyrma was an Anglican curate as well as a science fiction writer. Although born in England, he was the son of a Polish philosophy professor who fled the Polish-Russian War of 1830–1831. He concludes with a materialist interpretation of the legend that is built on numerous assumptions. Regardless of the origin of this story, it seems its function is to assert the power of Christian institutions over the dangerous nature spirits of the Polish landscape.

One story I have had narrated to me in the country about Gniezn, about a haunted lake, which I believe has never yet been published, and which is interesting to Englishmen as being in one point similar to a folk-belief of South Devon, i. e., as embodied in the proverb, "The River Dart every year claims its heart," i. e., somebody or other yearly drowned in the Dart.

A peasant was once cutting wood in a forest near Mogilno (the "town of tombs" or *tumuli* as its name implies). He penetrated depths of the forest glade never yet traversed by man. Suddenly between the glinting foliage, he perceived a castle—towers, massive walls, battlements—grander than he had ever seen even in his unfrequent visits to the "sacred city of the rest," Gniezn, or even to Posen, the other ancient capital, "the city of the recognition." In fact he had never before seen anything so grand.

The unselfish thought struck him, "Perhaps the lord of this grand castle is in want of workmen, and some of the men of my village may find good employment and pay with him." So with a parting glance at the noble towers of the forest palace he turned homewards and told the gossips of the village at the *karczma* or village inn that night of the grand castle he had seen and the excellent opening for well-paid work which it probably offered.

In the morning the village was early awake; the young men came out in numbers to seek new employment with the rich seigneur who had settled in their neighbourhood. They started into the forest. They followed the path pointed out by their guide. Lo! to their chagrin and grief only a deep blue lake appeared. The castle was a magic castle of the nymph of the lake, only visible in twilight.

Their hopes were disappointed, but the mystic lake was no longer unknown or unfrequented. A path was made through the forest to it, linking two villages. Then the spell worked.

Year after year some benighted peasant was caught in its deep blue waters, the more mysterious because half shrouded by the green foliage. The Rusialka claimed her offering of a human heart, some human life sacrificed to her Circe charms. But this could not be endured. The magic lake was held accursed. Again and again, in broad daylight, did the peasant try to sound its depths, just as the Cornish moorsmen say they have tried Dosmary Pool, in vain. At length something, every one felt, must be done. A deputation of peasants waited on the parish priest. It was a scandal to the Church that this demon of the water should thus hold sway in the parish. Persuaded by his parishioners he sallied forth with all the paraphernalia of exorcism to exorcise the spirit. He came with a long procession of villagers to the lake. He solemnly adjured the Rusialka to depart for ever. The service of exorcism was performed. Since then the peasants say the fatality of the lake has diminished, if not ceased. The story of the exorcism was, I was credibly assured, no legend but an historic fact.

As to the story itself, it may be explained easily on natural grounds. The evening twilight has strange effects in forest glades. Perhaps the mists of the lake in warm weather might have produced an effect on the mind of the peasant, full of fancy and folk-lore, to make him imagine a castle. Day dispelled the delusion. The idea of its being fathomless here as at Dosmary was due to no better sounding instruments than long poles being available. The exorcism was a fact. Its result possibly was due to peasants now avoiding the dreaded spot.

MARIANNHILL MISSION SOCIETY, AN EXORCISM OF A ZULU WOMAN[1]

1906

The exorcism of Clara Germana Tele of Natal, South Africa, is among the most spectacular ever recorded. Tele (or Cele in later accounts) was a Zulu girl who was baptized and sent to school at the St. Michael's Mission, run by the Catholic Mariannhill Mission Society. On August 20, 1906, Tele began showing the first signs of possession. An exorcism was ordered and was completed on September 13, 1906. Her symptoms returned the following year, and a second exorcism began on April 24, 1907. This time, another girl, Monica Mohletsche, was possessed as well. There is also a record of a third possessed girl at the St. Michael's Mission, named Engelberta; she was moved to another mission. The second exorcism was reportedly successful. Tele died of consumption on March 14, 1913.

The Mariannhill Mission Society gathered testimony from Rev. Erasmus Hoerner, who performed the exorcism; Henri Delalle, bishop of Natal, who authorized and witnessed the exorcism; and two nuns who worked closely with Tele. All of this was published in a pamphlet called Are There Devils Today? An Authentic Report on Two Cases of Exorcism Performed in Recent Years, with Signed Testimonies of Numerous Eye-Witnesses.

The cause of Tele's purported possession is unclear. One account records that on July 5, 1906, she publicly handed Rev. Hoerner a slip of paper pledging her service to the Devil. Rev. Hoerner's account implies that her parents, who practiced indigenous Zulu religion, somehow cursed her. Hoerner also makes a disturbing reference to Tele committing "sins again the sixth commandment" (in the Catholic tradition, this would be adultery) when she was "a girl of six of seven," suggesting possible sexual abuse. Bishop Delalle demanded to know the demon's name. Tele would not answer but spelled out the name D-I-O-A-R.

The most extraordinary feature of Tele's possession was her levitations. She is said to have floated to a height of five to six feet, almost daily. Rev. Hoerner describes multiple people attempting to pull her down, only to be lifted as well. Tele also reportedly walked up walls, a feature later attributed to an exorcism in Gary, Indiana, in 2012. Curiously, Hoerner's report notes that her clothes also defied gravity, clinging closely to her body during levitation. This detail echoes a letter from the fourth-century theologian Saint Jerome. Jerome described demoniacs near the tombs of the prophets in Jerusalem, writing, "Women hung upside-down in mid-air, yet their skirts did not fall down over their heads."[2]

Tele's native language was Zulu and she had learned some English, but while possessed she reportedly understood Latin, German, Polish, and other languages. She exhibited superhuman strength, and when a doctor administered opium pills to make her sleep, they had no effect. Tele was described as having a strange ability to extend her body to incredible lengths, particularly her limbs and neck.

Rev. Hoerner describes her as exhibiting a form of telepathy. She reportedly knew things about other people she should not have been able to know, including the location of clergy who had since traveled to Rome, down to their current street address. She exhibited an ability to sense holy objects and foiled numerous attempts to trick her by telling her ordinary water was holy water.

Weirdest of all, she could reportedly pick up dust and throw it on the ground, where it would turn into solid "bowling balls," seemingly larger than the original hand-ful of dust.

For all of this, there were those who doubted the pos-session was genuine. Rev. Hoerner's account mentions that Tele was highly intelligent, with a good memory, and "fond of playing tricks." There was also an incident when her clothes appeared to spontaneously catch fire, burning a hole in her skirt. Some speculated she started the fire herself, and one account noted that her clothes were sud-denly "soaked in kerosene." However, there is no skepti-cal interpretation of her levitations. It seems that either the various clergy were not credible witnesses or else that something truly extraordinary occurred.

FATHER ERASMUS DESCRIBES EXORCISM

Beginning the exorcism proper, I grasped in my left hand the stole which had been placed about Germana's neck and drew it firmly under her chin. With the right hand I held the Ritual. Father Apollinarius had hold of my shoulder to steady me. Sev-eral Sisters had come into the sanctuary so that seven or eight were present and there were also the eight large, strong girls. All who could, clung to the raving and howling Germana and all, together with Germana and her chair, were lifted up free of the floor. I was witness to this myself, as well as the Sisters in the chapel and the school children in the main body of the church.

Germana presented a terrible sight, her face being horribly distorted, and her savage howling and wild blows rendering the scene still more awful. Sister Luitgardis received a power-ful blow that left a blue mark on her arm. Meanwhile I contin-ued the exorcism with all my strength so that the perspiration rolled down my face.

The poor girl became increasingly violent. Her entire body swelled out as if distended by bellows; her eyes fairly pierced me with rage, and some invisible power lifted both her and those holding her up from the floor. Finally I ordered her hands clapped in handcuffs and her arms and feet tied together. But this proved a gigantic task.

Meanwhile Sister Hilaria and Sister Servatia, the superiors of the mission schools at St. Michael's and Himmelberg, had arrived, saying that even at a distance the air seemed filled with sounds of wild howling.

Though everyone who could possibly approach Germana assisted in trying to put her in bonds, we succeeded only after three hours in finally handcuffing her. Her arms were stiff and almost unbendable, and she was continually being lifted up with her chair by the evil one, amid ear-deafening noises and pandemonium. Finally Sister Anacleta succeeded in seizing the raving girl, with both arms clutched about her waist, while Sister Luitgardis and Sister Servatia, with the aid of the girls, bound her feet and limbs.

While Germana's right arm was being clapped into the handcuff, she suddenly jerked the arm from the two girls holding it and clutched Sister Anacleta with such an iron hold about the throat that she was nearly choked. At the same time Germana and the chair on which she was sitting soared so high into the air that the Sister, though quite tall, touched the floor only with the point of her shoes. Only a concerted effort of all present freed the Sister from Germana's throttling clutch.

Hardly had the feet been tied, than the rope broke. But when the Sisters, in their efforts to bind her still more securely, placed their weight upon her limbs to hold her down, they were lifted up from the floor together with the possessed girl. Continuing, however, the prayers of the exorcism, I commanded the evil spirit in the name of God and of the Church, to abandon his victim.

Completely bound, she lay with her back slightly leaning against the chair, like a perfectly rigid trunk of a tree. Again, together with the chair, she was elevated from the floor, while Sister Anacleta still clung to her waist. I myself continued to hold the stole as prescribed by the Ritual.

When I came to the passage, "I conjure thee, thou old Serpent!" she stormed and screamed pitifully, and sought to bite

Sister Anacleta's arm. I cautioned the latter, but she replied: "Then let him bite. I won't let go any more. I'll not be conquered by the Devil."

In a second the possessed girl twisted her head dexterously over my hand which held the stole and sank her teeth into Sister's arm with diabolical rage, causing a sharp, piercing pain. It was an astounding bite. The sleeve of Sister's habit showed not the least cut; only some foam marks of the teeth were visible. The arm itself had only red, blue, and green marks corresponding to the two rows of teeth; but between them appeared a small red wound, such as is caused by a snake's bite or by a needle. Large blisters filled with yellow fluid appeared on all the marks by next morning, and the arm gave pain for days.

At this exhibition of rage I continued with renewed faith and confidence. Satan bellowed louder and more frequently. "Wo! Wooo! Woe, Woe!" The awful sound pierced through marrow and bone. I felt that finally the decisive moment had come. Once more Germana plainly soared aloft above all those about her. She screamed and howled in a manner beyond words to describe, and again sank to the floor. There she writhed and twisted like one in the agony of death and then stretched out full length. All was over: Germana was freed from the terrible demon. The struggle ended at half past nine in the morning, September 13, 1906, in the Mission Church of St. Michael.

We let the poor girl rest for some time, loosened her bonds, and then offered a short prayer of thanksgiving before the Blessed Sacrament. She herself, so far as she had perceived and was aware, bore witness to the time and manner of the spirit's departure. Her soul, she said, was at peace again and she could pray with the fervor of her first Communion day. Voicing her gratitude again and again, she retired to her room for the rest so greatly needed.

To make absolutely certain that she was free, we renewed the exorcism in the evening; but Germana remained calm, singing and praying heartily with the rest, and declaring repeatedly how exceedingly happy and peaceful she felt to the very depths of her heart.

The following day was the feast of the Elevation of the Cross and we sang a solemn Te Deum with exposition of the Blessed Sacrament and recited the prescribed prayers of thanksgiving. The children sang and celebrated all day, and since that terrible affair a new and better spirit, filled with earnestness and fear of the Lord, rules in this mission.

[. . .]

ADDITIONAL REPORT OF
FATHER ERASMUS

Clara Germana Tele lived six years after the first exorcism and died of quick consumption on March 14, 1913, peacefully and resigned to the will of God.

The exorcism was witnessed by three priests, three Brothers, fourteen Sisters, and more than one hundred and fifty natives. During the exorcism the possessed girl repeatedly floated freely in the air, and sometimes four, five, or six persons, Sisters and adult girls, holding her were raised up with her.

The howling and raving were simply indescribable and most uncanny. They sounded like the roar and tumult of great armies battling in the air, now closer and then at a distance. At times it seemed as if all these noises emanated from Germana; then again the uproar seemed to be in the church and in the air outside. Germana would stretch and raise herself so that she often seemed half again as tall and strong as she actually was. Now her neck appeared two and three times its normal length; then her head expanded and her chest swelled up as if inflated with gas. Yet Germana was quite slim. At times her arms and limbs would stretch amid cracking noises as if they were about to break. When the exorcism finally prevailed she fell unconscious at the foot of the altar and lay motionless for some time. On recovering consciousness she rose, assisted by one of the Sisters and joined in singing the Te Deum. During her first possession Germana, or rather the demon, declared again and again that he would return, and the second siege would be more terrible than the first. She also predicted various extraordinary things that would come to pass.

For the present all was well, and Germana enjoyed comparatively good health and conducted herself like other native girls of her age for several months.

Toward the end of January, 1907, Germana stated that she would be possessed again, as the demon had announced his coming.

On March 6, 1907, I left for Europe, and Father Leonhard Siller assumed my duties at St. Michael's. Germana's condition grew worse so rapidly that on April 24, 1907, Dr. Delalle, Bishop of Natal, and two Oblate priests came to St. Michael's to conduct a second exorcism. Our mission congregation was represented by Fathers Leonhard, Cyprian, Mansuet, and two neighboring priests.

This time the exorcism concerned two persons, Monica Mohletsche and Germana. Concerning the latter Bishop Delalle wrote an accurate report for a periodical in Rome, the article being reprinted in English and American newspapers and causing great astonishment. Also *The Mercury* in Durban published the entire report.

The Bishop and the five priests were engaged in the ceremony from early morning until late at night. They succeeded in freeing Germana on the afternoon of the second day. In the case of Monica some awful scenes were witnessed. From eight to ten persons could scarcely manage her. Finally after much praying and conjuring the evil one began to depart amid terrifying bellowing.

Bishop Delalle, who took particular note of Monica's eyes, stated afterward that seven demons left in succession. From my own observation I might add that a weird fire often gleamed from the eye of the possessed person, a fire that sent hot and cold streaks down one's back. The diabolical rage, the hateful stare, that uncanny glow in the eyes of the possessed speak volumes—more than human tongue can utter or pen depict. There you learn to believe in the powers of darkness and their diabolical work.

Before possession Germana was healthy, vivacious, very talented, quite adept in feminine handiwork, including knitting and sewing. In appearance she was attractive with a comparatively noble countenance for a Zulu, slender but well built. At times she was fond of fun and playing tricks. Blessed with a good memory, she knew every thing that went on at the school and mission, and her judgment of others was generally correct.

As far as her public conduct was concerned, she was well disposed and acted honestly and candidly toward the priests and the Sister Superior. Though possessed of a deeply passionate nature, she was open-hearted and never found guilty of falsehood.

Unfortunately, her parents might have led a much more edifying life. Swearing and cursing of each other and of the children were a common occurrence. Perhaps this conduct contributed to bring much misery on their child. A parent's curse is something terrible, and even the pagans here dread it more than they fear any other evil.

Who can judge as to the manner and degree in which the unfortunate maiden was seduced into sins against the sixth commandment, even as a girl of six or seven years of age? Germana herself told me casually on one occasion that an aged sorceress had initiated her into vice and had urged her to seduce other school girls.

As for her interior, spiritual life, she was frank and candidly exposed her soul with her passions, struggles, sufferings and temptations. Often she wept bitter tears when she noticed how others evaded her or confronted her with past conduct! Great were her faults and heavy her penance. God grant her the crown of life!

You may ask: "Did her conduct after the exorcism offer any basis for a conclusion as to whether she was actually possessed or merely suffered attacks of delirium or insanity?"

In view of the foregoing, it seems to me that the assumption of insanity is contrary to all logic and common sense. Protestant missionaries, also, who read reports of the occurrences, were convinced that it was actual possession. The fact that she was liberated and remained so after the second exorcism would confirm that view.

Attacks of delirium are not stopped by sprinkling with holy water, or touching with particles of the Holy Cross.

Again, how do you explain the following facts and occurrences connected with the second possession:

I—Germana understood every language in which she was addressed—Latin, Polish, German, French, or any other tongue though she had studied none and though she had never heard a syllable spoken in most of these foreign languages. She generally answered questions very correctly in Zulu. She also replied in Latin when I commanded her to do so after having obtained permission to conduct the exorcism. During the ceremony she frequently recited in advance entire Latin sentences of the formula of exorcism which the priest was about to use. She would call attention to mistakes and at times made fun of certain words, stressing them in a peculiar manner and singing them mischievously in an effort to disturb the priest.

II—Germana frequently floated freely in the air at a distance of three, four or five feet from the floor. Sometimes she was lifted up in a vertical position; then again in a horizontal line, however, in the latter position her dress clung closely to her body and limbs instead of hanging down in accordance with the law of gravity. Sprinkled with holy water, she would immediately sink to her chair or bed. This occurred frequently in the presence of many witnesses. Some tried to pull her down, but without success. But as soon as Brother Medard sprayed her with holy water, she came down of her own accord, trembling and weeping.

III—She would also glide from the bed to the floor like a snake, as if her entire body were of rubber, now on her back, then on her stomach, and in all possible serpentine twistings. Here, too, her clothes would cling to her body. As soon as a drop of Holy Water touched her, or I ordered her to cease, she would return to her normal position.

IV—Her response to my orders was marvelous. Even when I was in my room and merely gave such a command in thought, she would comply, although she was in her own room and could not see me. I tried this rarely and only by way of experiment. She always knew when I left my room to go over to the house where she was staying. She would say to her nurse and attendants: "Father is coming; he is just leaving his quarters." How could she know this by natural means? I lived in a remote corner of the mission with several buildings hiding my room from view of anyone in the infirmary.

V—She always reacted when sprinkled with holy water; but only laughed when sprayed with ordinary water. We demonstrated this repeatedly, and the Bishop also tried the experiment. Sometimes we secretly emptied the holy water font and filled it with common water. Then while she looked on someone filled the holy water vial with this water. When this was applied to her she showed no reaction; but as soon as the priest would use real holy water from another flask which he had in his pocket, she would scream: "Quit, that burns!" In spite of all sorts of tricks we could not induce her to drink holy water. She would do so only under strict orders and under protest. Her conduct towards relics was the same. No matter how well I wrapped up particles of the Holy Cross, she would always detect their presence.

VI—Again, she publicly charged many young men and girls with all their secret sins, giving complete details as to place, time, number, etc. She also revealed things that happened in remote places which she had never visited or been told of. Her charges were confirmed by admission on the part of the guilty ones. But as soon as the sins had been honestly confessed, she would keep silent concerning them. She also revealed sins that had been concealed in confession. After the exorcism, however, she was entirely ignorant of these revelations.

F. J. BUNSE, S.J.,
THE EARLING
POSSESSION CASE[1]

1934

*One of the most famous exorcisms in American history
occurred in a convent in Earling, Iowa, in 1928. The American public learned of this event through a German pamphlet that was translated in 1935 as* Begone Satan! A
Soul-Stirring Account of Diabolical Possession. *It described the successful twenty-three-day exorcism of a
woman by a Capuchin monk named Theophilus Riesinger
(1868–1941). William Peter Blatty describes reading Begone Satan!* while researching The Exorcist.[2] *Many details
will be familiar to anyone who has seen that film: the
woman is tied to a bed; she speaks multiple languages; she
can tell whether food has been blessed; she exhibits a preternatural ability to leap and cling to walls that borders on
levitation, and she exhibits feats of projectile vomiting such
that the author notes, "These came in quantities that were
humanly speaking impossible to lodge in a normal being."[3]*

*While the case has become famous, little is actually
known about this event, including the identity of the
woman, who has been referred to variously as "Emma
Schmidt," "Anna Ecklund," "Mary X," or simply "The
Woman." Few people are aware that there was a second,
unpublished account of the Earling exorcism written in
1934 by Riesinger's associate, a German-born Jesuit named
Frederick J. Bunse (1863–1935). This account, excerpted
below, reveals that the exorcism never actually ended:
"Mary" (the name Bunse uses) became possessed again
almost immediately and was still being exorcised when*

this second account was written. Furthermore, Mary was being visited by Jesus, the Virgin Mary, the archangel Michael, and other heavenly personages as well as demons. Riesinger used her trances to question all these beings about various doctrinal matters. He came to believe that Jesus would return in 1955 and that the events in Earling would play a pivotal role in the final war between heaven and hell. The rite of exorcism in The Ritual Romanum *specifically advises exorcists not to ask about "future or hidden matters." However, Bunse asserts that demons are not able to lie during an exorcism. Mary effectively transitioned from a demoniac to a mystic and seer, a shift that has not been uncommon for possessed Catholic women since the Protestant Reformation.[4] In the text below, she compares herself to "Teresa of* Konnersreuth*" (Therese Neumann), a famous German mystic and stigmatic.*

Another controversial feature of the exorcism is that the various possessing entities include Mary's father, Jake (or Jacob), and a woman named Minnie, variously described as either Jacob's lover or Mary's aunt. The possession is attributed to witchcraft used on Mary by Minnie. Both texts state that Jake "attempted" to commit incest with Mary, leading one to wonder whether Mary's symptoms are a result of sexual abuse. Some clergy objected that possession by spirits of the dead contradicts Catholic theology. An Italian priest named Albert Bandini wrote his own pamphlet debunking the exorcism and pointing out that if damned souls can escape hell and possess the living, this contradicts the sovereignty of God.[5]

Bunse's unpublished account provides more clues about Mary. She was born in 1882, which would have made her about forty-six in 1928. She apparently met Riesinger in New York City, and he first exorcised her on June 12, 1908. This was preceded by a radical change in behavior. Bunse writes, "Some described this sudden change to an operation she had undergone." It seems as though the sentence ought to say either that the change was "described as an operation" or that it was "ascribed to an operation." The sentence appears this way in both copies of the Bunse text obtained by the author. If Mary indeed underwent an unspecified operation, could it have been an abortion?

The two seem to have had a close relationship, during which he exorcised her repeatedly, in multiple states, between 1908 and 1934. Riesinger's interest in exorcism brought him into conflict with the diocese of New York, and in 1912 he was transferred to Appleton, Wisconsin. Mary apparently traveled to Wisconsin for further exorcisms. An interview with Riesinger that appeared on March 8, 1936, in The Des Moines Register *describes Riesinger exorcising Schmidt "in 1926 and again in 1928." In fact, Riesinger claims to have exorcised twenty-two people. An article that appeared on March 4, 1973, in* The Post-Crescent *interviewed the son of a physician who observed one of Riesinger's exorcisms in Milwaukee. The physician also asked to observe an exorcism Riesinger was to perform in Texas, but Riesinger forbade this. Riesinger may have used mission work as an opportunity to perform exorcisms, or he may have taken numerous trips like the 1928 visit to Earling, and this is simply the only case that was documented. In the final analysis, Bunse's text points to a strange relationship between a rogue exorcist and a woman who seems to have enjoyed his attention for nearly thirty years.*

N. B. The following facts concerning the famous "Earling Case" are culled from the German manuscript of the case written by Rev. Father Theophilus Riesinger, O. M. Cap.

THESE ARE NOT TO BE PUBLISHED THROUGH THE PRESS OR FROM THE PULPIT

At the command of Our Lord the case has been sent to the Holy Office. The translation and discussion of the facts are hereby submitted by Rev. F. J. Bunse, S. J., Buffalo, New York, February-March, 1934. Rev. F. J. Bunse, S. J. died last year.

THE SO-CALLED EARLING CASE

Remark: This case concerns a person who is possessed by the
devil and favored by God with many translations. Her real name
and the place of her home may not be mentioned at the present
time. Our Lord forbade it. "If people know your name and
place, they would come to see you as they visit Teresa of Konnersreuth; but that is against my Will." Let us call her Mary.

MARY'S PERSONALITY

Mary was born in 1882; is small of stature, and of a weak
rather than strong constitution. She has a clear mind, but a
merely elementary education. She always was truthful and obedient, cheerful and companionable, and led an exemplary life.
Even when dangerous situations were forced on her, she remained virtuous. She preserved her virginity and never kept
company. Mary was truly pious and wanted to become a nun,
but was prevented by her mother from carrying out her resolution. It was, therefore, a consolation for her to be able to go to
Mass regularly, to frequent the Holy Sacraments, and to attend
the afternoon and evening services. She also was a member of
the Third Order of St. Francis and of the Young Ladies' Sodal-
ity. Then, while engaged at her work in factories, she heard
priests and the Church belittled, she had courage enough to
take their part, and she often inquired of her confessor what
she should say in their defense.

There was no happiness in her home. Her father cursed very
much, and used smutty language, and her brothers neither worked
nor went to church. Their sinful conduct aroused her indigna-
tion, and she was frequently at war with them.

When she was about 26 years old, she, suddenly gave up her
pious Christian life completely. She became melancholy, avoided
company, and finally went to places and persons that cast a
shadow on her good character.

She threw blessed articles away, smashed crucifixes, and had
thoughts of despair. People were amazed and scandalized. Some

described this sudden change to an operation she had undergone. Others thought it was "Hysteria"; after examination they found her healthy. In fact, Mary had become possessed by evil spirits and was not responsible for her actions.

POSSESSION BY EVIL SPIRITS

A test made on her person showed all the signs of possession mentioned in the Roman Ritual, Tit. XI, Cap, 1. No.3, and others. Besides her German and English, which she had acquired in early childhood, she understood Latin and Hebrew, the Italian, Polish and other Slavonic languages which she had not learned. She knew hidden things; e.g. the evil spirit who was in her predicted that the auto of a certain priest would be smashed on a definite day when he would be using it on a sick call, and that in such a way that no cause would be detected. The prediction came true. At the beginning of a certain exorcism the spirit threw her upon the floor and made her so heavy that Father J., O. M. Cap. who was "as strong as a bear," tried in vain together with three other persons to lift her from the floor. She heard voices in herself coming up from below—curses and blasphemies. The spirits tormented her every night from 12-3 by arousing her passions and tempting her to commit sin. During the exorcisms an infernal stench was created around her and she was thrown into convulsions; she intermittently roared and bellowed and barked and mauled and moaned and shrieked so that it was impossible to keep her condition secret. Her abdomen would either move up and down with terrific rapidity beyond the power of a human being or swell up to the immense volume of a big barrel on which no weight would make an impression.

It was these wicked spirits who blinded her and drove her about the city so that, when she intended to go to church she at last found herself in a clairvoyant's room; or when she was in church standing in line to go to confession, she was, when her turn came to enter the box, pushed away back to the last place.

Much more could be said to show how mary [sic] became a plaything of the devil, not responsible for her actions. One more sign of possession; when she received Holy Communion in the state of possession, one could see how the spirits withdrew from the presence of the Lord as far as they could—into her foot. These signs of possession were not only testified both by Father Theophilus, her spiritual guide, but also by other priests, physicians, nuns, and others.

THE CAUSE OF HER POSSESSION

The most natural question now suggesting itself is "What was the cause or occasion of such a terrible possession?" To be very brief, the cause was "Minnie," Mary's aunt, who was known among the people as a witch. This woman had put a spell upon some herbs and put them in Mary's food and drink, thus creating a condition in her body which gave the spirits, as they interpreted it "a Satanic right" to enter her. This condition is described in the Ritual Romanum, loco cit., No. 20. The spirits with the permission of God, made use of this right and, under the leadership of a certain Beelzebub, one of Lucifer's generals, took possession of Mary's body. Their purpose was to get her either to commit sin of impurity or at least to consent to the most impure carnal pleasures they would cause in her as "incubi" or at least to consent otherwise. Mary never consented!

After four years' possession, Beelzebub was forced by Father Theophilus' exorcism to leave Mary on June 18, 1912.

You now ask how we know that it was bewitched herbs that established the relation between hell and Mary's body. We know it from answers given in exorcisms. You may listen to these questions and answers. But that you may beforehand judge of the reliability of these answers, remember that an exorcism performed according to the precepts of the Ritual, loco cit. No. 15 will compel the spirits to give these answers. Thus, Father Theophilus found out that there were demons and damned souls in Mary; he learned their number and names, the cause of their damnation and many other things connected with the case. . . . It is true that the evil spirits are liars by habit; but they are compelled to tell the truth by the exorcism of the Church; when, under the ordeal of the exorcism they attempt to lie, they feel great pain and soon cry out, "I have told a lie."

Now listen to how Minnie was questioned by Father Theophilus, and you will at once see how much can be elicited by an exorcism. Father Theophilus had been listening to the deep voice of Mary's father, Jake, who was likewise damned, and like Minnie, ordered into the body of Mary, when on a sudden he heard a woman's voice:

QUESTIONING OF MINNIE

Q. Is there a woman here?	R. Yes.
Q. I command you to tell me your name.	R. My name is Minnie, Minnie, Minnie.
Q. Are you living or dead?	R. I am dead.
Q. When did you die?	R. Twenty-two years ago.
Q. Are you damned?	R. Yes, I am damned.
Q. Why have you been damned?	R. I did devilish deeds.
Q. How long have you been in the body of this girl?	R. Twenty-one years.
Q. Did you give some thing to the girl by means of which the relation of this girl to the devils was established?	R. I have done that.
Q. How did you do that; by food or drink?	R. Both ways.

REMARK: While Father Theophilus was continuing the exorcism, he was suddenly interrupted by the damned souls who cried, Murder, Murder: This explains the next question.

Q. Have you killed anybody?

R. Yes.

Q. Have you killed your own children?

R. Yes. (She was known for that.)

Q. How many?

R. Five, and another one, six in all.

Q. Are you baptized?

R. Y—e—s. (Hesitatingly)

Q. Have you been baptized in the Catholic Church?

R. (After an unintelligible sound)

Q. What do you mean by that?

R. I was baptized a Lutheran.

Q. Which faith is the saving one?

R. Only the Catholic Faith is the saving one. (She repeated the words several times.)

Q. Do you believe in Jesus Christ?

R. No, I do not believe in Him.

Q. You, therefore, put that bewitched stuff into the person on account of which hell can carry on its mischief with her?

R. Yes, it is I. I am to blame for it.

Q. You must render this stuff. You must get it out; I will compel you no matter how hard it is.

R. This is difficult, for it is spread over the whole system.

Since I mentioned also the name of Mary's damned father, the questioning of this damned soul may be inserted here.

QUESTIONING OF MARY'S FATHER

Q. What is your name?

R. My name is Jake, Jake, Jake.

Q. Are you the father of this child?

R. Yes, I am the father.

Q. Who sent you?

R. Lucifer sent me.

Q. Are you damned?

R. Yes, I am damned.

Q. What do you want to do here?

R. I want to lead my child to hell.

Q. You wretched dog, you want to ruin your child forever? I have known you in life, miserable hypocrite.

R. Yes, you have known me.

Q. You wanted to seduce your own child to sin in her young years. You went to church, and in the presence of your family, you have made fun of and ridiculed the sermons, the sacraments, Holy Mass; you have represented every thing to your children as the greatest stupidity. How often have you received the two Sacraments of Penance and Holy Communion sacrilegiously, even on your death bed?

R. Yes, I have done that.

Q. And last of all you have given your own children to the devil. Wasn't that a terrible crime?

R. Yes, it was the most terrible crime.

Q. What have you gained by this malice?

R. Nothing, I have merited hell, to be in hell forever; yes, forever; to be in hell forever through my own fault. (Saying this, Jake kept increasing his voice.)

Q. You are in hell, but your daughter will never go to hell with you.

R. Yes, she must go with me.

Q. Who has given you the right to ruin your daughter forever?

R. Am I not the father of the Child? Can I not do with her as I please?

Q. No.

REMARK: During this exorcism, Mary was insensible to the other world; she heard nothing of the dialogue between her damned father and the exorcist, though her father shouted loud enough to be heard and understood far away. The scorn and devilish laugh of the father was provoking. He did not bulge at all at the Sacred Heart.

It seems that he had taken the daring with which he had received the holy Sacraments unworthily on earth along into eternity. That first possession lasted from 1908 to 1912. The new possessions which took place after June 18, 1912 have, except for a short interval—not found their end yet.

"REPORT OF A POLTERGEIST"[1]

1949

On August 20, 1949, The Washington Post *ran a story with the headline:* priest frees mt. rainier boy reported held in devil's grip. *The article was read with interest by William Peter Blatty, then a student at Georgetown University. Blatty recalls thinking, "If there were demons, there were angels and probably a God and a life everlasting."[2] Through the Jesuits at Georgetown, Blatty obtained a diary of the exorcism, which became the basis of his novel* The Exorcist *in 1971.*

A cottage industry has sprung up attempting to uncover the true details behind Blatty's novel. The boy is now believed to have been Ronald Hunkeler of Cottage City, Maryland.[3] In February 1949, the family approached Rev. Luther Miles Schultze of Saint Stephen's Lutheran Church in Washington, DC, and reported the strange activity in their home. Schultze was at a loss to explain the phenomena and eventually directed the family to Father Edward Albert Hughes of Saint James Catholic Church in Mount Ranier, who sought permission to perform an exorcism.

In March, Schultze wrote to Joseph B. Rhine, director of the Parapsychology Laboratory at Duke University. Rhine believed the reported phenomena were scientifically significant. In the report below, a parapsychologist (possibly Rhine himself) relates the paranormal activity described by Schultze and discusses the problems in studying such phenomena scientifically.

* * *

Among the various claims of spontaneous psi phenomena, one of the less common is that of poltergeist activity, which consists of physical manifestations usually occurring in the form of knocks, raps, the hurling of objects, etc. Since these alleged occurrences, because of their spontaneous nature, do not easily lend themselves to scientific investigation, they have been noted in the literature, but they are not generally regarded by research workers as offering conclusive evidence of parapsychological activity. It is especially necessary, however, in a field so full of unexplained and unorthodox facts as parapsychology that all phenomena be examined in a spirit of open-minded inquiry. The following case of a reported poltergeist is presented, therefore, not as an established fact but as a possibly genuine occurrence with sufficient precedent to warrant thoughtful examination.

This review of the case is based on a report made by the Rev. Luther Schulze, a Lutheran minister in Washington, D.C., who received the following details from the D. family:

In January, 1949, scratching noises were heard continually in the walls and ceilings of Mr. D. 's home. An exterminating company was called and was unsuccessful in locating any signs of rodents, and the noise finally centered in the vicinity of Mr. D.'s thirteen and one-half year old son, Roland. From day to day the scratchings increased, and other manifestations appeared, such as the sound of squeaking footsteps in the hall, the moving of furniture with no visible cause, the flying-about of dishes, and the violent trembling of the boy's bed. The disturbances followed the boy when he stayed in neighbors' homes. After some weeks, the mother and father were convinced that an evil spirit, possibly that of a recently deceased relative, was the cause of the trouble, and it was then that they called in the Rev. Schulze who in turn enlisted the aid of one of his colleagues, Rev. L. At the suggestion of the two clergymen, Roland was sent to a mental hygiene clinic for examination, prayer circles were held, and at various times the family

took communion in an effort to rid themselves of the phenomena.

Rev. Schulze was frequently present when the disturbances
occurred, and he observed that in many instances it would
have been possible for the boy himself to have produced a particular effect, though he did not see him do it. On February 17,
1949, under close scrutiny, however, the following events took
place:

Rev. Schulze took the boy, weary from lack of sleep, home
with him for the night, but the manifestations continued even
there, though nothing of the sort had ever been known to occur
in that house before. About midnight, unable to sleep because
of the shaking of the bed, the boy "sat in a heavy armchair with
a very low center of gravity. The chair moved several inches;
then he placed his knees under his chin with his feet on the
edge of the chair. The chair backed up three inches against the
wall. When it could move no farther in that direction it slowly
tipped over . . . throwing the boy to the floor." This took place,
Rev. Schulze maintains, while the light was on and while he
himself stood in front of the chair watching.

At about three the same morning, with the light still on, the
boy was lying on the floor between two blankets spread out in
the center of the room in a space about six by eight feet where
Rev. Schulze had placed him to get away from tipping furniture. Twice he and his bedding moved slowly to a spot under
the bed. His head and hands at that time, Rev. Schulze reports,
were in full view, his body appeared to be rigid, and there was
no wrinkling of the bedding such as would be expected if the
boy were hitching himself forward by muscular effort of some
kind.

On March 5 Roland and his mother left for St. Louis to visit
relatives and, if possible, to shake off the phenomena. There
they enlisted the religious aid of some Jesuit priests, an Episco-
pal priest, and a Lutheran minister who separately conducted
rites of exorcism. The phenomena persisted periodically for some
time thereafter, and finally, after the boy's return to Washington in April, they gradually subsided. By the time the matter

was reported to the Parapsychology Laboratory by Rev. Schulze, the opportunity for observing the effects had passed.

Such cases as this are very difficult to evaluate, as has been remarked above. It is hoped therefore, that readers who may have similar experiences will promptly contribute written accounts of them to the Parapsychology Laboratory. In this way it may be possible to make an investigation while the effects are still present. Even if the unexplained events have ceased, however, a full description will be of value for the collection of spontaneous cases which is being made. From this collection some clues may be picked up as to the nature of these uncommon effects and how to go about investigating them.

LESTER SUMRALL,
THE TRUE STORY OF
CLARITA VILLANUEVA[1]

1955

The exorcism of Clarita Villanueva—the Filipina girl who was "bitten by devils"—was quickly forgotten by the media, yet it marked an important moment in the emergence of a global culture of deliverance ministry that Protestant missionaries have spread throughout the Global South. While Lester Sumrall's story of casting out demons may have been unusual for a Protestant missionary in 1953, casting out demons is now a common feature of Pentecostal and Evangelical churches throughout Asia, Africa, and South America. In 2019, director Roderick Cabrido released the Tagalog-language film Clarita *about the possession.*

Villanueva was eighteen (or seventeen in Sumrall's pamphlet). She was Visayan, an ethnolinguistic group of the Philippines that is predominately Catholic. Her native language was Tagalog, and—according to Sumrall—she spoke no English except during fits of possession. Clarita's parents had died when she was young, and she described her two brothers as abusive. She traveled to Manila, where she was arrested on May 6, 1953, for vagrancy and suspected prostitution. She awaited trial in Bilibid, a massive prison that had been used by the Japanese during World War II to house American POWs. In 1953, it was still housing Japanese war criminals.

While awaiting trial, Villanueva described being attacked by an entity she called "The Thing," which only she could see. The Thing was actually two entities: one a tall, hairy man dressed in black with enormous feet, the other short and furry (in some reports its fur was white, in others black).

In her cell she began experiencing fits and trances during which the entities would attack and "bite" her. Numerous people, including medical doctors and Manila's chief of police Col. Cesar Lucero, reportedly saw the "bites" appear spontaneously on her skin. In one account, an examiner removed his hand from Villanueva's body to discover a bite had formed under his palm. According to some reports, they were still wet with saliva. Photographs were allegedly taken, although descriptions of what the bites looked like vary slightly. At least some medical professionals suggested that the "bites" were actually bruises that Villanueva's body was somehow manifesting as a result of extreme stress. Dr. Mariano B. Lara, the chief medico-legal officer for the Manila Police Department, became convinced the bites were supernatural and wrote a report that is excerpted below. According to Lester Sumrall's pamphlet The True Story of Clarita Villanueva, *during one fit Villanueva began wrestling with an invisible entity, and when she opened her closed fist it contained a clump of coarse black hair. Dr. Lara collected samples of the hair and examined them under a microscope.*

While the phenomenon received little international press, it was widely reported in the Philippines. The media descended on the prison and observed Villanueva's fits. Sumrall reports that he became involved after he heard a forty-five-minute radio broadcast of one of Dr. Lara's examinations. Lester Sumrall was a Pentecostal missionary who believed in the power of miracles. He describes asking God to deliver Villanueva. In reply, he heard God's voice "in his heart" tell him, "If you will go to the jail and pray for her, I will deliver her."

Sumrall already had important connections in Manila and was able to get an audience with Mayor Arsenio Lacson, who had already been seeking a Catholic exorcism for Villanueva.[2] Lacson agreed to let Sumrall pray over

Villanueva, pending approval by Dr. Lara. Lara was reportedly convinced, telling Sumrall, "Reverend, I am humble enough to admit that I am a frightened man."

Sumrall describes fasting for twenty-four hours before confronting the demon on Friday, May 22. The deliverance was successful after three sessions. Sumrall allegedly asked reporters not to write about the affair, yet after they inevitably did, Sumrall noted, "It gave us [Pentecostal missionaries] recognition that otherwise would have taken many years to receive." Villanueva finally went before Judge Almeda-Lopez, who assigned her to the Welfareville institution for wayward girls, for observation. Sumrall got an attorney and petitioned her release. What happened to Villanueva afterward is unknown.

Sumrall's pamphlet went through several editions and eventually helped inspire a revival of Protestant demonology. As is common with such pamphlets, it is a narrative of triumphant evangelism. Sumrall regarded Catholicism as a false religion from which the Philippines needed saving. He reports that Catholics refused to help Villanueva and that when he visited her, "I was the only Protestant in the entire group." One female prisoner who did not heed his warning to be silent during Villanueva's deliverance and mocked the proceedings became the expelled demon's next victim and was bitten. Sumrall also writes, "This was the miracle that opened the hearts of the people of Manila to the full gospel and prepared the way for the great revivals which followed." The following year, Sumrall founded Bethel Temple in Manila, where his family still ministers.

"THE STRANGE CASE OF 'THE THING,'" *THE PHILIPPINES FREE PRESS* (30 MAY, 1953)

This is about the strange phenomenon of what has been arbitrarily called "The Thing" which the first couple of weeks of her confinement at Manila's city jail as vagrancy suspect, brought much suffering and misery to eighteen-year-old Clarita Villanueva, an unlettered Visayan girl from Bacolod City. Clarita claimed the "The Thing"—invisible to anyone else but herself—bit her in various parts of the body and generally made her life miserable. "The Thing," according to the girl, was really composed of two "things," a big one and a small one.

But, you would ask, could this be possible? Qualified authorities, including medical experts and psychiatrists, hold widely divergent views on the phenomenon. A member of the medical staff of the Manila Police Department at first diagnosed the case as one of plain insanity and claimed the girl probably bit herself during her epileptic fits. An army psychiatrist of V. Luna General Hospital in Quezon City came out with the view that it was a case of "hysterical fugue." One medical authority claimed that it was a case of malnutrition. Still others insisted that it was a case outside the realm of medical science: that the girl was under the influence of diabolical spirits and must be exorcised of "The Thing."

Not all of those who advanced their views on the strange case actually saw Clarita being bitten by the invisible "Thing." The medico-legal officer who first thought that the girl was insane changed his mind later when he saw with his own eyes teeth marks on the arms of the girl after the attack. He also saw for himself that the girl did not bite herself as he suspected.

When the girl is attacked, she appears to cower before an invisible monster. Stark terror is mirrored in her dilated eyes. Then she screams in blood-curdling agony. Tears stream down her face and then "The Thing" apparently lets go as she literally wilts to the floor. Sometimes, she does not need to point to the fresh teeth marks on her arms or neck because the bites are too pronounced to escape notice.

The strange case caught popular fancy and people were talking about it in the buses, in the jeepneys and in their homes. To satisfy our own curiosity, we decided to look into it. Before we set out, however, we were almost determined NOT to believe "The Thing." Why, it was too fantastic, we thought.

We went to the women's detention building in the prison compound Thursday morning in the company of Dr. Abelardo Lucero, of the Manila Police Medico-Legal Department. Just as we were mounting the steps of the squat concrete building, we were startled by blood-curdling screams from within. "The Thing" had struck again!

We went with all possible haste to the cell occupied by Clarita but before we reached it, the screams had stopped. In the cell we found Clarita seated on a wooden bed, with tears still flowing down her cheeks. An American civilian who we later learned was Rev. Lester Sumrall, a Protestant minister, was kneeling on the cement floor before the stricken girl. He was holding both of Clarita's hands by the wrists. He was praying. Manila Police Department's chief medico-legal officer, Dr. Mariano B. Lara, was standing to one side, wiping tears away from his own eyes. Prison officer Capt. Antonio Ganibi stood speechless behind Dr. Lara. Holding Clarita by the arm was Mrs. Dominga Reyes, a professor of psychology and philosophy in a local university. There were a few other people in the cell, but just then we were too occupied by the engrossing scene to notice them.

We could see immediately that the other people in the cell besides Clarita had gone through an experience they could not easily forget. They looked wild-eyed, perhaps from a little fear and also from a sense of bewilderment. Dr. Lara, who has become accustomed to opening cadavers in the Manila Police Department morgue without batting an eyelash, was shaky. He held the left arm of Clarita and pointed out to us the fresh bite on it. As if accusing us of disbelief, he asked in a quavering voice, "Don't you believe that?"

We drew closer and took a hard look at the bite. The sight sent a cold shiver down our spine. It did not, in any way, resemble a human bite. In the first place, it was too large for human teeth. In the second place, the bite was completely round. (Anybody may find out for himself by actual tests on his own arm that a human bite is elliptical.) And finally, we were awed to discover that all the teeth marks appeared to have been made by molars. Clarita seemed exhausted and so was Rev. Sumrall.

He was visibly shaken and his hands trembled. It would seem that "The Thing" won the first round.

Early the following morning, we returned to find out more about "The Thing." Rev. Sumrall had two other Protestant ministers with him when he showed up at 9 o'clock. Before going into the cell of Clarita, he pleaded with the people around to keep us away as "exorcising the evil spirits" was not a show. Only Dr. Lara went into the cell with the ministers. After a while, we also sneaked in.

Rev Sumrall knelt before the girl and took her hands into his. He asked her if she knew him and she said she did. But after a moment, while the minister was invoking the Lord to "liberate this little creature from the devil," Clarita's countenance changed. She became wild-eyed and screamed at the minister before her, telling him to go away.

The minister alternated prayer and sacred song with invocation for the Lord's help and exhortations against the devil, but Clarita continued to scream. When Clarita seemed to cower away from him in unrestrained fright, he covered her eyes with his hands and told her not to be afraid as he was going "to bind the hands and feet of the devil this morning."

The struggle continued. At intervals, Clarita was as meek as a lamb and, at the prodding of the minister, said that she liked Jesus Christ. The very next moment, however, she grew violent and cursed God and told the minister to go away. At one stage of the proceedings, Clarita became so violent and hysterical that she fainted.

The minister then turned around and informed those present that they had better go down on their knees and pray "for your own salvation." Everybody was on his knees in a jiffy. Perspiring and growing visibly weary by his efforts, Rev. Sumrall resumed the task at hand. He slapped Clarita a couple of times and she came to, but in no time at all she was screaming again.

After about an hour, Clarita's face seemed to soften. She became more attentive to the minister before her. In reply to a question, she told him that she liked Jesus Christ. At this state, the minister recited the Lord's Prayer and Clarita followed him. Then the minister asked if Clarita was still afraid of "The Thing" and she replied in the negative. She indicated that "The Thing" went out the window. And then three ministers sang a joyous "Hallelujah!" Clarita appeared worn out and she slowly stretched herself on her wooden bed to sleep.

The following day (Saturday) we saw Clarita again. She appeared happy. She told us that the night before, she had another struggle with "The Thing." She related that she seemed to be losing the fight when, in desperation, she exclaimed, "Dios ko!" (My God!) and "The Thing" took to flight.

According to Clarita, she has three brothers in Bacolod City, but she has no father nor mother. Both parents died when she was still very young. She said that her brothers were not as loving as they should have been and she came to Manila two years ago to shift for herself. Clarita served as a maid for a few months and then eloped with a man who turned out to be married with four children.

When she discovered the bitter truth, she abandoned him "for the sake of the children" and became a dancer. One evening some three weeks ago, she saw a late movie, she said, and on her way home she was picked up by police and booked on suspicion of vagrancy. She was committed to the city jail on May 6th. The first few days and nights in the women's detention building were uneventful.

Then on Saturday night, May 9th, something unusual happened. Without her knowing it, she said, her right leg got wedged in her wooden bed. She said it was only with great difficulty that she was finally able to extricate her leg. She said she did not attach any special significance to the incident but, after a while, she noticed that small pebbles were being thrown into her cell. Her cell mates also noticed the stones.

Clarita and her companions thought that perhaps somebody was only having a little fun. Then bigger stones came pelting into their cell. The women began scolding their unknown tormentor. They raised so much noise that the guard came around and ordered them to bed. She related that it was while she was sitting on her bed preparatory going to sleep that she first saw "The Thing" (the big one) perched on a beam overhead.

Clarita said that "The Thing" made a move to jump on her

and she froze with fright. "The Thing," she said, actually jumped on her and sat on top of her. Then the big one, which she described as big, black and covered with curly black hair, started biting her. Because of her fright at the sight of the supposed monster, she did not immediately notice the presence of the small one, which she described as small, spindle-legged and with a beard on its round face. She said that the small one helped the big one in biting her.

According to Clarita, she thought that the cell guard, as well as the other detention prisoners, did not believe her when she told them what happened. But when her screaming was brought to the attention of Capt. Ganibi, the prison officer, he ordered them to pray before the improvised altar in one of the cells. Clarita complained to the prison officer that she could not see the altar as the big one was obstructing her view. She told us later that Capt. Ganibi even slapped her because she insisted on turning her head away from the altar.

Sunday night, May 10th, was the most horrible night she had spent so far. Because of the almost continuous attacks of both the big one and the small one, Clarita kept screaming and Capt. Ganibi was fetched from his home to handle the situation. Ganibi had the girl taken to his office and had her surrounded by a human ring composed of jail guards and other persons. But the attacks continued and she showed them fresh bites on her arms and on her neck. Ganibi decided that "The Thing" was a matter for higher authorities. That was how the phenomenon came to public notice.

Fact or fancy? Published reports say that cases similar to that of Clarita are "nothing new in Japan." According to the Japanese belief, a bewitched woman is usually the object of the jealousy of a deceased or estranged wife. The "spirit" or "The Thing" (as in the case of Clarita)—so the Japanese version goes—assumes various forms unseen by anyone except the victim and bites her in different parts of the body until she gives up the surviving spouse of the deceased wife.

An old employee of the Manila city jail, with a philosophical turn of mind, explained the strange manifestations in the following manner: It is like the wind. The wind cannot be seen.

But it can inflict physical damage. "The Thing" may be likened to the wind. "The Thing" also cannot be seen. Like the wind, it also can cause physical damage. The wind is real. How about "The Thing?"

DR. MARIANO B. LARA, "AN OFFICIAL ACCOUNT OF CLARITA VILLANUEVA AND 'THE THING'"

At the time Clarita arrived, she was unconscious and was carried into my observation room seated on a chair. She was placed in front of the class of interns and myself. The body of Clarita was soft and entirely insensitive to all stimuli. Her arms lifted by me would fall without resistance. Pointed needles and pens touching her skin gave no response throughout her body surface. After several minutes in this condition, Clarita began to come out of this state of insensibility and trance.

Meanwhile, I was like Sherlock Holmes of the detective stories or Dr. Cyclops, the film character. Equipped with magnifying lens and with an unbelieving mind about this biting phenomenon, I scrutinized carefully the exposed parts of her body, the arms, hands, and neck to find out whether they had the biting impressions. I saw the reddish human-like bite marks on the arms. She was still soft in the entire body and could not stand up by herself. One of my assistants, a cadaver technician, Alfonso by name, helped carry her to a bed for her to rest during this state of partial trance. Alfonso got hold of her body and deposited her on the prepared bed, placing both her hands over her in order that they would not hang downward. At that very instant, this girl in a semi-trance loudly screamed repeatedly the word "aruy" (a scream of pain in Tagalog), and when I removed Alfonso's hand from Clarita's, I saw, with my unbelieving eyes, the clear marks or impressions of human-like teeth from both the upper and lower jaws, it was a little moist in the area bitten on the dorsal aspect of the left hand, and the teeth impressions were mostly from the form of the front or incisor teeth. Seeing these with my unbelieving eyes, yet I could not understand nor explain how they were produced as her hand had all the time been held away from the reach of her mouth, and that the place where the bite-impressions occurred, on the dorsal on the left hand, was the very place held by my assistant Alfonso. I knew she could not bite herself nor could Alfonso, who does not possess a single tooth, having recently had them extracted by a dentist. I am also sure that I did not bite the girl causing the impressions to appear on her hand! Not finding any possible explanation insofar as my human experience in medical training is concerned, I kept my mouth shut, but not my mind.

Clarita kept on screaming for about fifteen minutes with this bite on her left hand, and she turned bluish in the face and legs as if being choked. There were also a few reddish whelps in the front of the neck occurring with this phenomenon. After about twenty minutes of the attack, accompanied by stiffness and screaming, her body became soft and in a trance-like condition which was a repetition of the observation made when she was first brought into the room.

After about ten minutes of this trance and softness of the entire body, she gradually recovered consciousness and shortly thereafter, became normal again.

LESTER SUMRALL, *THE TRUE STORY OF CLARITA VILLANUEVA*

Clarita screamed these words at her invisible enemies and as she did, she lurched forward and grabbed with her hands which seemed to have been instantly freed. She went into a coma. The prison authorities who were in the compound and many prisoners had gathered. They laid her on a table, but her hands would not open. The doctor pried her hands open and to his uttermost astonishment, there was some long, black, coarse hair. It was in the palm of her hand and under the fingernails. Dr. Lara placed this hair in an envelope and put it in a guarded place. Under the microscope, Dr. Lara found that the hair was not from the head, nor from any part of the human body. I personally saw this hair under the magnifying glass. It was about two inches long, coarse, had no root and showed no signs of having been cut.

The doctor has no answer to this mystery. How an invisible being, presumably a devil, could have lost hair from his chest by a visible being pulling it out is one of the strangest facts of history!

This phenomenon we must leave unanswered at the present.

ALFRED MÉTRAUX, A
VODOU EXORCISM IN HAITI¹

1959

Vodou (or Voodoo) is an Afro-Atlantic religion that developed in Haiti when enslaved Africans attempted to continue practicing the traditional religions of West Africa while living under a French Catholic regime. The word "Vodou" is derived from vodun, *an Ewe-Fon word meaning "god" or "worship." An initiated Vodou priest is called a* hungun, *and a priestess is called a* mambo. *Many Catholic traditions have found their way into Vodou and some practitioners consider themselves Catholic. Vodou entails maintaining a relationship with supernatural beings called* loa, *who can be called upon for help. The* loa *belong to particular "nations" of spirits, each of which has its own music and ritual elements. For example,* loa *belonging to the* petro *nation are said to enjoy the sound of a whip cracking. Each* loa *also has one or more* vèvès, *geometrical designs traced on the floor using flour, ash, coffee grounds, or brick dust to call the* loa *during rituals.*

Alfred Métraux (1902–1963) was a Swiss anthropologist who conducted an ethnographic survey of Haiti's Marbial Valley from 1948 to 1950 under the auspices of UNESCO. In his book Voodoo in Haiti *(1959), he describes witnessing a Vodou exorcism. Spirit possession by the* loa *is a normal part of Vodou ceremonies. But in this case, the sufferer was believed to be experiencing possession by* l'envoi mort *("sent" spirits of the dead), who had been conjured by a sorcerer (boko or bokor). He is taken to a* humfo *(temple), where a* mambo *can perform the exorcism. At the center of the* humfo *is a wooden staff or tree*

called the poteau-mitan, *which symbolizes the connection between our world and that of the* loa. *The mambo
is supported by an initiated practitioner called a* hunsi, *as
well as an assistant called a* confiance. *She begins by casting cowrie shells as a form of divination to determine the
cause of the patient's illness. This reveals that she will
need the help of the* Guédé, *an especially powerful family
of* loa *associated with the powers of death and fertility.
Among the most powerful of the* Guédé *is Baron Samedi,
a* loa *of the dead, to whom the* mambo *offers sacrifice.*

*Vodou traditions are adaptable by nature, and Vodou
rituals often have elements of improvisation. Métraux
notes that this was a particularly elaborate exorcism. The
reader should not assume that contemporary Vodou ceremonies will closely resemble this one, especially if they
are performed outside of Haiti.*

SENDING OF DEAD ("EXPÉDITIONS")

The most fearful practice in the black arts—the one which
the ordinary people are always talking about, is the "sending of
dead" *(l'envoi morts* or *expéditions).* Whoever has become the
prey of one or more dead people sent against him begins to grow
thin, spit blood and is soon dead. The laying on of this spell is
always attended by fatal results unless it is diagnosed in time
and a capable *hungan* succeeds in making the dead let go.

The dead are sent under the auspices of Saint Expedit who is
invoked after his image has been placed upside down, in the
following prayer:

Almighty God, my Father, come and find so-and-so that he may
be "disappeared" (s*ic*) before me like the thunder and lightning.
Saint Expedit, you who have the power to move the earth, you
are a saint and I a sinner. I call on you and take you as my patron from today. I am sending you to find so-and-so: rid me of
(expédiez) his head, rid me of his memory, rid me of his thought,
rid me of his house, rid me of all my enemies, visible and invisi-

ble, bring down on them thunder and lightning. In thine honour
Saint Expedit, three Paters.

The success of this curse still depends on the goodwill of
Baron-Samedi, the all-powerful master of the dead. The *boko*
strikes his matchet three times against the stone consecrated to
this god and at each blow utters the god's name. He is then
possessed by Baron-Samedi who, through his mouth, orders
the person appealing to him to turn up at midnight at a cemetery and there offer bananas and potatoes, chopped small, in
front of the cross which symbolizes him. There too he must
take a handful of earth for each of the "dead" whom he wishes
to send and must spread it on some path frequently taken by
his victim. Whether the unfortunate man shall step on or step
over the earth makes little difference: the dead will enter his
body and hold him close for ever. A client may also take as
many stones from the tombs as he wishes in the knowledge
that each will become "a dead" ready to do his will, as soon as
he has thrown it against his victim's door.

There is another way of rousing the enmity of "a dead"
against someone to whom you wish harm. When a member of
the victim's family dies, two nails are surreptitiously driven into
a beam of the house in which the decease took place. The dead
person then cannot leave the precincts and in revenge begins
to persecute his kin, in particular the person against whom the
spell was cast. Atenaïze, who complained a great deal about
the persecutions she had suffered from her dead husband, had
discovered two suspicious nails in a beam of her hut and had
had them removed. Unfortunately in the process one of them
fell to the ground and was never found. She attributed all her
troubles to this lost nail.

The presence of "a dead" in someone can affect not only his
health but also his character. Milo Marcelin tells the pathetic
story of a father, good and honest, who overnight became a
drunkard and even an assassin because one of his subordinates had dispatched against him a drunken, vagabond "dead."

Those who "send dead" risk the wrath of their messengers if
they fail to feed them.

Cattle no less than human beings are vulnerable to *expédi-tions*. It often happens that out of jealousy or vengeance sorcerers put "dead" into a cow or a pig which soon seems afflicted with madness. Since an animal possessed is as dangerous as a human being in the same condition, its master is unable to sell it, and so must slaughter it.

TREATMENT FOR "EXPÉDITIONS"

According to *hungan*, illnesses resulting from *expedition de morts* are not easily cured. The dead embed themselves in the organism into which they are inserted and it is very difficult to make them let go. That this is no exaggeration may be seen from a description of an exorcism of "dead" which I had the chance of witnessing in all its complexities at Lorgina's sanctuary. The patient who was put through this treatment was a certain Antoine who had been taken into the *mambo's humfo* ill. With earthy complexion and wasted body he lay on a mat motionless as though eking out what little remained to him of life. A few weeks earlier this same man was a sturdy stevedore in the Port-au-Prince docks. His story was simple: he was taken suddenly ill and then went into an alarming decline. His family sent him to a *hungan* at La Salines who diagnosed an *envoi morts*. The magician was confident he could save him. In spite of the high fees he demanded Antoine took him on and endured a cruel and complicated treatment of which burning with seven matches was not the easiest part.

Antoine, seeing the dead would not yield, fell into such a state of prostration that he could no longer swallow. His parents then decided to take him to Lorgina and implored her to do anything she could to save him. She only agreed to take on his treatment after the *loa* Brisé whom she had invoked had promised her full co-operation. She threw shells and learnt that there were three dead in Antoine and there was no time to lose.

Given the nature of the illness the treatment had to be carried out not only under the aegis of the Guédé but even in the house which is reserved for them. There, the Guédé symbols had been traced out in ashes and coffee grounds.

On these *vèvè* the patient's mat had been placed in order to establish a more intimate contact between him and the Guédé. Various ceremonial accessories were put on the table, the stone of Brisé (blackish with a mirror inset), five bunches of leaves and three calabashes containing maize and grilled peanuts. In each of these a candle had been planted (one black, one white and one yellow). Two *gamelles* (wooden troughs) under the table contained a brownish liquid. This was the "bath"—that is to say bits and pieces of plants left to soak in water with bull's bile.

Lorgina ordered her *hunsi* to go and fetch the patient who had been sitting in the peristyle, clad in a nightshirt, with his back against the *poteau-mitan*. He was so weak that it was almost necessary to carry him. From what people said later it seems that on the way the "dead" inside him continually defied the *mambo* and swore they would not let themselves be driven out. The patient was stripped of his clothes and with nothing on but his pants, was laid out on his mat, his head resting on a stone. Washing and "tidying up" was now carried out as though the body were already that of a dead man. His jaw was bound up with a piece of stuff, his nostrils blocked with cotton-wool, his arms crossed against his body, palms uppermost, and his big-toes firmly tied together. On forehead, chest, stomach and in the palms of his hands were arranged small piles of maize and peanuts. Lorgina, taking a *zinga* (spotted) hen and a "curly" cockerel, orientated them and invoked the spirits. She gave the birds to her acolyte who brought them to the patient and made them peck at each pile of food, beginning with the head. The cock's refusal to touch the grain was taken as a bad sign: another cock was fetched. This one attacked the grain with such gusto that the man's eyes had to be shielded from his greed. Now the birds were placed on the body of the invalid, two on the chest and the third between his legs. Meanwhile Lorgina, who had never ceased mumbling Credos, Aves and Paters as well as a long prayer to Saint Expedit, launched into a series of

invocations to *loa* and magical formulae which invariably began
with "In the name of God the Father, God the Son, God the
Holy Ghost, in the name of Mary, in the name of Jesus and all
the Saints and all the dead . . ."

She got up, took the hen and a cock and passed them at
length over the body of the patient starting with his head. Into
this business she put a certain roughness and repeated several
different incantations of which I only picked up one sentence:
"All that is bad is to come out, all that is good is to go in." The
mambo and her aide broke off to emit little noises something
like the hissings of the snake-god Damballah. The assistant
with a bird in each hand went through the whole thing again.
He lingered when he came to the chest as though trying to
sweep up something tangible. The patient trembled from time
to time but the *mambo* cautioned him in commanding tone to
keep still. She listed the names of the *loa* of her *humfo* and addressed herself to Brisé, to Agirualinsu and to her other protectors, but she also invoked the ancestors and root-*loa* of her
client. She asked them to save him and to give him back his
health "with the help of God." For one last time the cock and
hen were passed over the patient and were then left beside him,
so dazed they did not move. It was the spotted hen which had
taken *l'expédition*. As to the curly cock, he it was who had taken
upon himself the patient's *mauvais-air* (malific emanation). He
would be set free. He was supposed to disappear mysteriously
a few days later.

Each of the three calabashes with the candles was passed
over the patient from head to foot. The same was done with
the stone of Brisé. Lorgina continued praying and making the
"*tététété*" noise. She dipped her cupped hands into the bath and
raising as much of it as she could, threw it brutally into the patient's face. The latter terrified, trembled, shuddered, grunted
and tried to get up. He was persuaded to keep still. Lorgina
explained that it was not his fault that he moved but merely
that the dead were on the move inside him and disturbing him.
More of the "bath" was thrown at him with the same violence
as before and now several people took turns at it so the proce-
dure might be continuous. The man was now streaming and

covered with leaves and bits and pieces of half decomposed vegetation. This shower bath was a veritable offensive against the "dead," an attempt thoroughly to drive them out. Their resistance took the form of incoherent movements which they imparted to the body of the man they possessed. Faced with the spectacle of such brutal treatment, a relation of the patient, who till then had remained quiet, burst into tears, and crying out that she could stand it no longer, tried to escape. She was constrained to sit down. The *mambo* ordered the dead to depart and told them that if they persisted in their obstinacy she would find a sure way of expelling them. Garlic was put in the patient's mouth who, in the violence of his reaction, threw off his chin-bandage and bonds.

Finally he fell back on his mat visibly exhausted. The *mambo* called him several times by his name: "Antoine, Antoine, is it you there? Is it you?" The patient replied faintly "Yes"; whereupon the assistant set fire to some *clairin* [cheap white rum] round the stone of Brisé on a plate and seizing the flames in his hand, ran them all over the body of the patient. Lorgina, filling her mouth with *kimanga* [rum mixed with herbs], squirted it roughly into Antoine's face. He tried to shield his eyes but was prevented. The *confiance* rubbed him vigorously and struck him with the edge of her hands on the shoulders, the inner crook of the arm and under his knees.

Baths, rubbings and general massage now brought to an end this first part of the treatment which had taken place in the "house of Guédé." The second act took place in the court, where a ditch had been dug. The patient was led there leaning on two *hunsi*, still walking with difficulty. Seven lamps made from orange peel were burning round the ditch and with them might be seen the three calabashes. The patient was helped into the bottom of the trench and handed a young banana palm which had just been uprooted. This he held in his arms. The chicken which was used earlier in the treatment was once again passed over all his body. Lorgina recited the formula "By thy will Good Lord, Saints and Dead, by the power of Papa Brisé, Monsieur Agirualinsu, Monsieur Guédé-nuvavu, Tou-Guédé, I ask you for the life of that man there, I *mambo* Yabofai, I ask you for the life of that man there, I buy him cash, I pay you, I owe you nothing." Once the prayer was finished the *mambo* poured the contents of the calabashes into her hands and with it rubbed the patient's body. She poured the water from a jug over his head and all over his body and then broke it against the parapet of the trench. She anointed his body with oil from the lamps. The speckled hen, all huddled up, was put at the bottom of the trench against the roots of the banana palm. It was this hen which, buried alive, must buy back the patient's life. If Baron-Samedi accepts the deal the banana palm dies; but if he refuses it the tree prospers and the man dies.

Quickly the loose earth on the edge of the ditch was pushed in and the patient helped out. The filling-in of the trench was completed as quickly as possible. The surface was leveled out and then crowned with three "perpetual lamps."

Now came the most dramatic moment of the treatment, the moment which must bring about the final defeat of the dead. The patient was rubbed vigorously with blazing rum and three small charges were let off between his legs. Lorgina and her assistants squirted *kimanga* over him, blowing some to the four cardinal points—all this done to the cracking of the *petro* whip. A white *maldyoc* shirt with red facings was brought. One of the flap-ends was slightly burnt. With the blackened edge signs were marked on the face and chest of Antoine. The latter put on the shirt and over it the night-shirt which he was wearing at the beginning of the treatment. Lorgina told him to spit as much as possible and go in under the peristyle alone. He did so, stepping almost firmly. There a cloth was bound round his head and his feet were washed with an infusion of medicinal herbs; then he was given tea to drink. He said he was feeling much better.

And indeed the cure was almost miraculous. A few days later Antoine was a changed being. He ate well and having got some of his strength back wanted to get up and move about. Soon he resumed his arduous work as stevedore.

It is not always necessary to endure such a spectacular treatment to get rid of "dead." The daughter of a certain Florilon was suffering from a serious illness. Florilon put it down to "dead" which his own brother had sent against the child to be avenged of the death of his son—an event for which he held Florilon responsible. Florilon first went to herb-doctors, then to the town doctors who all said they could do nothing. He decided—much against his better feelings since he was a fervent Catholic—to consult a *hungan*. The latter diagnosed the illness, prescribed ablutions *(bains)* with herbal infusions and gave the child's father an *arrêtement,* that is to say a talisman to stop the dead. This was a bottle full of magic herbs which he had to bury near his house. The girl was made to wear a *chemisette paman* (chemisette with facings) made of many coloured strips on which had been drawn indigo crosses. The child recovered but ever since then Florilon has felt an implacable hatred of the brother who had thus involved him in heavy expenditure and put him in debt to a *hungan*. At the time when I met him he had not yet finished paying off the fees of the *hungan* who, he feared, would unleash the *mort*s which he had succeeded in "stopping" if faced with further delay.

E. MANSELL PATTISON,
AN EXORCISM ON A
YAKAMA RESERVATION[1]

1977

Regarding Native American religions it is often true that "those who know do not tell, and those who tell do not know." The United States is home to 573 federally recognized tribal nations, each of which has its own beliefs and practices that, like all traditions, change over time. Many of these traditions are passed down only to initiated members of the community. Tribal nations generally do not explain their traditions to outsiders unless there is a need to, such as in court battles over government use of tribal sacred lands. The case below, recorded by psychiatrist E. Mansell Pattison, is significant because it provides a snapshot into the traditions of the Yakama (or Yakima) nation during a period of cultural transition in the 1970s.

One problem with discussing "Native American religion" is that these cultures often do not draw a distinct line between the secular and the sacred as Western culture tends to do. Similarly, it is debatable whether certain rituals can be meaningfully characterized using the Western term "exorcism." Several tribal nations, however, have healing rituals designed to remove evil spirits that plague the body and, sometimes, the mind. John Brown Jr. was a Navajo code talker who served during World War II. In an interview for the Museum of the American Indian, he alluded to a tribal ritual known as the "Pattison Enemyway" ceremony that he underwent to cope with the aftermath of his military service:

"I had nightmares thinking about the blood. The Japanese and the smell of the dead. Rotting Japanese and they probably got into my mind. And they had a Squaw Dance for me in Crystal. And I imagine they killed that evil spirit that was in my mind. That's what it's about. There's a lot of stories there. It takes a long time to talk about it. It usually takes a medicine man to explain everything properly. But it works."[2]

Likewise, "Mary" and her mother came to Pattison describing spirits—identified as ancestor spirits—that were adversely affecting Mary's mental state, perceptions, and behavior.

Pattison was a psychiatrist, not an anthropologist. He described his intervention with Mary and her family in an article in The Journal of Operational Psychiatry entitled "Psychosocial Interpretations of Exorcism." Pattison did not see belief in spirits as a sign of mental illness; instead, he argued that exorcism can be an effective form of therapy. He argued that cultures have their own systems of symbols and rituals that facilitate healing, and that the language of ancestor spirits and "witchdoctors" is not so different from that of psychoanalysts. He wrote, "Both engage in powerful rituals that are symbolizing exercises of their culture. Both are exorcists."

Pattison had his own psychodynamic interpretation of the problems Mary and her mother were experiencing, based on Freudian theory of repressed sexual jealousy between mother and daughter: Mary's mother described her father spitting on her, which could represent semen; Mary hallucinated blood, which could represent menstruation, etc. But instead of relating his theory to the family, he encouraged them to solve the problem using their own cultural traditions. Pattison felt the success of this approach had larger implications for how mental health professionals should interact with religious cultures.

A CASE STUDY

To illustrate some issues raised thus far, the following case from my own experience highlights the psychological meaning of possession and the function of exorcism from a comparative therapeutic view.

This experience occurred during a period when I served as the psychiatric consultant to the public Health Service Clinic serving the Yakima Indian reservation. The Yakima are located on several thousand acres of farming and lumbering land in central Washington amidst the rich agricultural Yakima valley. As on many Indian reservations, these Indian people live in close proximity to white Western culture. Although they have relatively good economic resources, life on the reservation is isolated from the world in which it is located. The reservation culture is in the midst of cultural disintegration. The "long hair" Indians cling to the traditional Yakima mores, while their middle aged children flounder in bewilderment, not part of the white culture, not part of the Indian. Meanwhile the grandchildren attend the local white schools and watch television in the homes of their grandparents. Here in the middle of two cultures we find our case.

Upon arrival at the reservation, one snowy December morning, the young public health doctor grabbed me for an emergency consultation. He had been called to the home of an Indian family the previous night to see an adolescent girl. The family stated that she was crying, frightened, incoherent, running around the house in a state of panic. He reported that upon arrival at the home he found the girl incoherent, babbling, agitated, muttering about ghosts and stated that she was afraid of dying. He gave her an intramuscular injection of chlorpromazine which calmed her down, and she went to sleep. He made a diagnosis of acute schizophrenic psychosis. Since I was due to arrive the next day, he requested that the family bring the girl to the clinic for my evaluation and recommendation for further treatment.

Precisely at the appointed time, the mother and daughter appeared. I had worked on the reservation for several years at this time, and was known to the Indian people. I had found good rapport and little difficulty in establishing working relationships with my Indian clientele. But this was a different situation from my usual clinical consultations. Both mother and daughter were sullen, guarded, withdrawn. The girl was a pretty, well developed, adolescent, thirteen years old. She was dressed like a typical high school girl. But she hunched herself over, eyes downcast, speaking in barely audible tones. With great difficulty and much patience her story was told.

The problems began the prior August when Mary (her pseudonym) had gone off to a week-long summer camp for Indian girls, sponsored by the local O.E.O. program. One night, as children are wont to do at a summer camp, after lights were out and the counselors were in bed, Mary and several of her girl friends went sneaking out of their cabin to frolic in the moonlight among the tall fir trees. As they ran about in the moonlight they looked up in the trees and saw human figures. These ghost-like figures drifted down from the trees, and the girls recognized them as their tribal ancestors. The girls talked to the ghosts and the ghosts talked to the girls. But after a few minutes the girls became frightened, ran back to their cabin, jumped into bed, and hid under their covers.

All seemed safe now. Except for Mary. A ghost followed her into the cabin, jumped on her as she lay in bed, and tried to choke her. She fought and struggled against the ghost, she gasped for breach, she screamed for help. The counselors came running into the cabin, but they could not calm her. Mary was sure the ghosts would kill her, she sobbed and screamed. Finally, the counselors bundled her up in a car and drove back home to the local hospital. When seen in the emergency room she was still in an agitated state and was given an intramuscular tranquilizer shot before being taken home to her parents.

The stage was set, and the pattern from then on to December was rather routine. Mary would go off to high school everyday with ratted hair and teenie-bopper clothes. She would participate in her daily high school activities like any teenager. She was on the honor roll, was a cheerleader, and a student body officer. But when she came home a different Mary appeared.

She combed her hair into long Indian braids. She put on long-skirted traditional Indian clothes, and wandered about the house as if in a daze. She would see ghosts at the window and cry out in startled fright. She went walking in the fields and saw blood on the ground. She thought the ghosts had killed one of her girl friends. She thought the ghosts would attack and kill her younger brothers and sisters. She would become so frightened and worried that at times she would cry, and scream, and run around the house. At times the parents could not calm her, and they would take her to the hospital for a shot to calm her down. But the next morning she would always get up and go to school like a normal adolescent girl.

The mother and the girl had no explanation for this behavior. They were bewildered. The mother turned to me and asked what I, as a psychiatrist, thought of this behavior. Was her daughter crazy? What I observed was a withdrawn sullen girl. But she spoke in a coherent manner; she was logical and realistic in her conversation with me. I stated that I did not know what this all meant, but perhaps the mother might have some ideas.

The mother said she had heard that psychiatrists did not believe in religion. Did I believe in religion? I told her that I thought religion was very important in the lives of people. Did I believe that she had been healed? I told her that many people experience healing, and that she too might have had a healing experience. She smiled, relaxed and leaned toward me. Look at my face! Do you see any scars? No, I don't. Well, my father healed me. Do you believe that? Yes. Well he was a witchdoctor; he used to care for the whole tribe. And when I was a girl I fell in a fire and burned my face. And he made a pack of mud with his spittle, and anointed my face and said his prayers. And said I would be healed and have no scars. He said I would have a beautiful face. Do you think he was right? Is my face beautiful. Yes.

The mother was satisfied. She sat back. Then she tensed up again. Doctor? Yes? Should I say this? Maybe I shouldn't. I've never talked about this before. My daughter doesn't know about this. I've never told her. Well. You see, my father, the witchdoctor, he told me that his powers would be passed on when he died. But not to his children, not to me. His power would be passed on to his grandchildren. And the oldest, this daughter, this girl, would have his powers.

By this time my thoughts about the clinical situation had been stirred. Do you think that Mary's experience has something to do with your father? Oh yes, she answered. But we don't talk about those things any more, because, you know, we're Presbyterians now, and people don't believe in witchcraft any more. But what if they did, I asked. How would you handle something like this?

The mother was now animated, and the daughter was listening intently. Well, we knew what to do. You see, in the old times, when someone was going to be given the powers of the spirits, was to be given the gifts of the witchdoctor, you had to struggle with the spirits. You had to prove you could rule them. Well, what would you do? I asked. Oh, there's nothing we can do. If this were the old times we would just open the door and let Mary wander out of the house at night. And she would go out and meet the spirits. And she would have to fight with them. And then she would come back with the powers. . . . Or maybe we would just find her out there after a few days, but that's the way it happens. . . .

I see, Well, what do you think about this now? Since this is not the old days, what do you think might be the best way to help Mary now?

Well, you know doctor, I've been thinking about that. You can't really practice much as a witchdoctor these days. It might be better if Mary were a Presbyterian and didn't accept the gift her grandfather left her.

Well, how would you work that out?

You see, doctor, we have to get rid of the spirits. We have to tell them that Mary doesn't want to want to fight with them. And then they'll go away and leave her alone. And she'll be O.K.

H'm. Well what do you have to do?

Oh, I don't know how to do that.

Who does?

Oh, Grandma does. She and other old women know the ceremony. We all have to get together. And we would dress Mary up in the ceremonial dress, and we have to have prayers, and offerings, and we would anoint her, and say the prayers. . . .

Lest I leave the reader in suspense, at the end of one of the most fascinating experiences of my professional life, I reached an agreement with Mary and her mother. We agreed that it was not appropriate for Mary to attempt to achieve the mantle of power her grandfather bequeathed her. That would be looking backward. So we agreed that Mary should renounce the legacy and look forward to becoming part of the modern world. The mother agreed to call the grandmother and see if she and the other tribal women could conduct a ritual of exorcism that night. I would return in one month. They agreed to see me again in that time.

Now it was January. With some trepidation I awaited their arrival. They came early! They were delighted to see me. I was a great doctor. They had followed my advice. The ceremony of exorcism had been conducted. It had been successful. Mary was healed.

Indeed, since that night of exorcism, the strange behavior had disappeared. The mother was happy, Mary was happy, I was happy. Because of my ongoing contact with this tribe, I had the opportunity to follow this family for many months thereafter. Mary remained healthy and happy. No more was she bothered. In contrast to her mien that first cold snowy December morning, when I saw her thereafter she was bright and bouncy, talkative and enthusiastic, like any other energetic adolescent girl beginning to become a woman.

SOME RELIGIOUS OBSERVATIONS

As I listened to this story, I thought of an Old Testament story that was almost identical, and I thought of the universality of human experience.

In the following passage, we read of Jacob wrestling with the angel of the Lord, in order to obtain power over the spirits:

And Jacob was left alone; and there wrestled a man with him until the breaking of the day. And when he saw that he prevailed not against him, he touched the hollow of his thigh; and the hollow of Jacob's thigh was out of joint, as he wrestled with him. And he said, Let me go, for the day breaketh. And he said, I will not let thee go, except thou bless me. And he said unto him, What is thy name? And he said, Jacob. And he said, Thy name shall be called no more Jacob, but Israel: for as a prince hast thou power with God and with men, and hast prevailed . . . And Jacob called the name or the place Peniel: for I have seen God face to face, and my life is preserved . . . and he halted upon his thigh. (Genesis 32:24-31)

What is remarkable is that over a span of perhaps six thousand years and over three continents we find the same interpretation. The man gains power over spirits by fighting with the spirits. If man wins, he then has special powers, he can command the spirits. He is a shaman, a healer, a witchdoctor. But it is a dangerous business, for to acquire the special powers requires a mortal combat. Jacob won, but he was crippled for life. And as for Mary, she feared her own death, or that of her siblings, if they got in the way of the combat.

In this case, we have the reenactment of an age-old saga: Man in quest of power over the forces of his life.

[. . .]

In this instance we can note that the diagnosis of acute schizophrenia is understandable, but inappropriate. However, the family itself was caught in an interesting and pathetic cultural bind. If they had been living within the traditional Indian culture, they would have followed the prescribed patterns of response. We may assume that the deviant behavior would have been appropriately resolved. However, the family was caught between the cultures, between two belief systems. And so the family was immobilized. The behavior of the patient, Mary, was congruent with the belief system of the old culture, while the treatment of the hospitals was congruent with the new belief system.

[. . .]

SUMMARY

This study started with an exploration of the current social interest in demonology and exorcism in western society. We have seen that beliefs in demonology are part of a larger supernaturalistic cosmology. However, acting out of demonology beliefs occurs only in times where there is social oppression and loss of social integration. Modern demonology can be seen to be part of the social repudiation of the scientific determinism of rational man, coincident with the rise of existential irrationalism. The practice of exorcism is but one example of the powerful use of symbolic transformations in healing rituals. Seen in terms of symbolic actions, psychoanalytic psychotherapy is also a practice of exorcism. This leads us then to examine the symbolic systems of society that incorporate both the client and healer. It is seen that western psychotherapy is just as much a part of its culture as other healing systems. We close with an eye to the future, can there be a psychotherapy that is not supernaturalistic?

MICHAEL L. MAGINOT, "REPORT SEEKING PERMISSION OF BISHOP FOR EXORCISM"

2012

Although the rule is often bent and sometimes broken, Catholic priests may not perform an exorcism without the approval of their bishop. Priests are expected to make their case that exorcism is warranted, and if the bishop is not persuaded they may not proceed. For many reasons, such discussions are normally not shared outside the Church hierarchy. The letter below is a rare example of a priest's letter requesting permission to perform an exorcism. It has been redacted to protect the identities of those involved. This was the first exorcism ever approved by Bishop Dale J. Melczek. In the copy obtained for this anthology, someone has underlined the detail of an object levitating.

The exorcism of Latoya Ammons of Gary, Indiana, in 2012 is perhaps the most famous exorcism in recent memory. The case involved strange activity reported in Ammons's home and the erratic behavior of her three children. The alleged possession was especially noteworthy because social workers and law enforcement appeared to endorse claims that unexplainable events were taking place. While the children were hospitalized for uncontrollable behavior, a case worker from the Department of Child Services and a nurse reportedly saw one of Ammons's sons walk backward up a wall. Although he was

holding his grandmother's hands the entire time, wit-
nesses described the boy's feat as "impossible." It was the
hospital chaplain who first reached out to Father Michael
Maginot. Maginot's request for an exorcism was approved,
and in 2012 he exorcised Latoya Ammons. The family
moved, and the problems subsided soon after. In 2014,
Zak Bagans, host of the show Ghost Adventures, *pur-*
chased the house in Gary. This led to weeks of sensation-
alized media coverage about the Ammons case. Ammons
and Maginot gave interviews on cable news shows. Bagans
finally had the house demolished for his documentary
Demon House *(2018).*

In the letter below, Maginot describes watching police
excavate detritus from the soil of the house's basement
and formulates a theory that the strange phenomena may
have been the result of previous tenants holding necro-
mantic rituals in the basement. Despite his concerns for
the family, Maginot emphasizes that he would not per-
form anything resembling an exorcism without his bish-
op's permission.

On Friday Morning, April 20, 2012, in the midst of my weekly
Bible Study Group, I received a call from Chaplain David Nev-
ille of Methodist Hospital, since I was on call for Fr. Joseph
Uko, to come to the North Campus to perform an exorcism on
a boy witnessed by many as walking backwards up a wall. I
told him that I would need the bishop's permission to do so,
but that I was willing to conduct the necessary investigation. I
gave him permission to pass on my contact information to
anyone interested in being involved.

I arranged to meet with the mother and grandmother at the
home they rented to bless it and investigate that Sunday Evening, April 22nd at 6:30 pm. Following Friday's incident, Child
Protective Services became involved and 2 of the 3 children
were placed in foster care with the Carmelite Sisters in East

Chicago, and the youngest boy was undergoing a psychological evaluation at another facility in Wheatfield, IN.

After I blessed the home at [redacted] Carolina Street in Gary, I interviewed the mother, Latoya Ammons [redacted] and her mother Rosa [redacted] who lived with them. The first time they noticed anything strange was shortly after moving into the house last November of 2011. After midnight, they would hear footsteps walking up the stairs from the basement and open the door into the kitchen, but when they would come out of their bedrooms, they would see nothing except perhaps when they would turn on the light in the room, it would flicker making a crackling sound for a time and then stop. When this continued, they later would leave their bedroom doors open to see if they would notice anything further, and one night after 3 in the morning the grandmother was awaken [sic] to see a shadowy figure of a man pace back and forth in the living room, and when they got up the next morning they saw on the wooden floor of their living room what looked like muddy footprints like from a boot. After this, they put a lock on the kitchen door to the basement, and when they would hear the footsteps come up the stairs and tried to open the door, they would hear pounding on the door.

Shortly after this, the kids would be affected during the day after school. One day, the daughter ([redacted]—just recently turned twelve) tried to get into her bedroom and the door was closed and she couldn't open it as if someone was holding it shut, and after several tries it flew open. One night, Rosa was watching television and heard what sounded like a dog barking in the kitchen, when she went in to investigate she didn't see anything but heard scratching on the door, but still didn't see anything when she finally opened it. The boys (especially [redacted]—just turned 8 and [redacted]—recently turned 10) would see a young boy around their age and he would talk and play with him especially in the closet, but they were scared in seeing an elderly lady like walking death with red eyes usually seen in the backyard. There seemed to be mechanical difficulties: the TV getting messed up, static on cell phones interrupting

calls, the engine lights on their cars turning on and off, ther-
mostat settings getting changed, things being hidden and other
such annoyances. Occasionally, they would see the sticks that
adjust the venetian blinds rock back and forth move from one
window to the next. During the winter, the porch was filled
with horseflies and later some 2 buckets of dirt from underneath the stairs had to be swept up.

Soon the children seemed to be affected physically by becoming sick with vomiting, diarrhea and fever, with a lot of
bleeding around the mouth and nose that would be left on
their pillowcases and the mother had three different kidney
ailments back to back. In early March, things would be ratch-
eted up to an unbearable level forcing the family to leave the
house before Easter. [The rest of this paragraph is redacted.]

That weekend, there was a family get-together at the house.
[Redacted] was sitting on the couch when something pulled
her off the couch. [Redacted] was in the bathroom and something threw him into the middle of the room, he complained that
something was pulling on his limbs and genitals and then they
saw his stomach go in and out. Next [Redacted] is picked up
and thrown into the freezer that is in the living room next to
the kitchen door. Afterwards, the kids become sleepy and go
to bed. [Redacted] is then awaken [sic] that something is pulling her off the bed. Family members and friends begin leaving
and some complain that something has followed them giving
them a heavy feeling or a headache that may take a couple of
weeks to finally dissipate. No one wants to come to the house
anymore.

Rosa tries to contact her mother Ruth over the phone about
what has occurred, which takes several tries due to bad connections, static, one can hear the other while the other can't,
except for cursing which both would hear. When Ruth tried to
call back, 10 o's appeared on Rosa's phone, which left a gar-
bled message. Eventually they were able to communicate to
the point that Ruth would talk to her neighbor who belongs to
a church that deals with deliverance more than their Baptist
church which was reluctant to get involved in such a way.
Early that week, Ruth brought in an Evangelist to pray over

the kids. When she went into the basement, she felt a lot of activity that was confusing and felt that Latoya was the one being attacked and would attack others through her and that she would need an exorcism. She was so overwhelmed that she had to leave the house. But she did suggest anointing all the doors and windows with oil, go through the house with bleach and sage incense, sprinkle salt throughout the basement, and she also set up a small altar in the basement with an open bible and a candle and incense burner. This did seem to work for three days. Then they discovered that the statue of the Holy Family that was placed on the altar had been thrown across the room breaking off the top part.

The kids now seem to be affected outside the house, where the crazy behavior would jump from one child to the other as they would get into the car, one would run to the car and start kicking it, and when restrained the other would be thrown to the grass, then one would start cussing, or saying it is time to kill, or doing some sort of demonic chant, where one would stop and the other would pick up where the other left off. Once inside the car, one would be rolling his head and stop and the other would start banging his head on the arm rest and stop, and then the crazy demonic talk would start moving from one to the other. When the entity leaves they fall asleep.

The last straw was when they witnessed a Febreze bottle levitating and moving back and forth in the living room before being thrown into Latoya's bedroom that sounded like an explosion which knocked the lamp to the ground breaking it. When Latoya went into the bedroom to investigate, she saw a large dark shadow figure at the closet. With that, the family quickly got some clothes and went to a hotel, but the entity seemed to follow them there. They eventually went to stay at Latoya's brother's house refusing to go back to their house especially at night, but the entity seemed to follow them there though it would be more active once outside the house.

When it was time to go back to school, the kids were so affected that they stopped going to school, which got the authorities involved. She was taking the kids to the doctor's when they were under a severe attack where one would act crazy and then fall asleep and then go to the next. When the doctor witnessed this, he told her to take the kids to the hospital to run a series of tests, which she would do the next day, where the infamous incident occurred. The way it is described was that Rosa was holding [redacted] by his hands while he was growling back at her, and she was trying to coax him back and saying "You are not [redacted]. [Redacted] come back." She was walking him back up against the wall when he continued to walk backwards up the wall until her hands were over her head and he immediately flipped over her head to land on the other side where she never let go or got twisted up. The psychologist and the social worker from Child Protective Services left the room to eventually get security getting the Police involved as well.

Toward the end of the interview [Three lines are redacted.] Rosa interrupted us pointing to the bathroom light that was flickering and making an electric type of noise. I then got up to take a closer look and it stopped the moment I got to the door. I returned back to the couch to continue the interview when the flickering started up again and again I got up to investigate and again it stopped just as I got to the door. I returned and mentioned that it must be scared of me, when it started up again, and this time it continued even after I entered the room to take a look. I then went back to get my crucifix and it still continued even after I touched the light fixture with it. I then ignored it to continue the interview.

Soon we were interrupted again when Rosa pointed to the venetian blinds in the kitchen and the stick that opens them was rocking back and forth about a 1/4 of an inch. When I was looking at the other blinds, I noticed the one in Latoya's bedroom had what seemed to be like a couple of ounces of water poured down the middle of them. I pointed that out to them and she mentioned that it was oil and that she made the sign of the cross on all the windows, doors and blinds about a month ago where it had dried. I felt it and it was wet and oily, and I didn't remember seeing it before when I blessed the room. I then heard the furnace kick on and went to look at the blinds, and in the kitchen, you can see the effect that the vent had underneath moving the tags at the end of the cords that open them.

When I pointed that out to them, they mentioned that is the only place below a window where there is a vent, where they manly [sic] run along the wall in the middle of the house. I also don't remember seeing any of the tags move. When the furnace kicked off, the tags stopped moving, but the stick continued rocking from one window to the next, while the tags remained still ruling out the cause being air currents of any sort. When I tried to resume the interview again, we were interrupted by Rosa pointing to the floor to what appeared to be wet footprints throughout the living room and concentrating around the chair [where] Latoya was sitting. I felt them and they were wet and when I tried to smear them with my foot, I was able to. Even though I sprinkled the floor with holy water as I went through the house, you would almost have to walk through a puddle to reproduce what we were seeing and I don't recall seeing that before. Soon Latoya began complaining about having a headache. I got my crucifix and placed it upon her head and she began to quiver and convulse. I immediately took it off since I was only prepared to conduct an investigation and didn't want to go any further. She then said she was freezing and went into her bedroom to get a blanket and then threw it off saying she was burning up. I was surprised since I only heard stories of how it was affecting the children. I asked if it affected Rosa also, and she said that it never affected her. Latoya was then becoming light headed and finding it difficult to concentrate and talk. I then looked at my watch and was surprised to see that it was 10:30 pm. She could call me later that week and we can finish talking [redacted]. I also gave them permission to give my phone number to other witnesses and they could call me. I then gave her and her mother a blessing as requested and left the house with them.

The next day, Rosa called me to say that Latoya was sick as a dog and that she was sleeping in the same room when they woke up to something moving the covers off their feet. [About ten lines are redacted.] She then mentioned that her brother is moving to Indianapolis and that there is another place available there with the same landlord. I told her that I would be willing to go out there and bless her new home since that could avoid going through all the hassle of procuring an exorcism, [the rest of this paragraph is redacted].

That Tuesday, I got a call from her friend [redacted] who was present at the March 10th get together seeing the daughter mysteriously be pulled off the couch and complaining about being pulled off the bed. After he left the house, he had a headache that lasted about 2 weeks and will never go back to that house again. That same day, I got a call from her brother [redacted] who confirmed the same event. When they were staying at his house, he witnessed the kids acting strange like he never saw before doing demonic chants involving numbers where one would pick up where the other left off and being thrown around and flipped by unseen forces, slamming their heads against the car and having to be restrained once in the car and then fall asleep immediately.

Friday afternoon, I got a call from the Lake County Police detective handling the case, [the rest of this sentence is redacted]. He told me they were examining the house that past Wednesday during the middle of the day, and we exchanged experiences. He said that the Gary Police Officer, Charles Austin, was experiencing strange phenomena on his radio as he approached the house with the channels changing rapidly hearing kind of a voice in the static until the battery went dead suddenly even though it was fully charged that morning. He mentioned that he took a lot of pictures and voice recordings and that [redacted] brought a videotape recorder that didn't work since the battery was dead despite being fully charged when he left. He had to use his phone to video record the visit. He was interested in contacting me.

On Wednesday, May 2nd [redacted] of the Hammond Police Department called that [redacted] was consulting with him as the former local expert on crimes involving the occult with the present one. He said that he would send me his report along with the DVD of the investigation of the house if that would help my report to the bishop, which I said [I] would indeed. He asked me if I saw the photographs taken by [redacted] and I said I hadn't, and he told me there was one I need to look at and that he would contact [redacted] to send that to me. He did call and sent me the photograph by email which looked like a white face underneath the stairs to the right and perhaps a darker greenish face in the middle. He later reviewed his audio recording while he was taking those pictures in the basement and after he mentioned that noises would be heard in the basement, it picks up someone whispering, "Hey." I mentioned that I was told that the youngest boy liked to play and talk to an unseen boy around his age. He mentioned that he found it strange that the poured cement floor appeared to be cut underneath the stairs and that there was dirt. He was going to procure a dog. He was going to ask the family and the landlord if you could dig underneath and if I wanted to be there, and I told him if it wasn't a crime scene, I would like to see if anything was buried there and pour blessed salt over that area. They were also going to check if there were any unsolved crimes, missing persons involving children in the area and the history of who owned and lived in the house.

On Saturday, May 5th I received the promised police report. In looking at the DVD, there was no trace of footprints or of the oil I saw on the blinds. On Monday, May 7th, I drove to Indy [Indianapolis] to bless the apartment before they would move in that Friday. On Wednesday, May 9th, [redacted] called that they procured a dog (however, not a cadaver dog since there is only one with the Chicago Police Department used for looking over a wide area) and that they would revisit the house the next evening. In their research, they discovered that the house was built in 1926 and a newlywed white couple moved in and lived there all their life. After she died, it was sold and the new owners never lived there but would rent it out to various tenants. The present owner bought the house in 2004 and rented it out to various tenants. On the block, there was one murder, a domestic dispute that was solved.

The next day when the house was revisited, I was there. There was no reaction by the dog. The Police began digging slowly and at two feet deep many disturbing things began to turn up beginning with a fingernail, then a pair of woman's underwear, a heavy metal object that seemed to be there a long time and was thought to be a weight that would hold down a drapery cord, hair beads, the tops of various candy bar wrappers, a pair of socks with the bottoms below the ankles cut off, a strange oval red lid from a tea kettle perhaps, and what we thought was a bone turn out to be a plastic broken piece from perhaps a shoe horn. After about three feet deep you can see a pristine layer of sand indicating that no digging went any deeper. Ruling out a possible crime scene, the hole was filled in with its contents and I poured blessed salt over it. A possibility that back in the 30's the couple's son may have accidentally been killed when he was playing around by swing[ing] the drapery cord when he was conked over the head by the ten pound weight. The grieving mother may have turned to the occult to conger [sic] up her son with having her husband's involvement who liked the energy boost from candy bars while burying the personal items surrounding the death. If this worked once, perhaps is [it] was tried other times with people close to her like her mother. If further research turns up some names that can be verified it may be worthwhile to have a Mass said for each to move on and enter the light of Christ's redeeming love.

Unfortunately, when Latoya entered the house for the first time since my first interview with her, her headache remained. Oil seem[ed] to condense and drip unto the steps from the crosses she made above. It also appeared all over the blinds in her bedroom. The police officers wiped down the blinds, and closed and sealed the door for 1/2 hour and when opened again, more oil appeared. Last Tuesday, May 15th, Rosa called and said that Latoya was getting worse. When I talked to her, she was having nightly dreams of [redacted] raping and intimidating her, which seems to be a new phase in her experience. I told her that I will be wrapping up my report and try to see the bishop as soon as I can.

Submitted to the Most Reverend Dale J. Melczek, Bishop of Gary on this Monday, the 21st day of May, 2012 signed by

Rev. Michael L. Maginot, Pastor of St. Stephen, Martyr Parish, Merrillville, IN

[Handwritten note adds: Permission granted by phone at 3:30 pm Wednesday May 30, 2012]

Notes

AN EXORCISM FROM
THE LIBRARY OF ASHURBANIPAL

1. Excerpted from R. Campbell Thompson, *The Devils and Evil Spirits of Babylonia* (London: Luzac and Co., 1904).
2. The translation of this line is doubtful.

THE BENTRESH STELA

1. Excerpted from James Henry Breasted, *Ancient Records of Egypt*, vol. 3 (Chicago: University of Chicago Press, 1906).
2. Gaston Maspero, *Manual of Egyptian Archaeology* (New York: G. P. Putnam's Sons, 1895), 109.

HIPPOCRATES, "ON THE SACRED DISEASE"

1. Excerpted from Francis Adams, trans., *The Genuine Works of Hippocrates* (New York: William & Wood Company, 1891).

LUCIAN OF SAMOSATA, THE SYRIAN EXORCIST

1. Excerpted from H. W. Fowler and F. G. Fowler, *The Works of Lucian of Samosata*, vol. 3 (Oxford: Clarendon Press, 1905).

TERTULLIAN, THE NATURE OF DEMONS

1. Excerpted from T. Herbert Bindley, trans., *The Apology of Tertullian for the Christians* (London: Parker and Company, 1890).
2. According to Herodotus, King Croesus of Lydia sent messengers to oracles to see if they could accurately report what he was doing on a given day. The oracle of Delphi (the Pythia) successfully

reported that Croesus was having tortoise and lamb cooked in a bronze pot at that moment. According to Tertullian's theory, this story only shows that daemons can be in two places at once. Pyrrhus was a Greek general who also consulted the oracle.
3. These are deities that were worshipped in Tertullian's homeland of Carthage.

PHILOSTRATUS, *THE LIFE OF APOLLONIUS OF TYANA*

1. Excerpted from F. C. Conybeare, trans., *Philostratus, The Life of Apollonius of Tyana* (New York: Macmillan Co., 1912).

ATHANASIUS, *THE LIFE OF SAINT ANTHONY*

1. Excerpted from Ernest Alfred Wallis Budge, *The Paradise or Garden of the Holy Fathers*, vol. 1 (London: Chatto and Windus, 1907).

CYNEWULF, "JULIANA"

1. Excerpted from Charles W. Kennedy, trans., *The Poems of Cynewulf* (London: G. Routledge & Sons, 1910).

THOMAS AQUINAS, THE POWERS OF ANGELS AND DEMONS

1. Excerpted from *The "Summa Theologica" of St. Thomas Aquinas, in English. Literally Translated by Fathers of the English Dominican Province, Vol. 5: Part I QQ. CIII-CXIX* (London: Burns Oates & Washbourne Ltd., 1922).
2. Desirable.

DESIDERIUS ERASMUS, "THE EXORCISM OR APPARITION"

1. Excerpted from N. Bailey, trans., *The Colloquies of Desiderius Erasmus Concerning Men, Manners, and Things,* vol. 2, ed. E. Johnson (London: Gibbings and Company, 1900).
2. Gerald Brittle, *The Demonologist: The Extraordinary Career of Ed and Lorraine Warren* (Los Angeles, Ca.: Graymalkin Media, 2013).

3. *Phasma* is the title of a comedy by Menander in which a young woman is mistaken for a goddess.
4. This would have been a small block of wax stamped with the image of a lamb bearing the banner of the cross.
5. Greek, literally an evil spirit.
6. The translator has rendered "Empyrian" as "Imperial." The Empyrian heaven is a reference to Renaissance astronomy, which imagined the heavens as a series of spheres encompassing the Earth. Ptolemy first described the Empyrian as the furthest of the spheres and therefore the highest heaven.

A POSSESSED WOMAN ATTACKED BY A HEADLESS BEAR

1. Excerpted from Ernest E. Baker, ed., *A true and most dreadfull discourse of a woman possessed with the devill, at Dichet, in Sommersetshire: a matter as miraculous as ever was seen in our time. A.D. 1584* (Weston-super-Mare: Robbins, 1886).
2. Erika Gasser, *Vexed with Devils: Manhood and Witchcraft in Old and New England* (New York: New York University Press, 2017), 13–15.
3. John Foxe, *The Acts and Monuments*, vol. 5 (London: R. B. Seeley and W. Burnside, 1838), 454.
4. Richard Baxter, *The Certainty of the World of Spirits Fully Evinced* (London: Joseph Smith, 1834), 24.

"A TRUE DISCOURSE UPON THE MATTER OF MARTHE BROSSIER"

1. Excerpted from "A True Discourse Upon the Matter of Marthe Brossier of Romorantin, pretended to be possessed by a Devill," trans. Abraham Hartwel (London: John Wolfe, 1599).
2. Sarah Ferber, *Demonic Possession and Exorcism in Early Modern France* (New York: Routledge, 2004), 40.
3. Brian Levack, *The Devil Within: Possession and Exorcism in the Christian West* (New Haven, Conn.: Yale University Press, 2013), 147.
4. The advice to wait three months before passing judgment is based on a famous case by respected sixteenth-century doctor Jean Fernel (Fernelius), in which a young man suffered a mysterious ailiment for six months before it was determined the cause was demonic possession. See Ferber, *Demonic Possession and Exorcism*, 51.

DES NIAU, *THE HISTORY OF*
THE DEVILS OF LOUDUN

1. Excerpted from Des Niau, *The History of the Devils of Loudun; The Alleged Possession of the Ursuline Nuns, and the Trial and Execution of Urbain Grandier, Told by an Eye-witness*, ed. and trans. Edmund Goldsmid (Edinburgh: Privately printed, 1887–1888).
2. Quoted in Aldous Huxley, *The Devils of Loudun* (New York: Harper & Row, 1971), 171.
3. Huxley, *The Devils of Loudun*, 171.
4. Moshe Sluhovsky, "The Devil in the Convent," *American Historical Review* 107 (2002): 1379–1411.
5. My thanks to choreographer Rebecca Whitehurst for her expertise on this question.

SAMUEL WILLARD, "A BRIEFE ACCOUNT
OF A STRANGE & UNUSUALL PROVIDENCE OF
GOD BEFALLEN TO ELIZABETH KNAP OF GROTON"

1. Excerpted from Samuel A. Green, *Groton in the Witchcraft Times* (Cambridge, Mass.: University Press, John Wilson and Son, 1883).
2. John Demos, *Entertaining Satan: Witchcraft and the Culture of Early New England* (New York: Oxford University Press, 2004).

THE DIARY OF JOSEPH PITKIN

1. Kenneth P. Minkema, "'The Devil Will Roar in Me Anon': The Possession of Martha Roberson, Boston, 1741," in *Spellbound: Women and Witchcraft in America*, ed. Elisabeth Reis (New York: SR Books, 1998), 99–120, sets the date as 1741. The autograph appears to say "January 1740." However the text describes Roberson attending a revival by George Whitefield, who did not preach in Boston until October 1740.
2. Minkema, 112.

AN EXORCISM IN THE NEW MEXICO COLONY

1. Excerpted from Robert D. Martínez, "Fray Juan José Toledo and the Devil in Spanish New Mexico" (Master's thesis, University of New Mexico, 1997).

GEORGE LUKINS, THE YATTON DEMONIAC

1. Owen Davies, *Witchcraft, Magic, and Culture, 1736–1951* (New York: Manchester University Press, 1999), 22.
2. Excerpted from Joseph Easterbrook, *An Appeal to the Public Respecting George Lukins (Called the Yatton Demoniac) Containing an Account of his Affliction and Deliverance; Together with A Variety of Circumstances which tend to Exculpate Him from the Charge of Imposture* (London: T. Scollick, 1788).
3. Excerpted from Easterbrook, *An Appeal to the Public.*
4. Excerpted from Samuel Norman, *Authentic Anecdotes of George Lukins, the Yatton Demoniac; with a View of the Controversy, and a Full Refutation of the Imposture* (London: G. Bourne, 1788).

FLAVIUS JOSEPHUS, *ANTIQUITIES OF THE JEWS*

1. Excerpted from William Whiston, *The Complete Works of Flavius Josephus* (New York: John E. Potter & Co., 1895).

THE SPIRIT IN THE WIDOW OF SAFED

1. Excerpted from J. H. Chajes, *Between Worlds: Dybbuks, Exorcists, and Early Modern Judaism* (Philadelphia: University of Pennsylvania Press, 2003). The original text contained acronyms known as *roshei teivot* (heads of words) to stand in for commonly used honorifics. For example "his memory for a blessing" is shorted to *z"l.* These have been removed for easier reading.
2. Yair Lior, "Dybbuk," in Joseph P. Laycock, ed., *Spirit Possession Around the World* (Santa Barbara, Ca.: 2014): 114–16.

EXORCISMS OF THE BAAL SHEM TOV

1. Excerpted from Dan Ben-Amos and Jerome R. Mintz, *In Praise of Baal Shem Tov: The Earliest Collection of the Legends About the Founder of Hasidism* (Bloomington: Indiana University Press, 1970), tale 20, 34–35; tale 84, 107–8.
2. Literally, he hath hid himself among the baggage, I Sam. 10:22.
3. "*Lekhah Dodi,*" a Sabbath poem written in the form of an acrostic on the name of the author, the Safed Kabbalist, Rabbi Solomon ha-Levi Alkabetz (about 1505 to about 1584). In the poem the Sabbath is personified as a bride.

"THE PROPHET MUHAMMAD CASTS AN ENEMY OF GOD OUT OF A YOUNG BOY: A TRADITION FROM AHMAD B. HANBAL'S *MUSNAD*"

1. Original translation by A. Richard Heffron.
2. Yusuf Muslim Eneborg, "Islam," in Joseph P. Laycock, ed., *Spirit Possession around the World* (Santa Barbara, Ca.: ABC-CLIO, 2015), 166–69.
3. Some commentators classify this *isnad* as "weak" (*da'if*) because one of the transmiters, Abd al-Rahman b. Abd al-Aziz, is unknown to them.

THE TRIAL OF HUSAIN SULIMAN KARRAR

1. Excerpted from "Two Murder Trials in Kordofan," *Sudan Notes and Records* 3:4 (December 1920): 245–59.
2. Lucie Wood Saunders, "Variants in Zar Experience in an Egyptian Village," in *Case Studies in Spirit Possession*, eds., Vincent Crapanzano and Vivian Garrison (New York: Wiley, 1977), 177–92.
3. G. P. Makris, *Changing Masters: Spirit Possession and Identity Construction Among Slave Descendants and Other Subordinates in the Sudan* (Evanston, Ill.: North University Press, 2000).

A HYMN TO DRIVE AWAY *GANDHARVAS* AND *APSARAS*

1. Excerpted from Ralph T. H. Griffith, *The Hymns of the Atharva-Veda*, vol. 1 (London: Luzak and Company, 1895).
2. Rupinder Kaur, et al., "Protective Effect of Lannea coromandelica Houtt. Merrill. Against Three Common Pathogens," *Journal of Ayurveda and Integrative Medicine* 4, no. 4 (2013): 224–8.

CHANG TU, "EXORCISING FOX-SPIRITS"

1. Excerpted from Jan Jakob Maria de Groot, *The Religious System of China*, vol. 5 (Leiden: Brill, 1910).
2. Judith Mageee Boltz, *Taoist Rites of Exorcism* (PhD diss., University of California, Berkeley, 1985), 21.

A FOX TALE FROM THE *KONJAKU MONOGATRISHŪ*

1. Excerpted from M. W. DeVisser, "Fox and Badger in Japanese Folklore," *Transaction of the Asiatic Society of Japan* 36, no. 3 (1908).
2. Richard Lloyd Parry, *Ghosts of the Tsunami: Death and Life in Japan's Disaster Zone* (New York: Farrar, Straus and Giroux, 2017).
3. Carmen Blacker, *The Catalpa Bow: A Study of Shamanistic Practices in Japan* (London: Routledge, 2004), 52.
4. Kiyoshi Nozaki, *Kitsune: Japan's Fox of Mystery, Romance, & Humor* (Japan: Hokoseido Press, 1961), 211.

HARRIET M. BROWNE'S ACCOUNT OF *KITSUNE-TSUKI*

1. Excerpted from "Fox Possession in Japan," *Journal of American Folklore* 13, no. 50 (1900): 222–25.
2. Shigeyuki Eguchi, "Between Folk Concepts of Illness and Psychiatric Diagnosis: *Ktisune-Tsuki* (Fox Possession) in a Mountain Village of Western Japan," *Culture, Medicine, and Psychiatry* 15 (1991): 421–51.
3. Kiyoshi Nozaki, *Kitsune: Japan's Fox of Mystery, Romance, & Humor* (Japan: Hokoseido Press, 1961), 213–16.

D. H. GORDON, D.S.O., "SOME NOTES ON POSSESSION BY BHŪTS IN THE PUNJAB"

1. Excerpted from D. H. Gordon, D.S.O., "Some Notes on Possession by bhūts in the Punjab," *Man* 23 (October 1912).
2. *The London Gazette* (January 2, 1931), 61.

GEORGES DE ROERICH, "THE CEREMONY OF BREAKING THE STONE"

1. Excerpted from Georges de Roerich, "The Ceremony of Breaking the Stone / Pho-Bar Rdo-Gčog/," *Journal of Urusvati Himalayan Research Institute* 2 (January 1931): 25–52.
2. In the prose introduction, Tibetan words are transliterated according to the Wylie system. Georges de Roerich utilized the older version of romanization developed by the Library of Congress. Although the Library of Congress updated its holdings to reflect a Wylie transliteration in 2015, I have maintained the older version in the primary text.

3. Pascale Dollfus, "The Great Sons of Thang stong rgyal po: The Bu chen of the Pin valley, Spiti," *Tibet Journal* 29, no. 1 (Spring 2004): 9.

4. Dollfus, "The Great Sons of Thang stong rgyal po," 11.

5. This is a trope in Tibetan Buddhist stories. In a more widely known tale, spirits are preventing the construction of a monastery in Lhasa, requiring the master Padmasambhava to subdue them.

6. Mahāsiddhas are individuals who have mastered supernatural powers (*siddhis*) through intense yogic practice. They are often said to flaunt social conventions.

7. Tibetan Buddhism features a variety of gods and goddesses as well as bodhisattvas—enlightened beings who have not yet become Buddhas. Avalokiteçvara is the bodhisattva of compassion. Vajrapāṇi is a bodhisattva who protects the Buddha and manifests his fierce or wrathful power.

8. In Hindu and Buddhist thought, the life span of the universe is divided into aeons, or "kalpas." A related idea is that each kalpa shall be marked by greater corruption and evil than the one preceding as the universe marches inexorably toward destruction and rebirth. Changes and innovations to Buddhist practice are sometimes justified by arguing that techniques that worked in previous kalpas are no longer effective in the current kalpa because the world has become too corrupt.

9. The "three kayas" are three different "bodies" that the Buddha possesses: his body that represents reality itself; his body of enjoyment; and his emanated body, respectively.

10. Sugata is an epithet for the Buddha.

11. Dollfus, "The Great Sons of Thang stong rgyal po," 12, reports that most villagers were apparently unaware of the interpretation that this character is the King of the North in disguise. They regarded the character as simply an unruly shepherd. A few described him as "hunter."

AN EXORCISM PERFORMED BY JOSEPH SMITH

1. Stephen Taysom, "'Satan Mourns Naked upon the Earth': Locating Mormon Possession and Exorcism Rituals in the American Religious Landscape," *Religion and American Culture* 27, no. 1 (2017): 57–94.

2. Quoted in Taysom, "Satan Mourns Naked upon the Earth,'" 60.

W. S. LACH-SZYRMA, EXORCIZING A RUSALKA

1. Excerpted from W. S. Lach-Szyrma, "Slavonic Folk-Lore," *The Folk-Lore Record* 4 (1881): 52–70.
2. Linda J. Ivanits, *Russian Folk Belief* (New York: M. E. Sharpe, 1992), 75–82.

MARIANNHILL MISSION SOCIETY, AN EXORCISM OF A ZULU WOMAN

1. Excerpted from Mariannhill Mission Society, *Are There Devils Today?* (Detroit, Mich.: Fireside Printers, 1927).
2. Quoted in Peter Brown, *The Cult of the Saints: Its Rise and Function in Latin Christianity* (Chicago: University of Chicago Press, 2009), 106.

F. J. BUNSE, S.J., *THE EARLING POSSESSION CASE*

1. Excerpted from F. J. Bunse, S.J., *The Earling Possession Case: An Exposition of The Exorcism of "Mary," A Demoniac, and Certain Marvelous Revelations Foretelling The Near Advent of Antichrist and the Coming Persecution of the Church in the Years 1952–1955* (Unpublished manuscript, 1934).
2. William Peter Blatty, *On* The Exorcist *from Novel to Film* (New York: Bantam Books, 1974), 18.
3. Carl Vogl, *Begone Satan! A Soul-Stirring Account of Diabolical Possession in Iowa* (trans. Celestine Kapsner), in *Mary Crushes the Serpent and Begone Satan!* (1935; repr., Gilbert, Ariz.: Caritas Publishing 2016), 65.
4. Moshe Sluhovsky, *Believe Not Every Spirit: Possession, Mysticism, and Discernment in Early Modern Catholicism* (Chicago: University of Chicago Press, 2007).
5. Albert R. Bandini, *Angels on Horseback: A Critical Review of the Pamphlet Begone Satan Which Relates an Alleged Case of Demoniacal Possession Occurred in Earling, Iowa* (1936; repr., Fresno, Ca.: Academy Press, 1950).

"REPORT OF A POLTERGEIST"

1. Excerpted from "Report of a Poltergeist," *Parapsychology Bulletin* 15 (August 1949), 2–3.
2. William Peter Blatty, *On* The Exorcist *from Novel to Film* (New York: Bantam Books, 1974), 6.

3. Leo Ruickbie, "Hunkeler, Ronald E.," in Joseph P. Laycock, ed., *Spirit Possession around the World* (Santa Barbara, Ca.: ABC-CLIO, 2015): 156–57.

LESTER SUMRALL, *THE TRUE STORY* *OF CLARITA VILLANUEVA*

1. Excerpted from Lester Sumrall, *The True Story of Clarita Villanueva: How a Seventeen-Year-Old-Girl Was Bitten by Devils in Bilibid Prison Manila, Philippines* (Manila: Sumrall, 1955).
2. "Mayor to Ask Archbishop to Exorcise 'Draculas,'" *The Sydney Morning Herald*, May 20, 1953, 3.

ALFRED MÉTRAUX, A VODOU EXORCISM IN HAITI

1. Excerpted from Alfred Métraux, *Voodoo in Haiti* (New York: Schocken Books, 1972).

E. MANSELL PATTISON, AN EXORCISM ON A YAKAMA RESERVATION

1. Excerpted from E. Mansell Pattison, "Psychosocial Interpretations of Exorcism," *Journal of Operational Psychiatry* 8 (1977): 5–21.
2. Quoted in M. M. Eboch, *Native American Code Talkers* (Minneapolis, MN: Abdo Publishing, 2015), 89.

Index

The Penguin Book of Hell

Edited by Scott G. Bruce

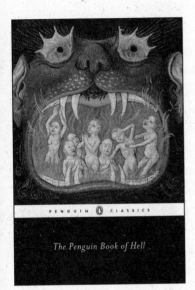

From the Hebrew Bible's shadowy realm of Sheol to twenty-first-century visions of Hell on earth, *The Penguin Book of Hell* takes us through three thousand years of eternal damnation. Drawing upon religious poetry, epics, theological treatises, stories of miracles, and accounts of saints' lives, this fascinating volume of hellscapes illuminates how Hell has long haunted us, in both life and death.

"A rich source for nightmares."
—*The New York Times Book Review*

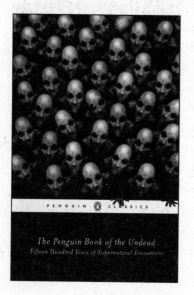

The Penguin Book of Ghost Stories

From Elizabeth Gaskell to Ambrose Bierce

Edited by Michael Newton

This selection of ghost stories brings together the best and most terrifying tales of the genre, from Elizabeth Gaskell's "The Old Nurse's Story" to Edith Wharton's "Afterward." With a thoughtful introduction and helpful notes, Michael Newton places the stories contextually within the genre and elucidates the changing nature of the ghost story and how we interpret it.